"Only the mediocre are always at their best. This book tells about the price a U.S. Army cavalry battalion paid in blood when a few senior officers were off form during the 1968 Tet Offensive."

—John Collins, Senior Defense Specialist (ret.),
Library of Congress

"Anyone who has fought will recognize this as a real story about some very tough battles, written by a real soldier who was there. Charles Krohn is a keen observer who with just the right amount of trenchant humor tells a tragic story, tells it extremely well, and lets the emperor appear unclothed whenever it is appropriate to do so. A superb chronicle about a handful of brave men who did what they were asked to do despite the odds against them—on both sides."

—General Donn A. Starry, USA (Ret.)

"Very interesting, often moving, and authentic. . . . This book calls to account those responsible for 'cutting loose' the 2/12th Cavalry to suffer grievous losses in the fighting north of Hue."

—Lewis Sorley, author of Thunderbolt

"Krohn calls for stateside training in which infantry battalions practice operations after vital support systems have faltered. His first-rate account demonstrates what can happen in combat when such systems do break down."

—Publishers Weekly

THE LOST BATTALION OF TET

BREAKOUT OF THE 2/12TH CAVALRY AT HUE

Charles A. Krohn

POCKET STAR BOOKS

NEW YORK   LONDON   TORONTO   SYDNEY

Pocket Star Books
A Division of Simon & Schuster, Inc.
1230 Avenue of the Americas
New York, NY 10020

Copyright © 2008 by Charles A. Krohn
Originally published by the Naval Institute Press

First Pocket Star Books paperback edition April 2009

POCKET STAR and colophon are registered trademarks of Simon & Schuster, Inc.

For information about special discounts for bulk purchases, please contact Simon & Schuster Special Sales at 1-800-456-6798 or business@simonandschuster.com.

The Simon & Schuster Speakers Bureau can bring authors to your live event. For more information or to book an event contact the Simon & Schuster Speakers Bureau at 866-248-3049 or visit our website at www.simonspeakers.com.

Designed by Richard Yoo
Photo © Associated Press

Manufactured in the United States of America

10 9 8 7 6 5 4 3 2 1

ISBN-13: 978-1-4391-0114-8
ISBN-10:   1-4391-0114-0

To Jeannie

ACKNOWLEDGMENTS

Many people helped me with this book and I want to thank all of them, particularly those who consented to interviews. In no case did anyone ask to express himself anonymously. I believe their collective testimony helped me find the essential missing pieces, and I am very grateful for their cooperation.

The many agents and editors who sent me rejection slips helped tremendously because they caused me to write and rewrite until I produced a manuscript that was finally worth publishing. I assume they will forgive me if I omit their names. Earlier versions were, I now admit, badly flawed, because they were personal chronicles of my first fourteen months in Vietnam. I figured what was interesting to me would fascinate everyone, so there was no point in being too selective. Consequently, there was no analysis of the events I so passionately described nor a focus on the Tet period. Everyone was either a hero or a flawless leader. Of course there were villains. Perhaps I was influenced by still being on active duty and subliminally concerned about my career potential. Yeah, I was. As the years passed, I added a lot of detail and some analysis to the diary, but the quintessential story stayed buried. After every rewrite I swore I would write no more, because there was no more to write about. The rejection slips still arrived as before, but they started to read a little softer. "We might have considered publishing this book a few years ago. . . ." Frustration grew, because I just didn't know how I could tell the story any better; everything I could remember or dredge up was in the manuscript, crafted as artfully as I knew how.

The first person to put his finger on what it would take to make *The Lost Battalion* publishable was Mark Gatlin of the Naval Institute Press. Like the others, he rejected the book; but he left the door open by suggesting how the manuscript might be fixed.* "Throw away the first

---

* Readers might find a certain irony in the fact that Naval Institute Press eventually published this revised edition that is being reprinted by Pocket Books, given that the press passed up an opportunity to publish *The Lost Battalion* in the early 1990s. This in no way diminishes my appreciation to (then) associate acquisitions editor Mark Gatlin (who is no longer with the press) for his incisive recommendations on how to improve one of my first drafts, which was ultimately accepted by Praeger.

forty pages," he advised, and "get to your story," because no one wants to read another "my tour in Vietnam." He advised me to "call a spade a spade," describing events and then translating them for the reader. I read the letter quickly and stuck it in a file drawer for a month, irritated that I still missed the point without knowing why. One sleepless night the answer hit me without warning. I was struck that I had missed the obvious for so long, and stayed awake until dawn scoping out a new approach. At first light I dashed off to my office with the early commuters to begin rewriting with a feverish vengeance. The result really surprised me. I recognized for the first time that I was describing a battle that took place in Vietnam but wasn't just about Vietnam. It took another year to finish the job.

Dan Eades, my editor at Praeger Publishers, worked countless hours with me to reach the final goal, publication.

Two in the Army's Center of Military History found documents for me that I would have never otherwise discovered. They are Colonel John A. Cash, USA, and Colonel George L. MacGarrigle, USA (Ret.). Colonel F. Clifton (Clif) Berry, USA (Ret.), a friend and author of many books about Vietnam and other military subjects, kicked me in the tail until I got it right. He has broad shoulders to match his sharp foot. Clinton N. Chadbourne provided the maps and sketches.

Gus Peleuses typed most of the manuscript and made compelling recommendations. He's a retired State Department official who's seen a lot of the world, and I learned to respect his judgment.

My wife, Jeannie, and our four sons, Cyrus, Josh, Alex, and Clay, think I've spent far too much of their time on this project. Even so, I acknowledge their role in helping me reach the finish line.

CONTENTS

Contents

Contents

THE BATTLE OF HUE

A Retrospective View and a Few Surprises

I AM PLEASED THAT POCKET BOOKS IS BRINGING OUT this updated Naval Institute Press edition of the book Praeger published in 1993. As soon as the book reached its original readers, it triggered a wave of comments, mostly friendly, wondering why I had failed to include a description of an event that, according to the correspondent, should have been included.

I was moved by letters, e-mails, and calls from next of kin, some of whom had learned details about the fate of their loved ones for the first time. This communication was one of the unintended consequences of writing a book about the war, and it was very gratifying for readers to reach out to me, whether their comments were supportive or critical. At least it proved my book was being read by interested and knowledgeable people who were willing to share their innermost thoughts. Many authors are not so fortunate.

My intent now is to make corrections or adjustments of interpretation, warranted by the receipt of new information. Later I'll share with you some of the comments I received.

First, let me correct the casualty figures. During the six-week period described in the book, the foxhole strength of the 2/12th fell from five hundred to fewer than two hundred. I originally said this included 60 killed in action and more than 250 wounded in action, a casualty rate of about 65 percent. Among the fallen were the battalion commander, Lieutenant Colonel Bobby Gregory, the operations officer, Major Larry Malone, a company commander, Captain Jim Stone, and my assistant, Sergeant Richard Keefe. Gregory's replacement was Lieutenant Colonel Dick Sweet, a Korean War veteran.

I now know the KIA figure was eighty-one, not sixty, including the crew of five who flew Gregory and Keefe over the Que Son Valley. It also included Captain John L. Barovetto, commander of B Troop, 1st Squadron, 1st Cavalry, attached to 2/12th Cav for the defense of Landing Zone Ross. When I wrote the battalion up for the Presidential Unit Citation immediately after Tet '68, I used the casualty figures available at the time. I assume that some of the wounded later died, increasing the total of friendlies killed in action.

In new appendixes at the end of this book I include the names of those killed and a list of the twelve who received the Distinguished Service Cross for heroic service during this period. I don't claim this is a record, rejecting notions of competition for heroism, but it does reflect the intensity of the combat described in this book.

While working on this new edition I received an e-mail from Dennis Moss, a friend of Captain Barovetto. "John Barovetto was a great leader who was very respected by his men, both for his knowledge and the way he interfaced with his men," Moss declared. "He was a great man." I endorse this observation. I also learned from Roger Kehrier that Jim Stone's remains have yet to be recovered, but the search continues.

Maybe the greatest surprise came in March 2006 from Dr. Erik Villard of the Army's Center of Military History. Dr. Villard told me he was writing "the official U.S. Army history of the period of the Vietnam War" and noted that *The Lost Battalion* has been extremely valuable to me in explaining the Army's role in the battle." It is flattering to know that significant portions of Villard's monograph are drawn from *The Lost Battalion*.

I recognize that Dr. Villard cannot repeat my speculations as historical fact in an official publication. But based on my examination of an early draft, close readers of my book will find no contradiction with his work.

Perhaps the person most affected by my publication was Dick Sweet, who took command when Gregory was killed. Sweet later suffered from post-traumatic stress disorder, manifested by sleepwalking and troublesome memories. He bought twenty-five copies of *The Lost Bat-*

talion, and I assume some of the recipients may have been contemporaries who had distanced themselves from Sweet after word leaked of what happened at Thon La Chu. Without knowing the details of why it was necessary to leave the bodies of eleven soldiers behind when we escaped encirclement, many, perhaps, considered his decision a monstrous lapse of judgment. Sweet saw the book as a vindication of his actions and orders. He died in 1994—at just sixty-five—soon after the book was published.

Some of the warmest responses I received were from the mothers of soldiers who read the book and wrote me that, for the first time, they understood what combat must be like. Consider the comments of Major Bill Scudder's mother. Bill was the battalion executive officer. She said her son's "deep respect for the flag and dedicated love for his country is a legacy from his father." She added, "I might never have known of his acts of courage except for your determination to tell the true story of The Lost Battalion. I am grateful to you for adding another flower to my bouquet of life."

David Moorhead from Plymouth, New Hampshire, called soon after the book was published. Sobbing, he related how he was with the battalion at Thon La Chu and was struck in the head by an enemy automatic weapon. He said he had total amnesia until he read my book, which restored his identity. He just wanted to thank me.

Max Cleland told me that he learned soon after being

commissioned that "others can doubt and argue; the soldier has to believe. For all those who doubted the Vietnam War and for all those who argued, there were those of us on the ground being shot at who had to believe." Lieutenant Cleland was the battalion communications officer until wounded by a grenade explosion.

Tom Dobrinska's sister from Landglade County, Wisconsin, found closure in a passage about a lieutenant who was killed during the battle at Thon La Chu. Frankly, at the time I wrote the book, I didn't know the lieutenant's name. Tom's sister told me that she and her mother had read the book and determined the dead officer was Tom. "My mother is on her death bed after two and one-half years in a wretched battle with cancer," she wrote. "We sort of feel that she was meant to live long enough to learn the real truth. Very interesting that your book is being published just before her death. I couldn't read the gruesome details to her." In her letter she enclosed Tom's DSC citation and a photo of a county monument on which his name is inscribed.

Some stories I heard later would make no one proud. Here's what Lieutenant Paul Becker, who now lives in Naugatuck, Connecticut, told me several years after *The Lost Battalion* appeared. "I left the 2/12th in late May of 1968 without so much as a hello, goodbye, or go to hell, and never heard from them again. When with the 2/12th I got a Purple Heart. It came through distribution, kind of comparable to a corporate inter-office memo. In April 1969 I received a Silver Star for actions that took place at

LZ Leslie just three days after I joined the unit. It made the Fort Dix paper. My wife attended the ceremony, but no one from my Fort Dix unit did. I have a son and a daughter. On many occasions when they were very little I would go into their bedrooms at night and just stare at them as they were sleeping peacefully, all comfortable and warm and marvel at the fact they were there because I hadn't been killed during the war."

But I heard some stories of quiet heroism, too. Here's what Richard Tulipano of Wading River, New York, told me about what happened to him when we tried to go back into Thon La Chu a second time:

We set up a perimeter that night and the next morning. . . . One of the guys . . . saw something moving. . . . Next thing I knew there was a huge explosion. . . . When I went to reach for my ammo . . . I saw my arm hanging off. I was never so scared, or felt so alone, in all my life. . . . Besides my arm, my lung was collapsed. I got hit in the throat and assorted other places. . . . When the medevac came, a group of us headed for it. I was the worst off so two guys were helping me walk. . . . I somehow ran but when I got to the chopper, it was full. The door gunner got off, put me in his seat, and stood on the skid and fired from there, shielding my body. I'll never know the man who saved my life.

Another soldier, whose name I'll not mention, sent me several letters a day for a while, along with his medical reports. It was clear that he had never recovered from his position being overrun in Que Son Valley. He was just eighteen at the time.

Daniel Griffin, former member of Company C, surprised me with a tale from the battalion's attack in the A Shaun Valley in May 1968. "We found an NVA headquarters and school," he explained. "In one of the classrooms was a blackboard with Vietnamese writing and 2/12th Cave 1st Cave. I told our Kit Carson Scout to read it." The scout translated that they were teaching their soldiers about our escape from TFP. "They wrote they [the NVA] used to own the night and that GIs would never move at night. And when they had them surrounded, they escaped. You no longer can trust the Americans not to move at night."

Perhaps the most extraordinary unintended consequence of my book's publication is the tale of Jim Cervera, now a deputy chief of police at Virginia Beach, Virginia. His brother—or half-brother—was among those we had hastily buried in the mass grave before we escaped from Thon La Chu. When his family was informed, they were so upset that, among other things, they stopped celebrating Christmas. Using my book as a guide, Jim went to Vietnam just a few years ago and found Thon La Chu. There, he discovered an old man who took him to what remains of the mortar pit where we had left the dead. It was the beginning of a healing process for the entire Cervera family.

I received a surprise e-mail from John Fazio, now a

college professor in Oregon but an 11 Delta (armor reconnaissance specialist) in Vietnam. "I joined the 2/12th on February 6th, 7th or 8th," he wrote. "I was literally rolled-pushed out of a chopper on a mercy flight to your location and dropped into a fog that never seemed to lift. . . . Thank you again for your work and the sense of peace it has at least brought to one who was there." He told me that he came home 50 percent disabled from small-arms and shrapnel fire but explained, "I made an excellent life in no small part by watching men under fire function with dignity and in some cases grace."

During a visit to Washington in July 2007, Mike Oberg recounted a well-known story of an NVA soldier who urinated on him while he was scouting enemy positions in February 1968. As Mike lay in the brush, an NVA soldier unexpectedly emerged and walked to the edge of a clearing to relieve himself.

"I just took it" in the face, Mike explained. "It was an embarrassment; it's humiliation, but I took it so I wouldn't give my position away." The NVA soldier returned to his foxhole, none the wiser. But a few minutes later, enemy soldiers started chasing Mike, forcing him to dispatch that soldier and several others with bursts from his M-16. They didn't give up the chase easily. "It was like being under a rotary mower with so many machine guns firing overhead."

Mike values his days with Company A. He explained that one of the defining moments of his life occurred when Captain Helvey asked if there were any sole surviving sons in the company. He marveled that Helvey cared enough to ask the question, perhaps to make sure they didn't get the riskiest assignments. Mike fit the category, but said nothing. He was determined to do his duty, not avoid danger or hardship. "For those of us who served in Vietnam, there's still an IV of blood between every one of us," he said. Mike now lives in Bellingham, Washington, and, at age sixty, is in good shape physically and mentally.

Finally, there is my own story. Based on my experiences in Vietnam, I was convinced that conventional light infantry has little chance of surviving contact with a superior force without artillery support. This conviction was never challenged until 2002, when I learned that the 10th Mountain Division was deploying to Afghanistan without any organic artillery. Wanting to learn why artillery was being left behind in the fight to liberate Afghanistan, contrary to Army doctrine and my own experiences in Vietnam, I made some hasty inquiries among my friends in the Pentagon; Fort Sill, home of the Artillery School; and U.S. Central Command, at the time headed by General Tommy Franks, who trained as an artillery officer.

My political contacts said the Army didn't see the need to take artillery, while my military contacts said the political leadership set the rules. Reaching out to several people closely affiliated with the secretary of defense, I sent the message that soldiers were being put at great risk without supporting artillery. Much of this book is about what happens to light infantry in the attack without artillery support. Steel was still cheaper than blood. I reminded them of what had happened to Secretary Les Aspin following the fiasco in Mogadishu. In short, if soldiers were killed or wounded in Afghanistan because there was no artillery to support them, blame would inevitably fall on the shoulders of the person perceived most responsible. Air-delivered precision weapons are useful, but they have limitations, a function of weather, response time, and availability.

The next division to deploy took artillery with them. Perhaps my reaction was impolitic, but it was clearly motivated by a desire to keep the faith with companions, alive and dead, my profession, and my conscience.

Regarding a couple of troublesome issues: in the book I describe the division commander's apparent nervous breakdown, an assertion supported by several sources, including the operations officer, then Colonel Collier Ross. Ross confirmed the essential details later, after he rose to the rank of lieutenant general; my other sources, still alive, remain confidential. My conclusion, however, is contested by the chief of staff, Major General George Putnam, now retired.

General Putnam also challenges my statement that Major General John J. Tolson ordered the 2/12th Cav to attack an entrenched North Vietnamese regiment at Thon La Chu without air or artillery support. He maintains the brigade commander, Colonel Hubert S. "Bill" Campbell Jr., was responsible because it wasn't Tolson's style to attack with air or artillery. General Putnam also believes Colonel Campbell was responsible for Sweet's mediocre fitness report.

I now would like to mitigate some of the unflattering things I wrote about Colonel Campbell—feelings that even prompted me to visit his gravesite at the Florida National Cemetery in May 2006. Major Phil Pons, then one of Ross's staff officers, believes Campbell was an officer of exceptional qualities who first refused General Tolson's order to air assault 2/12th Cav to the wall of Hue. Marching toward Hue was fraught with difficulties, but nothing compared to what would have happened had we landed within range of heavy machine-gun fire.

Colonel Campbell was one of the few brigade commanders who ended their career without a promotion to general.

General Putnam was helpful, however, when he noted that the order for the 2/12th Cav to attack toward Hue was not in the handwriting of Major General Tolson, although the order was copied on his personal notepaper. I later learned from (then) Major Don Bowman, Campbell's executive officer, that the handwriting belonged to Colonel Ross. I assume the order was dictated by General Tolson, but I can't confirm that. Bowman noted that his relationship with Ross cooled significantly later, for reasons that were unclear to Bowman. My suspicion is that Ross felt Bowman was too loyal to Campbell, in light of Tolson's displeasure. Ross died in February 2003.

"Candidly, the original book made the Old Man

[Campbell] out to be inept and timid and me to be dumb," Bowman wrote me. "Neither is true. Later, before Khe Sanh, I stood beside Campbell while Tolson screamed at him at a range of about two feet about our plan of attack. . . . Campbell was adamant that we should secure the dominating terrain before moving out. Tolson and Ross stomped out of the TOC [tactical operations center], but we did it the Old Man's way with minimal casualties. The 3d Brigade was chosen after Tet to lead into Khe Sanh. . . . If they had shit to step in they sent us in first, and you don't send losers into the tough stuff first."

While writing the book I tried to steer away from personality clashes, sticking to the facts as I found them. From an analytical viewpoint, this works fine. But I don't want to convey the impression that lines of authority in combat are seamless or harmonious, particularly when the dust settles.

Friends tell me that the value of *The Lost Battalion* is that it has timeless qualities, beyond the war in Vietnam, about men under fire. This wasn't my intent, but I'm flattered by the observation. My gratitude is boundless to those who lived through Tet '68 and contributed to this book by word, deed, or endurance.

THE LOST
BATTALION
OF TET

CHAPTER 1

AMERICA'S BEST

WE SAW THE CHOPPER APPROACH.

The bastard rocketed us instead of the enemy positions. One soldier died instantly, and four more were wounded. The enemy, in a treeline two hundred yards in front of us, were unscathed.

When the ARVN gunners, after shooting two rounds, refused our next request to fire because the hamlet in front of us was considered friendly, Lieutenant Colonel Sweet, our battalion commander, called Colonel Campbell, the brigade commander, to explain our dilemma. Campbell said he was under pressure from division to keep us moving and ordered us to continue the attack toward Hue. It was a legal order, so there was no point in arguing.

Every man present intuitively realized he was like a

sailor ordered to stay at his station on a sinking ship with no lifeboats. We were going to have to attack across an open field into foxholes and bunkers prepared solely for the purpose of discouraging anyone from getting closer. There would be no artillery support, air strikes, or helicopter rocket runs to soften the NVA positions, no smoke to conceal our attack. There was no possibility of pulling

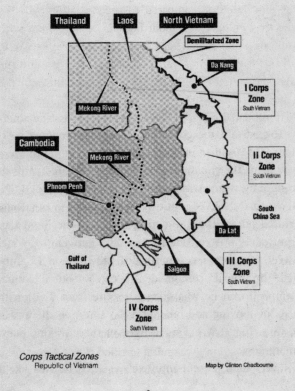

Corps Tactical Zones
Republic of Vietnam

Map by Clinton Chadbourne

2

back and selecting another route, or even attacking indirectly from a flank using firepower and maneuver. No, this was going to be a frontal assault where every man would be exposed to lethal fire from the instant he got up until the dug-in enemy facing us either withdrew or was killed.

The difference in size between the 2/12th Cavalry Battalion in 1968 and the Light Brigade in 1856 was slight: our four hundred compared to their six hundred. It's true they charged for about one and a half miles with cannons on the front, right, and left, and we only had to advance two hundred yards or so, but both we and the Light Brigade offered human-wave targets that put the defenders at little risk.

It was quiet when we began to move across the otherwise nondescript field.

The ground had been cultivated at one time, so there was no place to hide. There weren't even shell craters. From behind our trees we looked out over the mud to see the enemy reinforcing their positions, ready to receive us shoulder-to-shoulder. It was the first time I used the new binoculars purchased on a recent R&R in Tokyo.

I had the feeling it was going to be my last.

THIS INCIDENT ON FEBRUARY 3, 1968, JUST OUTSIDE HUE was something that should have never taken place. There was no satisfactory or compelling reason for a U.S. infantry battalion to assault a fortified North Vietnamese Army force two hundred yards away over an open field with no artillery or air support. The defenders had every advantage. The only support available was a helicopter gunship that mistakenly attacked the U.S. forces instead of the NVA. A steady drizzle and heavy, low clouds meant further support from the air was unlikely for the foreseeable future. As the Americans started moving across the field just before noon, every man was a target. The Americans fired their rifles furiously as they rushed to the other side, but the NVA defenders were barely scathed. The NVA commander—cool and firmly in control—allowed the U.S. battalion to reach the treeline and one hundred yards beyond, withdrawing his forces slightly so the Americans could gain a foothold. His blocking forces were under orders to let the Americans in, so they would be encouraged to continue toward Hue, believing the withdrawing NVA had been defeated.

In fact, the NVA commander set a trap. As Americans labored hard to establish a hasty perimeter and consolidate their force before moving on, the NVA closed in behind the battalion with a three-to-one combat advantage in manpower and firepower. In one horrible instant, Lieutenant Colonel Sweet, the U.S. commander, realized that he was surrounded and confronted by two devastating realities: he could neither move nor maneuver his forces, and any notion of reinforcement or resupply was out of the question. No field manuals, training, or previous experience prepared him for what was to become an ultimate test of human endurance.

Nine hours after first making contact with the enemy,

U.S. artillery units arrived and began firing to support the solidly surrounded infantry battalion. Ammunition available to the artillery was barely sufficient to ensure the outnumbered force was not instantly overrun, but as time passed and casualties mounted, annihilation was never ruled out by the youthful battalion commander, especially as he saw the perimeter shrink to ever-smaller circles. The size was a function of riflemen available to mount a defense. One of the battalion's four companies, normally 171 men, was down to 40.

During the next afternoon, the entrapped men saw that their fate was ordained: death or captivity. Help from higher headquarters was neither offered nor available in the time remaining. Artillery support became increasingly dangerous as the distance between attackers and defenders inexorably closed. Exhaustion, no food at all, and very little ammunition added to the despair.

The battalion commander, Dick Sweet, realizing now he was on his own to make whatever decision would save the most soldiers, pulled in his company commanders to give them a say in the options. After every commander spoke his mind, Sweet made the decision to make a run for it that night where encircling forces seemed to be the weakest. It was a gamble with high stakes. If the maneuver failed to take the enemy by surprise, the fight was over.

The dead and equipment were left behind to give those escaping every chance to succeed. Ruses were contrived to fool the NVA for a few needed minutes as the battalion started to move in single file toward a hilltop to the west. Failure meant every man for himself, an unspoken but understood reality. For the time being, the wounded would stay with the column. But they, too, faced an uncertain future.

That night, whatever force looks after infantrymen was with the remnants of the 2d Battalion, 12th Cavalry. The tattered, limping column made it to a mountaintop where the NVA could not follow. Although they didn't know it until much later, the Americans had stumbled into the headquarters of the NVA forces attacking and holding Hue. When the battalion set out toward Hue on February 3, it was supposed to take only a day to reach the city walls. It took nearly a month.

DURING THE VIETNAM WAR, U.S. SOLDIERS WERE PROvided more and better support than any previous fighting force in our nation's history. Supply systems pumped in countless tons of war matériel of every description, and a well-greased distribution network ensured there was always enough firepower on hand to support the commander's scheme of maneuver, regardless of what it took. So plentiful was the support that soldiers and commanders too, with just cause, came to take it for granted. Despite occasional lapses, there was always more than enough to feed the war machine as many beans and bullets as it could digest.

Artillery pieces could be blown up, helicopters shot down, and trucks destroyed, but there was always enough matériel in the pipeline to provide a replacement in a matter of days, if not hours. Ammunition dumps occasionally took a direct hit and filled the sky with incredible pyrotechnics, but the system was so robust that men fighting the ground war were rarely affected. A world-class supermarket chain couldn't do any better.

But when the system went haywire, it went truly and disastrously sour, triggering first surprise, then shock. On even rarer occasions, commanders who had the power to move battalions and brigades from one place to another momentarily forgot about the rupture in the pipeline and issued movement orders as if nothing had happened. The first order, such as sending us toward Hue, may have been innocuous enough, seemingly insignificant at the time. Yet the results after all events were played out were disastrous. Not merely sad or unfortunate, but tragic.

I use the word "tragic" advisedly, because ill-advised attack orders can trigger a chain of events that once started cannot be stopped. For many unfortunate soldiers at the end of the chain the result was death, often senseless death. That no single person could be held responsible adds to the tragic dimension.

In the case of Vietnam, all lives were lost in vain, but some more than others. If tragedy can be measured one life at a time, the story is indeed worth recording.

THIS TRAGIC TALE BEGAN ON FEBRUARY 1, 1968—THE beginning of the Tet holiday—when Major General John J. Tolson III, commander of the 1st Air Cavalry Division, was directed by higher command to send an infantry battalion toward Hue to help take pressure off besieged U.S. Marines trapped in the city who were holding on by the skin of their teeth.

Tolson alerted the commander of his 3d Brigade, Colonel Hubert S. (Bill) Campbell, who in turn called one of his battalion commanders, Lieutenant Colonel Richard S. Sweet, commanding the 2d Battalion, 12th Cavalry, or 2/12th Cav. Campbell read Sweet the order from a small sheet of Tolson's personal notepaper in the general's own handwriting.

Mission
(1) Seal off city on west & north with right flank based on Song Huong River.
(2) Destroy enemy forces attempting to either reinforce or escape from Hue Citadel.

Twenty-five years later Campbell still had this message among his personal papers saved from the war, folded in quarters so he could stick it in his pocket.

Until we received our order to move toward Hue, things were pretty quiet at Camp Evans, the new headquarters of the 1st Air Cavalry Division about fifteen miles north of Hue near Highway 1. Camp Evans was the new temporary station of the 3d Brigade. Just the day before, Campbell recorded in his diary several administrative matters, including the importance of "each day each man filling five sandbags." The Tet truce was just about

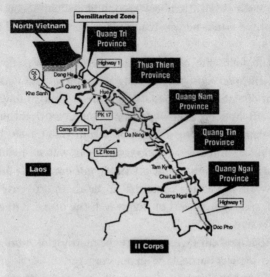

I Corps Tactical Zone

Map by Clinton Chadbourne

to begin, so it was hardly surprising that everyone acted as if the war would slow down for a few days.

At 3:40 A.M. on Wednesday, January 31, the NVA attacked and occupied Hue, bringing the same panic to the northern part of the country that had taken hold of the southern regions the day before when Nha Trang and seven other cities were attacked. These assaults were launched one day prematurely, due to an NVA command and control fiasco. By the end of January 30, many observers assumed that the NVA threat had come and gone. They were stunned by the attacks on January 31. Tolson got an inkling how serious the situation was in Hue by late Wednesday afternoon, and could not have been too surprised when he was requested to help out on February 1.

The following afternoon the 2/12th Cav was flown by helicopters to a tiny friendly Vietnamese base within sight of Hue called PK-17. We prepared to march toward the city as soon as the sun came up the next morning. The details of getting to Hue were left to Sweet. I was the battalion's intelligence officer, but there was no reliable information about enemy activity in our immediate area, so Sweet picked the route that made the most sense to him, staying just west of Highway 1, the Street Without Joy.

Because things were so quiet the morning of February 2, no one was particularly anxious or worried. We figured we'd be at the walls of Hue within a day and pick off the VC one by one with rifle fire as they scurried to get out of our way. By nightfall we'd be drinking beer in the Marine compound.

PK-17 was a fairly primitive place by U.S. standards, only about the size of a football field, no more than a few tin shacks and a couple of palm trees surrounded by some scraggly barbed wire. If I objected to the mud, trash, and garbage, I enjoyed the silence of the ARVN (Army of the Republic of Vietnam) compound. Camp Evans had been noisy. Men shouted and swore at the top of their lungs just to be heard over the cacophony of helicopters, generators, radios, and vehicles.

There were a couple of troublesome points, however.

The worst was that our packs, or knapsacks, had been left behind when we were airlifted to PK-17. The brigade plan called for the men to be moved in first, with packs immediately to follow. The purpose was to get all of the men forward as soon as possible. Leaving the packs behind meant we could get an extra soldier or two in each Huey helicopter. But by the time the battalion made it to PK-17, the weather had started to close in fast. Campbell decided to put off bringing in the packs until first light, when the flying weather might be better.

The weather was arguably the crappiest I'd ever seen in Vietnam. You could see only about fifty feet in any direction. Then it started to drizzle and the wind picked up. Wind-chill was unknown in those days, but it must have been in the low forties, making us miss our packs—and the sweaters in them—even more.

The infantry is accustomed to lousy weather. Under normal conditions it would have been no big deal to pull a poncho out of the pack and stretch it over a foxhole for a good night's sleep. But no packs meant no ponchos. And no ponchos meant sleeping in a bathtub with the cold water running.

Maybe the sun rose the next day, maybe not. We had no way of telling. The fog lifted slightly, but not much. The packs still had not arrived when we set out on foot for Hue. With luck, they'd be delivered before nightfall. We assumed we were carrying small arms ammunition to meet foreseeable needs.

The greater worry was that our supporting artillery

11

battery had not arrived at PK-17 the night before, again because of the weather. There were two tubes of ARVN 105mm artillery in the compound that we might count on in a pinch. They didn't belong to us, but we figured we could borrow them, especially since they weren't firing missions for anyone else. This seemed okay at the time, because we expected to walk into Hue unopposed. Besides, we could always count on rocket-firing helicopters to be overhead in a matter of minutes after we called them. If nothing else, the 1st Air Cav had plenty of helicopters.

We started moving toward Hue the morning of February 3, marching in a diamond formation like they teach at Fort Benning's Infantry School. We were confident, if a little uneasy. After walking just a few minutes, someone spotted what might be enemy positions in the woods before us, so we called for a rocket ship, or ARA for aerial rocket artillery.

It wasn't a good idea. As I explained earlier, the bastard rocketed us instead of the enemy. They call it "friendly fire."

We wished for artillery too, but the best we could hope for was that it would arrive soon by helicopter at PK-17. When the artillery battery finally arrived and started firing for us after dark about 6:00 P.M., we had been in face-to-face contact with the enemy for nearly nine hours. Until then, we had little to fight with beyond our rifles and fists. Is it any wonder we felt like naked pilgrims in a tiger cage?

CAST OF THE PAST

LOCATION IS IMPORTANT TO THIS STORY, BECAUSE THE closer you were to North Vietnam, the greater the threat from the North Vietnamese Army (NVA). The 2d Battalion, 12th Cavalry (or, more commonly, 2/12th Cav) operated in the northernmost area called the I Corps, Tactical Zone. The northern portion of I Corps abutted North Vietnam near Dong Ha, while the western part of I Corps was adjacent to Laos. The NVA had no problem moving forces into I Corps from the west, because they could move through Laos pretty much as they pleased. So far as I know, the NVA never came into I Corps over the fences separating the two countries near Dong Ha. Instead, they infiltrated into the area from the western flank where the border runs unmarked for several hundred miles through uninviting mountains, forests, and jungle territory, maybe best suited for the tigers who, during ordinary times, hunt and prowl unmolested there. Perhaps Special Forces operated on the border, but the terrain was considered unsuitable for regular forces like 2/12th Cav.

The nearest we got to the border was a camp on the eastern edge of the mountains and jungle separating Vietnam and Laos, a place we called Landing Zone Ross, named after our commander, Lieutenant Colonel M. Collier Ross. LZ Ross was an outcropping of rock in the Que Son Valley. The valley had been cleared for farmland; it was the last cultivated area our side of the border. The Que Son Valley was a strategic corridor. As such, it was a natural avenue for the NVA to move eastward, and a good place for us to stop them. Because LZ Ross was only twenty-five miles west of Da Nang, we were close to our supply base and brigade headquarters at LZ Baldy. A road connected Que Son with Da Nang, but I don't recall anyone anxious to travel by wheels when helicopters were so abundant. In fact, my assistant and I were the only ones to travel frequently by jeep between LZ Ross and the hamlet of Que Son, less than one-half mile away. Once a major from brigade came to visit and we took him to Que Son, but he vowed he'd never make the trip again.

Major A. Earle Spry was the brigade intelligence officer—my counterpart—and I respected him a lot. When he said "no more jeep trips with Krohn," I wondered if he knew something I didn't.

The real reason we went to the village was not to visit

the refugee center, but to trade with the U.S. advisory detachment, which seemed to have an endless supply of beer. I never revealed the source of my beer to anyone, especially anyone senior. What the advisory detachment wanted from me in return for the beer was assurance that I would help get them artillery fire if they were attacked, because the only defense they had was their own small arms—rifles, grenade launchers, and machine guns.

LZ Ross was on the western edge of the piedmont between the mountains and the South China Sea. About seventy thousand people lived in the Que Son region, but only one-third were under control of the Saigon government. Rice growing was the major activity with two crops a year, one in spring, another in fall. The worst weather for our operations was in December, when morning fog often reduced ceilings to five hundred feet and visibility to just two miles.

The brigade to which our battalion was assigned was commanded by Colonel Hubert S. Campbell, who later took a lot of heat over what happened to us at Hue. Campbell impressed me as a pleasant fellow, more academic than bellicose. In fact, he served in New Guinea during World War II, and spent three years in Korea during the Korean War with the 187th Airborne Infantry Regimental Combat Team as a battalion and brigade operations officer. He sported a thin moustache and always smoked a pipe, which made him look something like David Niven. Campbell was put in the job by the division commander, Major General John Tolson. The two knew each other from Fort Rucker, Alabama, the Army's aviation center, and apparently got along well. One former subordinate remembers Campbell as likeable enough, but not very assertive, an officer "who rose to high rank without really being tested." I never got to know Campbell well, because captains don't talk directly to colonels. Not unless the lieutenant colonel the captain works for knows about it beforehand or, better yet, is with him to make sure nothing gets screwed up.

The 2/12th Cav and the rest of the 3d Brigade were temporarily assigned to beef up the Americal Division, while the rest of the 1st Air Cavalry Division operated farther south in I Corps in the vicinity of Bong Son. The Americal was commanded by Major General Samuel J. Koster, who enjoyed fame of a sort when the My Lai story broke. The unit that shot up the My Lai civilians was part of the Americal. I recall seeing General Koster a couple of times at LZ Ross, but never spoke with him. If I had, I might have offered him some of the precious Smithfield ham that I kept in a pillowcase suspended from a tree. We always tried to show hospitality to visitors, whether they were VIPs or not. After the rest of the 1st Air Cavalry Division was ordered north into the I Corps area in January 1968, to counter the growing NVA threat through infiltration routes in the Khe Sanh area, I never saw Koster again.

Lieutenant Colonel Ross was a bit of an enigma. If I were asked then for someone to play the part of a battalion commander in the movies, I couldn't have thought of anyone better for the part than Ross. He was a West Point graduate, Class of '49, and spoke with a deep Missouri voice. At six feet five inches, he was only a few inches shorter than Peter the Great, but thinner. Ross was unfailingly diplomatic, polite but not condescending, and seemed to weigh every word carefully. Except for the captain he relieved, Ross was highly regarded by his company commanders for candor and understanding, particularly in combat situations. I was not surprised to learn that his external appearance masked a roaring fire of ambition. He ended up retiring from the Army as a three-star lieutenant general.

There were two majors in the battalion—the executive officer and the operations officer. The battalion XO was Don Bowman. Both he and Ross were parachute enthusiasts and seemed to understand each other's needs quite well. Tom Ritchie was the operations officer, or S-3. The thing I remember best about Ritchie was his fear of flying with Ross's eventual replacement, Lieutenant Colonel Bob Gregory. When the war heated up, Ritchie was at a significant disadvantage because of Gregory's dislike.

Captain Bob Helvey, of Charleston, West Virginia, was commanding headquarters company when I arrived in the battalion. At LZ Ross we became close friends, a relationship that has lasted nearly twenty-five years. I was a captain too, the battalion's intelligence officer, or S-2, having been discovered by Bowman in the division's public affairs office, a real pesthole. Helvey ran the day-to-day operations at Ross, a fairly difficult job, but one he had to perform until command of a line company opened up. The LZ was about the size of three football fields, a self-contained small city, and Helvey was a mayor of sorts. He juggled the competing interests as well as anyone, although not yet showing the stuff that made him a legend in both Tet battles.

Helvey was a small-town boy with strong country traces. He walked methodically, like a mountain man. It would be almost impossible to pick Helvey's face from a crowd as unusual in any respect. His height was average too, about five feet eleven inches. There was nothing extraordinary about his ice-blue eyes, unless they were squinting at you—usually a sign that a storm was brewing inside. His hair was ordinarily blond, but usually cropped too close to show much color. He never carried a comb. During periods of sustained combat like the Battle of Hue, when he was unable to get it cut, his disheveled hair made him look like a truant schoolboy just before going home to take his punishment. His face was neither pretty nor ugly. "Rugged" is the word I'd pick. As soldiers go, he was a natural.

Whatever I have to say about Bowman later, I'll never forget how he threw me a lifesaver when I needed it most by recruiting me into the 2/12th Cav from the public affairs office. Think of all the problems a military unit could have during the Vietnam era: the public affairs office had them all.

3

CURTAIN RAISER

LZ ROSS WAS ABOUT THE SAME AS ANY FIREBASE IN Vietnam—maybe a couple of football fields surrounded by barbed wire. Since we never stayed at one firebase very long, usually no more than a month, little care was put into tidiness. We pissed into tubes stuck into the ground just deep enough so they wouldn't tip over in a strong wind. The tubes were improvised from metal containers used to ship artillery ammunition. Urine collected near the surface in shallow ponds with an ineffable aroma that complemented the burning shit from the dozen outhouses sprinkled around LZ Ross. Burning was the most convenient way to dispose of human waste, although the oily fumes were gagging. It's no wonder that LZ Ross smelled like a latrine.

We moved into LZ Ross in October. Our brigade was

sent into I Corps so the Marines could concentrate their forces nearer Vietnam's northern border. We scoured the Que Son Valley adjacent to LZ Ross with thoroughness, occasionally making contact with the enemy. One day we uncovered an NVA training site and confiscated more than three tons of rice, twenty pounds of salt, and fifteen pounds of marijuana. We also found benches and a blackboard, evidence that the facility was not for the use of local farmers. We assumed the pot was for medicinal use, given the discipline of the NVA forces.

If October was quiet, November was even slower. The after-action report noted only one friendly killed and one wounded. We killed forty-two NVA "by body count" and captured fourteen tons of rice. While we were proud to be serving our country overseas, the results achieved scarcely justified keeping an infantry battalion on the frontier of civilization, regardless of how dangerous the Que Son Valley could be. We almost forgot the message— "The Que Son Valley can be dangerous"—that the Marines impressed on us before they departed.

Time went by slowly for me too, and I used to welcome the opportunity to spend time with the companies maneuvering in the valley, especially when they discovered a cave or tunnel. As the intelligence officer, I could claim the right to be the first one in. One day I crawled through a tunnel several hundred yards long, armed with only a flashlight and .45 caliber pistol. Just after making a ninety-degree turn, I found myself facing a bundle of several sticks of dynamite, with wires leading around the next comer. Withdrawing as fast as I could, I called for engineers to destroy the tunnel with explosives, and never claimed the right to be first in again.

The greatest danger I was in was not from the enemy but from Captain Bill Scudder, commander of Company C. After I berated him over the command net—a radio frequency monitored by everyone in the battalion—for not properly tagging a prisoner that several of his men risked their lives to capture, he was out to get me. If I had behaved with such rudeness face-to-face, he might have even shot me on the spot for pushing a bureaucratic response down his throat.

December arrived without notice or fanfare.

Late one afternoon in early December—just as the fog was beginning to collect in Que Son Valley, blowing in wisps over quiet fields and silent knolls—two senior NVA officers in neat khaki uniforms emerged from the bushes where they had waited patiently near a mountaintop for an opportunity to study at leisure the panorama that unfolded before them several thousand feet below.

As the two officers walked into the small clearing, they might have frightened a bird or two nesting in the peaks. No need to worry. Rolling out their maps on the soft, moist ground, they probably never considered the possibility that they were the first men to set foot on this soil. They knew what their task was.

Setting their caps aside in order to make it easier to adjust their Russian-made binoculars, hefty but eminently serviceable, the two were oblivious to everything but the task before them. They were professionals. Twisting the maps around to conform with the landscape, they compared the maps to their notes and scribbled hasty remarks in the borders. With the wind rising a little as the sun settled out of sight over their right shoulders, one of the slight, clean-shaven officers, probably the junior in rank, fell to one knee to keep the maps from fluttering while the other jotted his impressions in a notebook. Everything was precise. Wasting no time trying to complete the work before their view was obscured by darkness and fog, and knowing that there might never be another opportunity to continue the reconnaissance before making their report to superiors in an underground headquarters deep in the mountains to the west, they had only an instant to sense the presence of two helicopter gunships bearing down upon them from above.

It's not certain who saw whom first, but it didn't make any difference. It's probable that the two officers sensed the hopelessness of their predicament and accepted the inevitability of their fortune stoically, an accident of fate they couldn't avoid. They didn't panic. Considering the range of the helicopters, they may have had an instant to wince at the bright muzzle flashes from the swirling machine guns before darkness overcame them. The maps were covered with blood, but it didn't matter.

These pilots were professionals, too. While one of the helicopter gunships circled protectively overhead, the other pilot landed his ship next to the remains of the two intruders. There was just enough room to set the helicopter down firmly on its tube-like skids, but no time for hesitation. It was a courageous act, but not reckless.

These pilots were from D, or Delta, Troop, 1st Squadron, 9th Cavalry, the division's aerial reconnaissance force. They knew that if they kept to one side of a mountain, their engine noise could not be heard over the crest. The sound of the powerful turbojets bounced backward rather than flowing over the peak into the next ravine.

The names of the two dead officers from North Vietnam may have been known at the time to our intelligence officers. They have been forgotten now, although their skeletons probably still rest on the mountain overlooking the Que Son Valley. However, the trophies of the kill—the maps, the plans, the documents, and the highly prized pistols—are not forgotten, for they changed the course of history, at least as far as the 2/12th Cav is concerned.

The trophies—minus the pistols, presumably, which were spoils of war—were turned over to Major Spry at 3d Brigade headquarters at LZ Baldy for analysis. The pilots didn't know if they had captured anything important or not, and anyway, they needed sleep and relaxation before starting out on the next day's mission. Major Spry was one of the finest intelligence officers in the business and enjoyed the confidence of many people far senior in rank. More revealing of his character, he was idolized by those junior to him for his quiet ways and steady manner. He was almost always serious, which made us wonder what he knew that we didn't. He wore glasses, and his gray eyes never seemed to blink. The fact is, he was always concentrating. As a hallmark of his intelligence, he treated routine matters routinely and gave urgent matters the attention they deserved. John Paul Vann, the legendary counterinsurgency expert, was his half-brother.

Because the major's best interpreter was unavailable when the pilots turned over the materials they had just brought in, Spry asked me over the radio if he could send a helicopter to LZ Ross to pick up Sergeant Phung, my interpreter. "I'll get him back to you first thing in the morning," Spry said over the secure radio which scrambled our conversation electronically. "I think we killed the commander of the 3d Regiment, 2d NVA Division," he added. "I don't know yet who the other guy is, but he was carrying a sketch that looks an awful lot like LZ Ross." I sent Phung.

At first light the next morning, I called for a helicopter to take me to Baldy to see what he had. I met with Spry in his little office. He looked like he hadn't slept. His light beard made it hard to tell if he had shaved.

"Only once in a war do you find something like this," Spry said, motioning eagerly to the five pounds of documents spread over his desk. "I haven't translated everything yet, but in a nutshell we have here the plans for an attack on LZ Ross. After they hit you—or maybe at the same time—they intend to cut the country in two."

"Do you have an idea when?" I asked. "How much time do we have?" It was December 6.

"I haven't gotten to that yet," Spry replied. "But one

thing's for sure. Once they plan an attack, it's only a question of time until they try to pull it off. It could be tonight or it could be months from now." His private guess was that they'd be ready by December 23.

"Wow," I thought, "it sounds like real excitement." A juvenile but honest reaction. Neither Spry nor I made a connection with Tet, which was still weeks away.

"You know, Krohn, we hit paydirt last night," he added. "After we killed the first two officers, we sent in another team and they killed fifteen more. We positively identified one of these as the political officer of the 2d NVA Division. He was carrying identification, and his name matched up with our roster of their headquarters staff." What Spry didn't tell me was that one of the maps we captured was a U.S. Army map retrieved by the NVA from one of our helicopters when it was shot down earlier.

"The plan was in great detail, soundly conceived, and well supplied. And they alluded to the use of new and unusual support," Colonel Campbell recalled later. "At that time we had not encountered any extensive enemy use of rockets or automatic antiaircraft weapons. Analysis of the plan, of course, gave us great advantage. He [the NVA] had a detailed time schedule in the plan; this time schedule took him through December 23. We assumed that he would probably attack at that time and he would then take advantage of the Christmas truce to recover and withdraw. However, his plan stressed that he was to destroy the 3d Brigade and to secure the Que Son Valley.

25

Later events were to show that this offensive action was to tie in with the upcoming Tet Offensive."

I rushed back to LZ Ross and reported to Lieutenant Colonel Gregory, our new battalion commander, gushing out everything at once. The thought of an impending battle put him in a state of high excitement too.

Our security at LZ Ross was strengthened by an attachment of tanks and armored personnel carriers from B, or Bravo, Troop, 1st Squadron, 1st Cavalry. They arrived one day with a couple of dozen vehicles, which we sprinkled around the firebase inside our wire. The terrain outside the wire wasn't really suitable for mechanized operations. Tanks could move only single-file down roads that were scarcely more than cattle paths. Crossing flooded rice paddies was out of the question. It wasn't so bad during the dry seasons, but the terrain was nothing like the rolling plains that tankers like best.

The fact is, the B Troopers were like fish out of water. Tanks had no role in our end of the valley; they couldn't maneuver effectively in this terrain. Yet the troopers themselves were good people, and I came to like the commander, Captain John Barovetto, a Boston native. Once I sent a newspaper reporter over to B Troop to spend the night. As he departed the next day to go on an operation with one of our companies, he left Barovetto a bottle of Scotch to hold until he returned. Barovetto assured the young reporter that the bottle would be in good hands.

"Krohn, how good are your hands?" he asked me later in the day.

"Great. Why?"

"Well, if you've got good hands, you know what to do with this."

Gregory was not enthusiastically accepted into the battalion, even though he was the commander. At first, there was resistance that stemmed from lingering loyalties to Colonel Ross. Then, there was the matter of drinking: the battalion staff had to sign a pledge that we would not drink more than two cans of beer a day, and no hard liquor at all. I signed the pledge to make him happy, with no intention of honoring it, provided the opportunity arose—"Only a fool obeys a stupid order." In fact, we were lucky to have good drinking water, much less a can or two of cold beer.

Always wearing a pair of tight-fitting black gloves—a cavalry affectation, and no small feat in a tropical climate—Gregory would perform most of the battalion's reconnaissance missions himself in a helicopter provided for that purpose each day. He would persuade the pilots to fly at treetop level and zoom over the valley while he searched for targets of opportunity in the free-fire zone. Any targets.

The matter was brought home to me one day by Captain Helvey, by then commander of Company A. He called me on his radio from somewhere in the free-fire zone, using a special frequency which was not monitored by the battalion commander or anyone on the staff. I liked to conduct intelligence business privately.

"Charlie," he said, "I've got a big problem. The Old Man [Gregory] says he just flew over my area and complained he wasn't seeing enough smoke." It was the practice under Gregory to burn everything in the zone that could be used by the NVA, and to shoot almost everything that moved. "Worse yet," Helvey went on, "I saw an old man walking around near here and Gregory wants me to bring the old man in for questioning. I know damn well that the old farmer is not VC. We ran into him about an hour back and he told me that he would just as soon die as leave his home, which was pretty much destroyed anyway. I don't want to force him to move. What do you think?" I agreed with Helvey that there was no intelligence value to be gained by bringing in such people.

"Despite what the Old Man says, I'm not going to bring him in and I'm not going to burn him out. If anything happens, will you support me?"

"Bob," I said, "I can't think of a better issue to take a stand on, if it comes to that. Go ahead and leave him."

This one episode, seemingly so inconsequential, cemented our relationship for life.

A few minutes later Gregory reported to the battalion TOC (tactical operations center) that he had just shot a Viet Cong from his helicopter. Helvey heard the call and decided to move to the site to recover any documents. What he found was the old man.

Helvey was so angered by this event that he made plans to press charges against Gregory, regardless of the cost to his own career. My hunch is that Gregory would have beat the charges, because the man was in the free-fire zone, where, technically, anything goes. It would not have been a moral defense but it would have sufficed. But Helvey would have been badly tainted. After the court-martial, nobody would want him. Helvey would have been asked to leave the Army—an offer he was prepared to accept.

Why did Gregory commit this senseless act? Helvey feels that Gregory had been trained to fight Russians in World War II at the Fulda Gap, where situations are black-and-white. He was not prepared for the subtleties of a guerrilla war.

Before returning to Vietnam on his second tour in 1967, Helvey had studied everything he could get his hands on. "I read everything I could find about their tactics," Helvey remembered. "That's why I was comfortable. I knew what they were going to do." Gregory, on the other hand, simply wasn't prepared.

Gregory was spared the embarrassment of an investigation when he was killed before Helvey could carry out his plan. A fortunate side effect, however cruel, is that Helvey stayed with the battalion through the entire Tet campaign where his valor saved the lives of hundreds in the 2/12th Cav. Gregory was later awarded a posthumous Distinguished Service Cross. His bravery, after all, was incontestable.

4

REASONABLE WORRIES

BY MID-DECEMBER 1967 WE WERE DEEP INTO THE winter monsoon season. The days were short and the nights cold. I even had pajamas made from an old parachute, and the soldiers who guarded the perimeter were alerted not to fire on the "white ghost" who occasionally emerged from his hole in the middle of the night to scamper in bare feet toward the piss tube sticking out of the ground near the headquarters bunker a few yards away.

Contact became more regular as Tet approached, so we increased our alert measures by patrolling in a somewhat broader pattern and by firing more artillery into likely enemy approaches and assembly areas. One of my jobs was to pick targets for those nightly fire missions, based on my assumption of where the enemy might be hiding. Lieutenant Colonel Gregory made the final decisions, but he always accepted my recommendations. My guess was as good as anyone's. Normally, I selected mountain trails I thought the NVA would use for reconnaissance, trying to put myself in the place of the NVA intelligence officer with the same job I had. This was not a scientific activity. Major Spry would call several times a week on the secure radio with suggestions for me to consider. I never ignored his advice, because he had access to clandestine sources, probably radio intercepts that were often reliable. Anyone with a Zenith Transoceanic radio could listen to NVA broadcasts, but there was no point in trying unless you knew which frequencies to tune to and had someone standing by to translate and interpret. These radios were sold in the PX, and I brought one with me to the 2/12th Cav so I could keep up with what was happening in Vietnam and the rest of the world. The only other source of news was *Stars & Stripes*. But we could never count on getting copies on a regular basis. Moreover, we were always suspicious of censorship.

The nearer Tet got, the more everyone at LZ Ross started worrying about if and when we would be attacked. We showed the same preoccupation as marooned sailors waiting for a wisp of smoke on the horizon. As the intelligence officer, I was supposed to be the specialist, but I only knew that the 2d NVA Division was operating in Que Son Valley from bases deep in the mountains to the west. Everyone knew that much and demanded more details, which I couldn't supply. I knew that our battalion would be a threat to their supply lines if they tried to march unobserved around LZ Ross in the no-man's-land just outside our area of responsibility on their way toward Da Nang, where there were targets far more important than our tiny firebase. Our position meant they would certainly hit us before beginning any big offensive in the coastal area. We were in their way, and we knew it.

Still, as hard as we tried, we couldn't locate any signs of significant buildup. From time to time we made contact with small NVA units, but nothing serious. I was puzzled, and so was everyone, including Spry, the brigade intelligence officer. We knew the NVA units had to have a mission of some kind beyond keeping us guessing what they were up to. We considered and discarded all of the reasons that came to mind as either too weak or too timid to make any sense.

Now I know the NVA avoided major contacts because they didn't want to sap their strength before launching their big attack on LZ Ross later. Of course, they had recon parties keeping track of our movements, but their main force units stayed hidden in the mountains, training and rehearsing until the last moment. The 2d NVA Division commander hoped he could first destroy LZ Ross and the forces sent to reinforce us. Once our forces in the Que Son Valley were eliminated, he would have a chance to attack Da Nang and cut the country in two. It would be a history-making event, so he was anxious not to tip his hand too soon.

While it was impossible to evaluate the effectiveness of our H&I (harassment and interdiction) fires because we had no charter to patrol back in the mountains— and, frankly, we didn't solicit permission either—there never seemed to be a shortage of ammunition available for these missions. We had all we needed, thanks to the Americal Division. The Marines who had preceded us at LZ Ross were limited to two rounds per tube per day; we fired hundreds. This may sound wasteful, but the noise of artillery blasting away day and night provided a measure of psychological comfort.

We also hoped that the Air Force bomber runs would strengthen our defenses, particularly the B-52 missions that shook the ground with the thunder of a thousand volcanoes. Air Force Phantom jets came by occasionally, but they didn't fly in our area unless the weather was clear and they had nothing better to do. The bombing missions may have done some good, but considering the NVA forces available to attack LZ Ross, most of their effect must have been psychological too.

If we had the means to search the forests and mountains near the Laotian border, we probably would have found the 2d NVA, but on their turf, ready and waiting. That would have been far too big a task for our battalion, or even for all of the 3d Brigade, because it would have meant moving to the area on the ground, and flank security for a force that size would have had to be nearly as large as the force itself. The terrain lent itself to ambush. Maybe we could have moved smaller forces nearer the border by helicopter, but this was never considered, to the best of my knowledge, because such an operation was beyond our capabilities. Even if we had attacked in force, the NVA could have pulled back into Laos. We couldn't have followed. The policy at the time was to respect international borders with our main force units. In any case, the wisdom was to let them attack us, where odds favored the defender.

Ross was not the commander when the attack came, having been replaced in November by Lieutenant Colonel Gregory. Major General John J. Tolson III, the 1st Air Cavalry Division commander, selected Ross to be the division G-3, or operations officer. Everyone was fond of Ross, and if we regretted seeing him go, we knew the G-3 job called for an officer with a bright future, which meant a promotion was in store for him soon.

Gregory arrived by helicopter the same day Ross departed. The first thing he did was to call the staff together to give us his command philosophy. I listened with full attention. Afterward I had the sense that "this man is too anxious to succeed." His intention to fly regularly into the free-fire zone worried me. Later, he proved true to his word. Not everyone liked flying with Gregory, however. Several officers went to extraordinary lengths to avoid Gregory when he was in a flying mood. One major who went back to An Khe was so apprehensive about having to fly with Gregory again that he would not return to LZ Ross. The artillery liaison officer, Captain Dan Redner, was so shaken about having to fly with Gregory that he had to be replaced with another officer. Captain Dane Maddox, our artillery battery commander, was no more enthusiastic than Redner, but professionally he couldn't afford to let Gregory know his feelings. It didn't help his morale when Gregory told him one day, "Either I'll do well enough as a battalion commander to make general, or else I'll get killed." When Maddox flew with Gregory, he always carried extra ammunition.

Major Bowman, the S-3, also had to fly with Gregory, and wasn't any happier about it than Maddox or Redner. One day Bowman tried to caution Gregory that he was using his helicopter the way others used a tank. "But there is a difference," Bowman explained, hoping Gregory would get the point. "The skin on this helicopter is no thicker than your shirt." But his comment didn't change anything.

5

OPERATION RAWHIDE

ONE NIGHT THE CHIEF OF THE VILLAGE ADJACENT TO OUR perimeter fence was kidnapped, and we realized the NVA could move into the village and examine our defenses with little interference. The only reason for reconnaissance would be to prepare an attack. With the prospect of a Tet attack, we decided to dismantle the several dozen shops and stalls that comprised the civilian village adjacent to our perimeter fence. Our action forced the local merchants to take their unsold wares home each night to the refugee center at Que Son hamlet near the U.S. advisory detachment—a nuisance, perhaps, but it was our business that ensured their survival. The merchants provided necessary services, and we didn't want to get rid of them entirely, just to tear down the walls that kept us from getting good observation of the valley beyond. They sold candy and canned food, cut hair, and did laundry. Soldiers enjoyed walking just outside the main gate for the change of pace. I never got wind of any sexual services, but I wouldn't rule out the possibility. On the other hand, there was an active Baptist church nearby, and the Vietnamese minister kept a close eye on things.

The decision to remove the shops was made the day after the village chief had been kidnapped, which gave credence to the belief that the NVA were sneaking into the village at night to examine our defenses. No one really knew whether the NVA were using the village for cover, but it made sense to clear the areas around LZ Ross just to make sure that attackers couldn't move toward us unseen. If they could have gotten within a few yards of our fence before being discovered, they could have taken advantage of the confusion, pouring through the fence and lobbing grenades into the TOC (tactical operations center) without meeting much resistance. And if they could have gotten to our command and control, our piece of the war would have been over. We would not have been the first firebase to be overrun in the war, but the thought of being the last helped us make the decision to remove the shops.

The day after Gregory took command, he ordered a three-company sweep of Que Son Valley dubbed "Operation Rawhide." He commanded from a helicopter and flew low overhead in order to measure our progress. Using a helicopter as a CP (command post) was standard practice in the Cav. The purpose of the operation was to round up all the people and cattle remaining in the valley and herd man and beast toward the refugee center, with the idea of turning the valley into a free-fire zone. In a free-fire zone we could fire on anything moving without fear of hitting friendlies. Theoretically "Operation Rawhide" made sense, but the practical result was to deprive the Vietnamese of a means of livelihood, a situation they were unlikely to ignore. And with the locals having been alerted to our plans, the only results produced by the five-day operation were a few tons of rice, thirty-six lethargic water buffalo, and a couple of elderly farmers.

Given the meager results, I doubted the effort required to mount the operation was worth the alienation of the local Vietnamese. It is possible our operation saved the lives of several hundred people who might have been caught between our forces and the NVA when they finally attacked LZ Ross. After the operation, we continued to scour the valley making sporadic contact. During one skirmish, Company B killed four NVA while sustaining one friendly loss. There was little doubt that the tempo of enemy activity was increasing. Word came down through intelligence channels that a Tet attack was possible, even probable, any time from December on, but no one was sure if it would be before, during, or after the holiday. Newspapers carried Saigon-based stories predicting something was brewing, but most of us assumed they were generated by Saigon brass trying to keep our defenses up. We paid little attention to the warnings on that account.

Based on our own fears, however, we increased alert measures by adding more stand-tos, periods when everyone on LZ Ross would be awake in a foxhole or in a fighting position ready to repel an attack. Normally the stand-to was conducted just after dark or just before dawn, but we did vary the pattern. Sometimes we also fired a "mad minute," with every man firing his weapon through the fence to show the enemy just how much firepower we had. The actual stand-to may not have done much to improve readiness, but the fact that we did it made us more alert the rest of the time. We believed we were leaving no security stone unturned. I hated like hell getting out of bed at odd hours, but I was disciplined enough to recognize the wisdom of doing it.

I never doubted our ability to withstand an attack. I knew other forces could be brought to our relief, if necessary, by helicopter. There was plenty of artillery in the neighborhood to help put a wall of steel around LZ Ross. Furthermore, helicopter gunships could attack the NVA with rockets and machine guns as soon as it was light. We had so many radios that communications could never be threatened. Gregory may have been quick on the trigger, but he understood the principles of defense.

Christmas at LZ Ross was nothing special, although the cooks worked hard to put out the best meal they could. The battalion staff walked over to the neighboring church for a short service, the pews empty except for us. Maybe it gave the minister some comfort to know that he had not been abandoned. As the year 1967 ended, I felt the United States had held its own in Vietnam. Our presence in Que Son Valley proved the NVA were being successfully challenged on their borders. Not one of my confidants nor I had reason to question our being in Vietnam, nor did any of us harbor any doubt about the final outcome. Being away from home was inconvenient, of course, but none of us rebelled. One way or another, everyone at Ross was destined to spend a couple of years in the Army anyway, and most of us felt that what we were doing was more interesting than stateside duty—and a lot more important. Maybe our sentiments were strengthened by our isolation, but we were a team of like-minded people who understood each other. The bonds between us were strong and interdependent. The Army may have a benevolent dictatorship for its roots, but the system worked because it was in everyone's best interest to make it work. I feel a loss at not being able to describe our companionship better. Never did I see any signs of resentment or abnormal behavior in the ranks worth reporting. We knew the die to attack us had been cast early in the month, but this knowledge only strengthened our bonding and our pride.

CHAPTER 6

REHEARSING THE GLADIATORS

AS 1967 CAME TO A CLOSE, IT APPEARED THAT THE attack we expected at LZ Ross wasn't going to materialize until 1968, but we had to be prepared around the clock in any event, and this put a strain on everyone. We had at least one stand-to—our highest state of readiness—each night.

It was universally supposed that I, as intelligence officer, could predict to the minute when the attack would come. I had the same reply for everyone who asked me about it: "I'm the S-2, not the fortune-teller."

The weather stayed about the same, and reminded me of San Francisco. It was in the seventies during the day and the fifties at night. A little rain and plenty of fog.

One day in late December, Helvey's company killed an NVA soldier and found $6,500 worth of Vietnamese piasters on the body. We assumed he was a paymaster. "Mousie got 'im," Helvey told me, as he handed me the money. Mousie was the nickname of Company A's point man. "Mousie and the paymaster spotted each other at the same time," Helvey explained. "It was as if Mousie just looked at the other guy and he was dead. He has instant hand-and-eye coordination. I've never seen anything like it. He killed him with his first shot." Helvey put Mousie, whose real name has been forgotten, in for the Bronze Star.

Helvey thought twice before reporting the incident because, once he reported it, he knew that I would have to turn the money in to brigade to support the report. Otherwise, brigade wouldn't believe it. Of course Helvey's men could have used the money themselves to buy beer. I saw his point. As it turned out, it may have been the first and last time such a sum was turned in to the 3d Brigade, according to Major Spry. I couldn't keep it a secret from Company A.

At the first good opportunity, I told Helvey I understood how some of his men must feel about turning the money over to me. "Tell them that my reward is that in the future you'll get the pick of the best interpreters and scouts in battalion. You'll also be the first to hear of any intelligence coming from the brigade. That's a promise." I then told Spry I wanted to be the first to know of anything he learned so that I could keep the intelligence flowing. I was his best source, and he agreed to give me priority.

As a result of my relationship with Spry and our over-all familiarity with NVA operations, I took it upon myself to prepare a detailed scenario of what the attack would probably be like. Working with my assistant, Sergeant First Class Richard Keefe, and my interpreter, Phung, I drew up charts to explain how I thought the attack would unfold. After giving the briefing to the battalion staff, I asked for and received Gregory's permission to present the same information to every man on the firebase. We had about four hundred men at Ross, including our battalion, the cavalry troop, the artillery battery, and the other teams supporting us. A couple of companies stayed in the valley. Normally, I briefed from the pulpit in the chapel the Marines had left behind, nailing my charts to the cross, but sometimes the briefings were presented in bunkers, foxholes, or fighting positions—wherever I could talk to soldiers with minimum interference with their duties. Keefe held the charts and helped me answer questions.

It was easy to hold their attention as I described how the attack would begin with a barrage of enemy rockets and mortars, which would be fired to mask infiltration of the sappers. As the barrage lifted, the sappers would move quickly toward the command posts, artillery pieces, and fuel and ammunition storage sites. One team would attempt to blast a hole in our perimeter fence to enable the main attacking party to break through in some kind of combat formation. They would use bangalore torpedoes and satchel charges of powerful explosives, perhaps of American origin. I said that our barbed-wire obstacles might be a small impediment to the attackers, but they would not be decisive in aborting the attack.

There were always two points I stressed. First, when the attack came, everyone must stay put and fight from the position they occupied at the time, regardless—even if they were in the latrine. "If it's dark, the only way to tell who the enemy is is by who's moving and who's still," I said. "It would be foolish for any of us to move, because the enemy will be moving too. So, if it's moving, shoot it." The second point I made was that the soldiers protecting the perimeter must not take their eyes off the fence when the shooting started, even though the temptation to duck under cover would be almost irresistible. I agreed that the natural inclination would be to find protection behind sandbags or in a foxhole, but that is exactly what the attackers were counting on. It was their plan to send the sappers forward to penetrate our wire while our security force ran for cover when the rockets and mortar barrage started. "The only way to defeat this tactic is to keep watching, and you've got to think about this from now on. You may get wounded, but better wounded than dead."

I always left them with one closing point. "Don't worry about panic. If you concentrate on what you're doing, and think about it real hard, there won't be time for panic until it's all over." No one fell asleep during these briefings and I was never interrupted. Announcing that I planned to leave for R&R in a few days usually drew a few chuckles.

The first indication an attack on LZ Ross was imminent came on January 2, when Company C made contact with the enemy in the Que Son Valley. Lieutenant Jim Stone was the commander, and a good one. His men were prepared when they unexpectedly ran into elements of the 2d NVA Division. Company C killed thirty-nine NVA soldiers. There were two friendlies KIA (killed in action), a respectable kill ratio for those who keep numbers. (Several days later Jim Stone himself became a statistic.)

The action this day was the first we had seen in about twenty days, but it wasn't the major attack we were expecting. Still, we captured two prisoners with important information about the event we were waiting for. "These prisoners said they had just come out of the mountain area known to be the base area for the 2d NVA Division," Campbell (the brigade commander) recalled, and "that they had come forward with one thousand men and that they had seen six 122mm rocket launchers which were completely unknown to us, and also numerous antiaircraft weapons." It was a warning to get ready for the big one.

Spry knew the attack was imminent, although I can't be certain he told the 2/12th Cav the same thing he told Major General Koster. When Koster asked, "When will it be?" Spry said it could be within seventy-two hours after the NVA in our area went on radio silence. When they stopped broadcasting, Spry said, it meant the NVA were on the move. Spry later acknowledged that the NVA radios went silent just after New Year's Day, so there was some advance warning, but information like that may have been too sensitive to pass on to us. Of course there is irony in not being able to give information to the people who need it most, but that's the world of intelligence.

The long-awaited attack on Ross was launched precisely at 1:30 A.M. on January 3. We were rewarded for our preparedness: we killed 242 NVA soldiers with only 1 friendly KIA and 63 WIA (wounded in action). The best part was that the NVA weren't able to penetrate our perimeter fence. Not one sapper made it through. Bodies by the score lay in front of our wire, dozens dangling from the strands they could touch but not cross.

It was our finest hour . . . and I was not even there, having taken a few days' leave to rest in Japan. The only thing I remember now of the R&R is waking up with a terrific headache on the floor of a Kyoto hotel and watching the snow fall. When I got back, I was told that the attack—conducted by three NVA battalions—had developed precisely as I had predicted: first they fired hundreds of mortars and several dozen 122mm rockets, all carried by hand from North Vietnam. Recoilless rifles were also used to support the attack. By 5:30 A.M. the enemy had broken contact and withdrawn. It was a brave attack, certainly risky, but a complete failure. The prevailing wisdom was that it probably would have succeeded if we hadn't been prepared.

Sergeant Keefe was interviewed by a reporter just after the attack, while I was still on R&R. "We had a bit of a hard time keeping people up for the attack," he said, "but we just kept crying wolf."

Campbell agrees that the attack took place almost precisely as planned, even though the NVA knew we had captured the plan. If the 2d NVA Division commander didn't know the plan was lost when the regimental staff failed to return from the reconnaissance mission, he could have read about it in the December 15 edition of *Time* magazine:

"An Air Cav reconnaissance helicopter team got in a shooting match on the ground and killed the regimental commander of the 3d Regiment, 2d Division of the North Vietnamese army. On him and his party were five pounds of important documents, including maps showing all of the U.S. positions nearby and the NVA's regimental battle plans."

Of course I don't know for sure that the NVA had people in the United States gathering information and intelligence on their behalf, but I wouldn't rule out the possibility.

The attackers of Ross were soon buried without ceremony in mass graves outside the perimeter fence. We used a small bulldozer, ordinarily maintained at Ross to help with fortifications and to keep the roads repaired, to dig the burial pits.

At exactly the same time that Ross was attacked, another NVA battalion hit a company-size outpost we had established in the western end of Que Son Valley at a place we called LZ Leslie. The attack on Ross broke off about 5:00 A.M. on January 3, but the attack on Leslie went on until the end of the day. At noon the defending company (Company D) was reinforced by another company from a sister battalion, 1/7 Cav. The NVA had attacked Leslie with flamethrowers, satchel charges, and choking gas. When it was all over, fifteen cavalrymen were dead and fifty-five wounded. We later buried sixty-three NVA soldiers, including forty found inside the perimeter fence.

I can't say that I might have prevented Leslie's being overrun, but I never gave Leslie the same attention I gave to the defense of LZ Ross. I should have realized that LZ Leslie—being isolated and exposed in Que Son Valley—was at greater jeopardy than Ross, and given them equal attention. So should our battalion commander.

Later I was asked if the NVA really used flamethrowers, because they are not the easiest weapons in the world to employ. There are the matters of fuel, pressure, and ignition to contend with. During my Vietnam tour I recall seeing a couple of our own flamethrowers around our landing zone, but I don't remember ever using them. But my answer was, "Why be surprised?" Less than a month before the attack on Ross and Leslie, the Viet Cong had used flamethrowers with great effectiveness at a Montagnard village near Dak Son, some seventy-five miles northeast of Saigon. Flamethrowers basically spew out thickened gas—or napalm. It's an easy way to get someone's attention, offering a lesson in terror survivors tend not to forget.

Leslie might not have been overrun at all if Gregory had left Helvey's company defending it. Helvey ensured that every man in Company A understood the terrain and his precise role in the defense. They put up all the fences and erected all the barriers, including mines and booby traps. It was a full-time job. Gregory, however, felt that Helvey's men were having it too easy. So he made the decision that LZ Leslie would be occupied on a rotating basis so no single company "got over" at the expense of everyone else. Company D was barely in position when Leslie was attacked and nearly overrun.

With a little more luck on their part, the NVA attacks on Ross and Leslie might have succeeded. I can only speculate that the commander of the 3d Regiment of the 2d NVA Division was too new on the job and lacked the necessary battle experience to understand how difficult it is to attack prepared positions. However, an attack by his predecessor near the Que Son Valley on November 13 against another battalion of the Americal Division was wildly successful: fourteen helicopters were shot down. Spry thinks the commander of the 3d Regiment, flushed with victory, might have boasted to his division commander how easy it was to ambush the Cav, and hungered for a second opportunity to prove it against us.

"I think the success of the attack on November 13 was the battle that gave the 3d Regiment's commander the idea of how to ambush an Air Cav brigade, and he sold the plan to the 2d NVA Division commander, which resulted in the battles the 2/12th Cav had in January," Spry surmised.

THE DEATH BATTALION

PURSUIT OF THE NVA STARTED EARLY ON JANUARY 7, when Gregory had the four companies line up at one end of the valley. It took several days after the attack to rearm and regroup. The plan was to sweep through the valley and eliminate scattered remnants of the enemy, especially those who were still harassing LZ Ross with sniper fire. It was risky, and also ill-advised.

Shortly after Gregory made the decision to conduct a battalion-size pursuit, he realized he might have overestimated the destruction of the NVA force on January 3. Unfortunately, however, he did not commit the battalion into the pursuit in a battalion formation. Instead, he sent the four companies out independently. Once the companies got into trouble, Gregory had several battles to control all at once, which is what he was trying to do when his helicopter was shot down.

Helvey was in the middle of the fight from the first shot. It didn't take long for Gregory to arrive overhead in his command-and-control helicopter, flying at treetop level for a firsthand look. "I told Gregory to stay away from the fight, because he was flying too low and drawing a lot of enemy small arms fire," Helvey recalled. "I had a feeling that he would be shot down as soon as I saw what he was doing."

Helvey also had a premonition that something was wrong when the sweep began. He knew the valley well and sensed he was leading Company A into an ambush, so he moved cautiously—too cautiously for Gregory, who told him to pick up his pace and keep up with the other companies.

But Helvey had seen fresh overturned soil and shrubs with branches cut off.

It was extremely quiet. Helvey noticed branches moving along the treeline, which indicated the NVA might be using the greenery for concealment. Then the entire treeline moved. It was like a scene from *Macbeth*. Helvey reported this to Gregory, but Gregory was so excited the only thing he could say to Helvey was "move . . . move . . . move . . . keep moving." Casting aside his fears, Helvey obeyed orders. A few minutes later, the NVA sprung the trap. It took a whole day to break contact. There was information that Gregory's helicopter was down, but no details.

Jim Stone, commanding Company C, had been killed, and one of his platoons surrounded. Lieutenant Ronald S. Taylor was the platoon leader. Taylor kept the platoon together throughout the night and was later awarded the Distinguished Service Cross for his heroism. Battalion artillery fired some seven thousand rounds in support of the platoon during the night of January 7–8, which helped keep their morale up. Throughout the night, the artillery walked a wall of steel around the encircled unit. Nothing could have gotten in. Two helicopter crews also helped by resupplying them with ammunition, despite heavy enemy ground fire. Two pilots were wounded, but the ammunition got through.

Although it isn't mentioned in the official reports, the enemy was kept away from the encircled men by friendly artillery firing on top of the remnants of C Company. Putting all of the friendlies under overhead cover made this act rational.

"Don't make too much of this," I was advised by one who was there.

"Survival is more important than heroics."

BOWMAN WAS NOW THE 3D BRIGADE S-3 AT LZ BALDY, having been replaced as battalion S-3 by Major Lawrence M. Malone. Malone was a West Point graduate, Class of '58, who had been serving on the division staff for six months. When his time came to change jobs, he was assigned to the 2/12th Cav. I last saw him at Camp Radcliff while I was waiting to leave for the Tokyo R&R. We had a friendly conversation at the airfield, and I looked forward to working with him.

Bowman was busy one afternoon at Baldy when an assistant division commander—a brigadier general—of the American Division arrived unexpectedly to find out what was going on. The first thing he noticed was that the 3d Brigade was not reporting a very high kill ratio against the NVA. Bowman pointed out that he could only report to the American what the 2/12th Cav reported to brigade, and reports hadn't started coming in, because there was a fight going on. The brigadier general commented that the kill ratio would doubtless go up if the 3d Brigade air assaulted by helicopters to put more infantry into the middle of the fight. The general apparently didn't know about the NVA ambush plan. Campbell did and was understandably reluctant to react impulsively—along the lines the general was suggesting. "Finally," Bowman said, "I had to ask him to leave the 3d Brigade area before he got a lot of people killed." The general probably didn't like to hear suggestions from Bowman, but he departed.

WITH STONE DEAD, GREGORY MISSING, AND A PLATOON surrounded, the rest of the battalion started to withdraw toward LZ Ross. The remnant knew that they would have to fight their way back. Among the first killed was Captain Barovetto, who was trying to find Gregory. The immediate cause of his death was leading his armored unit from a tank, his head exposed over the turret.

As the survivors of Barovetto's B Troop approached Helvey's company with their tanks and armored personnel carriers, they mistook Company A for enemy forces and opened fire. Several of Helvey's wounded, who had been collected for medical evacuation, were casualties of B Troop's misjudgment. They were killed where they lay helplessly in an old bomb crater.

Meanwhile, company commanders tried to get some of B Troop's tracks to help carry out the dead and wounded, but there was no way to halt the panic: the drivers refused to stop, according to the recollections of Captain Philip E. Pons, Jr., the battalion's S-3 (Air), or assistant operations officer for aircraft support. B Troop lost three tanks and one armored personnel carrier to enemy fire.

Pons had been at LZ Ross in the battalion tactical operations center when Gregory boarded his helicopter at the beginning of the operation. He didn't think anything was unusual until he heard Gregory was in trouble.

"May Day . . . May Day . . . we've been hit . . . we've been hit . . . I've been hit." Those were Gregory's last words. It was 1:15 P.M. The fighting raged on the rest of the day. Finally, all battalion units broke contact, seeking refuge behind the fences of LZ Ross. Only Taylor's platoon was left behind.

Captain Dane Maddox was also at LZ Ross, having been left behind by Gregory. Maddox was scheduled to be on Gregory's flight, but was delayed by a radio call from the artillery battalion commander, his boss. Gregory didn't want to wait for Maddox to finish the conversation, so he left without him. As soon as Maddox finished talking to his commander, he raced to the helicopter pad, but it was too late. He could scarcely see Gregory's helicopter flying low over enemy positions. A moment later, Maddox watched the helicopter drop into the treetops, aflame.

"This was Gregory's style—to fly in harm's way so the enemy could engage his aircraft," Maddox recalled. Gregory would observe the enemy's location, then try to destroy those firing at the helicopter. Gregory told Maddox to carry extra ammunition for his rifle so he could help engage targets of opportunity that Gregory identified from the air. "He felt this approach—instead of pulling up and using artillery or other means—would enhance his reputation and improve his chance of promotion."

When Scudder realized that Maddox was not going to be able to make the ill-fated flight, Scudder begged Gregory to let him go instead of Maddox, since it was Charlie Company that was in contact. This was the company that Scudder had recently commanded before his promotion to major. Gregory turned down Scudder's request. "The three senior officers of a unit should not be in the same helicopter," Gregory declared, leaving Scudder behind as the senior officer at LZ Ross.

Bill Scudder heard the same radio message that Pons did, except Scudder heard it from the radio that was always left blaring on the porch of the battalion commander's hooch. He just happened to be in the area checking out defenses in case the attackers turned on Ross. Scudder rushed to the TOC and directed Pons to inform brigade. Until the whereabouts of Gregory could be confirmed, Scudder had to assume command. He knew instinctively that "Charlie Company was in serious shit."

Campbell, the brigade commander, arrived at Ross in a matter of minutes to help keep everything from falling apart. Scudder proposed air assaulting by helicopter one or two of the infantry companies laagering at LZ Ross. Campbell jumped back into his helicopter to check the feasibility of the proposal.

It didn't take long to recognize there would be no air assaults into Que Son Valley, as several NVA 12.7mm (.51 caliber) machine guns tried to shoot Campbell out of the sky. He started taking hits just as he lifted off Ross. He never made it over the encircled force. In fact, the machine guns were part of an ambush operation organized to destroy any and all helicopters flying into Que Son Valley, exactly as shown on the map we captured earlier.

Campbell returned to LZ Baldy, but he called Scudder every forty-five minutes until at last he returned to Ross about midnight with news that five companies would be available the next day to rescue the forty-five entrapped troopers.

Campbell's response earned him Scudder's lifelong respect, and formed the basis of a "special friendship" between the two. Scudder later confirmed that he always felt comfortable with Campbell and never hesitated to speak his mind to him. Only people who trust each other can afford to be that candid.

Earlier that afternoon, Lieutenant Colonel Richard S. Sweet had been flown into LZ Ross to become the new battalion commander. Sweet had been serving as deputy commander of 3d Brigade until a battalion command slot opened up. When word reached Campbell around 1:30 P.M. that Gregory's helicopter was down and a battle raging, Campbell ordered Sweet to LZ Ross to take command. Sweet had expected to get a battalion of his own, but not like this.

Sweet landed at LZ Ross about 2:30 P.M. carrying his pack, combat gear, and CAR-15, a collapsible version of the M-16 rifle. He was met by Lieutenant Colonel Edwin S. Townsley, the division engineer and his classmate from the Army's Command and General Staff College at Fort Leavenworth, Kansas.

Townsley briefed Sweet on the tactical situation and told him it was messy.

In the middle of the discussion Townsley surprised Sweet by asking him to hand over his CAR-15. Sweet did, responding instinctively to Townsley's whispered advice to stand absolutely still. With great casualness Townsley fired a burst into the grass on the other side of the fence a few feet from where they stood. It happened too fast for Sweet to react.

"I dispatched him," Townsley explained, pointing to a dead NVA soldier lying facedown with an unexploded grenade still clutched in his right hand. Many years later

I did some work with Ed Townsley and can confirm that he has the composure of an Oxford don. I can't imagine his showing emotion.

But this was no time to linger. Sweet ran to the TOC, where he was given a more detailed briefing by Major Bill Scudder. It was depressing to learn that one company was cut off and running out of ammunition, and that another company was streaming piecemeal back through gaps in the wire fence surrounding LZ Ross. The armored cavalry troop was disorganized and its commander dead. No one had any idea where the armored vehicles were heading or what the losses might be.

Communications between the companies and the battalion command post weren't very good either. Radio-telephone operators (RTO) scurrying for cover and protection had broken the antennas to their radios in their haste.

Sweet studied Scudder as he listened to Scudder's every word. Finally the memory clicked. "Billy, you don't remember me, but I knew your family at Fort Benning when I was there teaching tactics and you were a young teenager going to Columbus High School."

Scudder was only thirteen at that time and didn't remember Sweet, but it didn't make any difference. By that time Scudder had already decided Sweet was an officer to respect.

Sweet, with Campbell's blessing, decided to launch a counterattack against the NVA at first light the next day with three companies. The plan was simple but not easy. Scudder would be the task force commander. Sweet would control the effort from his command post at LZ Ross, where he could also direct the defense of the landing zone should the NVA launch another surprise attack.

Scudder was ordered to head south on foot from LZ Ross, then hook north and east toward the trapped platoon. Behind the encircling NVA force was an east-west dirt road. As Scudder made the turn north, the armored cavalry troop was deployed to deceive the NVA by appearing to attack behind them along the road from east to west. The hope was that the NVA feared our armor so much that they would pull out of their encircling positions to defend against an armored attack. Unfortunately, it was drizzling. There was no dust cloud to tip off the NVA, which would have helped with the deception. Still, the armored force fired its machine guns and made as much racket as it could by revving up their engines and driving around in circles. The plan worked beautifully. The NVA withdrew to more defensible positions.

Scudder and his command group accompanied the tanks and armored personnel carriers from B Troop to a high knoll. From there Scudder could see the encircled force and control the extraction. The knoll was too steep for the M-48 tanks to climb in a forward gear, so they had to climb the hill in reverse.

Once the tanks were in position, Scudder directed Taylor to mark the most southern and northern positions with smoke grenades. The tanks provided covering fire to the relief column by firing as close to the smoke as safety allowed, probably no more than ten yards away from the position of Wild Card, as C Company was called. (A Company was Ace High, B was Bad Bet, and D was Stacked Deck. The battalion net was Roving Gambler, so the scheme was easy to master, once you broke the code. The nicknames were developed for radio communication.)

The extraction was made a little easier by the arrival of a flight of B-52 bombers that dropped five hundred–pounders on the mountain passes to the west. Normally these "arc lights" were done after dark, but in this case a

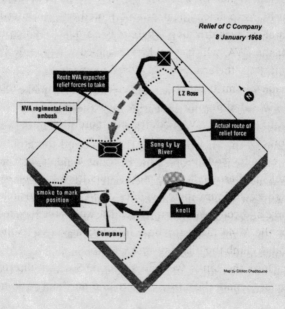

Relief of C Company
8 January 1968

Route NVA expected relief forces to take

LZ Ross

NVA regimental-size ambush

Actual route of relief force

Song Ly Ly River

smoke to mark position

knoll

Company

Map by Clifton Chadbourne

special mission was cranked up as a diversion. It was hard to tell how much damage they did, but the psychological benefit was terrific. I had earlier experienced going in by helicopter shortly after an arc light mission to evaluate the damage of the hundreds of bombs hitting the ground, almost simultaneously. Nearly everyone near the immediate impact zone was rendered unconscious, sometimes for days. Some never recovered their sanity and were found much later walking about like zombies.

Scudder and his men took advantage of the diversion to creep up to Taylor's encircled platoon and join forces. Together they returned to Ross.

All the while LZ Ross was under attack by rockets and mortars—more than one hundred, according to Sweet. The green tracers from the NVA machine guns ricocheted throughout the valley, showing everyone who was in control.

The people—heroes actually—who helped make the system work during the battle were the pilots and the crew of the helicopter who flew in late dusk to deliver ammo to the encircled men. The officer on the ground couldn't see the helicopter and the pilot couldn't see him. The only way to guide the helicopter was by its sound, which got louder or softer. Every time the helicopter passed overhead it took groundfire. Time was running out. The pilot came up with the only plan that had a chance to work. As he headed back for one final pass, the pilot told the officer on the ground, "I am running the stopwatch. Tell me when I calculate ten seconds, counting NOW. Counting 10-9-8-7-Our Father in Heaven, forgive us our sins-5-4-3-2-1-KICK IT OUT!"

At that moment, the helicopter was directly over the entrapped men, and the ammunition—kicked out of the helicopter by the crew chief—fell directly in their midst.

Machine gun fire tattooed a design across the helicopter as the ammunition fell into the middle of the encircled platoon. Both pilots were wounded but managed to keep control. A few minutes later they crash-landed at LZ Baldy.

The two pilots were Captain John F. Boyer, Jr., of Harrisburg, Pennsylvania, and Warrant Officer Dale H. Dobesh, of Savage, Minnesota. Afterward Boyer recalled that "we took some rounds that gave us a hell of a scare . . . I felt something slam into my back. I had no idea how bad I was hit."

I returned from the Tokyo R&R to find my popularity at an all-time high.

The soldiers recalled my earlier concern for their welfare, and how my predictions helped them survive the attack. The fact that I was absent when the attack came embellished my reputation for being someone who really knew what was going on—and who was smart enough to be somewhere else on January 3! They treated me like a good-luck piece, and as I made my daily rounds of the firebase, I found myself being invited into every bunker I passed for a cold beer. I didn't know where the ice or beer came from. I was flattered at first, but after a while I had to forgo inspections.

I told everyone I was sorry to have missed the big attack, so I could see for myself how good my predictions were. On the other hand, I did enjoy Japan. In fact, I was lucky to get away, because Colonel Gregory didn't want me to go. He did everything in his power to keep me at Ross, short of ordering me to stay. When I pointed out that I had been planning the trip for a long time, and was even meeting a friend from the States, he reluctantly agreed to my departure. I reminded him that I was only going to be gone for five days; besides, I was leaving Sergeant Keefe behind, and he knew as much as I did about the enemy situation.

Not only was Keefe good at his job, he liked Gregory—and Gregory liked him. Keefe was in the helicopter with Gregory when it was shot down. Keefe was the only one I knew who enjoyed flying with Gregory, and was close to earning an Air Medal, awarded after flying thirty combat missions—which Gregory's certainly were.

It was not a good time for 2/12th Cav, which was just beginning to be known as "The Death Battalion." Our intelligence about the enemy was still vague; virtually the entire command group had been killed in one helicopter crash. Altogether, eighteen officers and men were killed and forty-two wounded in the aborted pursuit. The bodies in the helicopter had still not been recovered. They included Gregory and Keefe, three helicopter crewmen, and the new battalion S-3, Major Lawrence M. Malone. Their bodies were recovered and identified in late March 1968, but I never did learn the details.

I got back to LZ Ross on January 10, about three weeks before the Tet holiday officially began. I had a lot to catch up on, and the battalion needed intelligence support more than ever before. The usefulness of everything I did earlier to prepare the battalion for the assault on LZ Ross ended when Ross was attacked. Now there was a new war facing us: a conventional war. Sweet and I barely knew each other, but he seemed to talk sense. We immediately agreed that the Communists would ultimately lose the war, although our victory would not come cheaply if our current predicament was a taste of things to come.

CHAPTER 8

SWEET TAKES CHARGE

SWEET WAS A VERY UNUSUAL OFFICER. EVERYTHING about him was wound up and tightly strung: his walk, his manner, his conversation. A good listener and not aloof to his staff, he was far more forceful than Gregory—some said vain and arrogant. For sure he was self-confident. He stood about five feet seven inches and wore glasses, but not all the time. He didn't crusade against drink. He smoked a pipe. Insisting always on being meticulous, he reminded me of how officers used to be in years gone by—either loved or hated, but always obeyed. Sweet, age thirty-six, acted as if everyone should have absolute confidence in him. He assumed it.

Sweet retired from the Army as a brigadier general and now lives in rural Maryland overlooking the Potomac River, just before it empties into Chesapeake Bay. Sailing is his main diversion. He seems much more human now than he did then, probably because time has eroded the distance between captain and lieutenant colonel. Sweet's one problem was one many would envy, unless they gave it serious thought: he was often the first to be right. In a profession of tremendous egos, being right, especially early on, is not often an asset. For every person who respects him, Sweet knows someone who still blames him for wrongs received, real and imaginary. Few are combat veterans, however. Several are officers who left the Army after Sweet discovered they wore medals for valor they never earned. Others are those who stood by as Sweet tried to save his battalion from extinction. Even today they know that Sweet knows.

When people ask me what Sweet is really like, I say he's like Gary Cooper in *High Noon*. Very right and very alone. The word "courageous" seems to be as good as any.

A week after I returned from R&R, Sweet took me aside and shared some reservations he harbored about how our country was conducting the war. He didn't go into the basic issue of the war itself—we were both convinced that we were engaged in a humanitarian campaign. However, he did question the strategy we were using to defeat the insurgency. Recognizing the heresy of our conversation, he swore me to secrecy.

Sweet went on to explain he was dumfounded that others had not recognized the changing aspect of the war brought about by the full-scale intervention of the

North Vietnamese Army. Instead of drawing lessons from the earlier experiences of the division in Vietnam, Sweet looked back further to the Korean War, where he served as a twenty-three-year-old company commander when the Chinese entered the conflict. He saw a lot of fighting there.

"We are now faced with a new war, and an old war, depending how you look at it. We're going to have to rely less on helicopters and more on conventional ground tactics," Sweet said. I had never heard anyone in the 1st Cav talk heresy like this. A month later, however, it was conventional wisdom. But not before the 2/12th Cav was nearly destroyed.

Within a few days of taking over, Sweet had his act together. "Get your gear on, Charlie," he said one morning after studying our maps. "Tomorrow the battalion is going into the Que Son Valley, and the command group is going with it. I'll lead this battalion into battle from the ground. I'll be damned if I can do it from a helicopter or by sitting here at Ross. It's time for commanders to get back on the ground with their troops. There's not much difference between this war now and the war we fought in Korea."

Into the Que Son we went before dawn, some four hundred of us—the battalion's "foxhole strength." It was a quiet morning when we left Ross, but in the distance I could hear an antique generator turning over. Ta-CHOCK-a-da. Ta-CHOCK-a-da. It must have been the mill in the village working around the clock. Our immediate mission was to find and recover the bodies of the seven who had been killed in the helicopter crash the week before. It didn't take long to reach the scene.

I moved forward to examine the burned and twisted wreckage of the helicopter, but I couldn't see much. I couldn't even tell where the doors were. The downed ship was about two hundred yards away in the middle of a dry rice paddy about the size of a football field. Several mounds next to the hulk suggested the presence of the bodies we were looking for. I supposed they were shallow graves.

If we were going to be ambushed, this was the place. Repressing the desire to reach the helicopter by the most direct route, Sweet deployed our forces wide to the right and left until our objective was encircled. Movement was slow after we discovered booby traps and took some poorly aimed sniper fire. I was surprised at this point to see Helvey literally kicking a young lieutenant across the rice paddies. This was not his style. Later I learned the young officer had been hiding behind a dike when Helvey found him. Although there wasn't any serious shooting going on, the lieutenant was scared. Helvey called it cowardice. Later that night, Helvey forced the lieutenant to board a helicopter with the orders, "Don't come back. I don't give a shit where you go." He never saw him again.

As our soldiers darted from tree to hillock, always looking for the best cover, Sweet and I waited anxiously until the area was secure on all sides. Neither of us felt inclined to talk. The silence ended when a helicopter gunship buzzed over the trees. The pilot offered to provide us support in the event we needed it.

"We're firing artillery into this area," Sweet radioed the pilot, "so don't go too far away. Stay over me and you'll be all right." However, the air strike that the Americal Division had requested several days earlier—and subsequently canceled, *we thought,* when we reported that we'd be operating in this area—arrived on schedule. The bombs dropped precisely on target. Miraculously no one was hit. However, one of the exploding bomb fragments struck the helicopter, which came crashing to the ground only a few feet from where we were. Stunned, the pilot checked to make sure his crew was safe. His crew saw he had a back injury and carried him over to Sweet. He spoke in a whisper: "'Stay over me and you'll be all right' . . . my ass."

We still had no plan prepared to recover the bodies, because we had no way of knowing before we left what to expect when we got to the wreckage. Since I was the only staff officer present who had known Gregory, I felt it was my place to volunteer to lead the mission. Besides, I expected to find Keefe's remains. I asked if there were any volunteers, and three soldiers stepped forward. We started moving across the field toward the helicopter, staying off the paths where the booby traps might be. We carried no weapons—just our shovels and body bags.

When we got to the hastily dug graves, two of us worked, while the other two stood well back, to reduce the damage a booby trap could inflict. Then we changed places to share the risk and the work. We worked with extreme caution, shoveling away the earth in small scoops. We found the first body after an hour of digging: we could tell it was Lieutenant Colonel Gregory by the black gloves he always wore. With dignity and reverence, we lifted him from the ground. I wiped the soil from his face.

When we found Gregory's body was not booby trapped, we uncovered the rest as quickly as we could. It was careless, but we appreciated that the enemy had honored our dead with suitable burial. We rarely did the same for them.

We could not find two of the bodies we were searching for, including Sergeant Keefe. Did this mean that they were prisoners? We simply did not know. Although we learned a month after we left LZ Ross and the Que Son Valley that their bodies had been recovered by the battalion replacing us, we had no way of knowing at the time if they had escaped into the jungle or if they had been taken prisoner.

When we finished digging, I had to ask for another detail of soldiers to help carry out the bodies. Lieutenant Colonel Gregory was left for my working party of four. After ensuring that the other bodies had been moved out of the way, we each took hold of a corner canvas carrying strap and started toward the edge of the field where the remains would be evacuated by helicopter. When the body bag brushed against the ground, I was shaken by our disrespect. "For God's sake, let's not let that happen again," I said.

After the bodies were flown out, we worked our way back to LZ Ross. While we earned solid claim to the ownership of LZ Ross, the price was high. During the month of January, we listed 40 killed in action and 194 wounded—a lot of friends by the wayside. My uniform smelled of death, and I had it burned.

CHAPTER 9

HISTORICAL MOMENT

WE STILL HAD ABOUT A WEEK TO GO BEFORE TET officially began when we were alerted that we'd be moving from LZ Ross to Camp Evans near Hue. We figured that our work in the Que Son Valley had been completed and looked forward to seeing some new territory. Helvey had been in Hue during a previous tour and said good things about it. I was going home in a few weeks and was glad to have the opportunity to see Hue before I left. I expected to visit the city, however—not attack it.

Although Tet had not yet officially arrived, we thought that the enemy had already tried to execute his Tet strategy . . . and lost. It was time to relax and enjoy the holiday. The war was not over, of course, but it was slowing down. We all knew the Vietnamese went to great lengths to celebrate Tet, regardless of their station in life or political persuasion. Our interpreters and Kit Carson Scouts anticipated the coming festivities and longed to be with their families and friends again. Although we suspected there might be a few small skirmishes during the Tet period, Sweet encouraged our Vietnamese companions to take their well-deserved leave. We couldn't send everyone home, so we let the Vietnamese draw lots to see who would stay and who would go. To be safe, we required two interpreters and two scouts to stay behind. There were long faces from those who lost, but they all accepted the results gracefully. The losers would have to wait until the others returned before taking their leave. To compensate for missing Tet, I told them they could take a couple of extra days. After all, they all worked for me.

Kit Carson Scouts were, bluntly put, VC turncoats. When the ARVNs captured a young Viet Cong soldier, he might be given the opportunity to acknowledge the error of his ways and agree to switch sides. Often, I suppose, the argument was very compelling, but in fairness some former VC did rally to the government's side because they had become disillusioned with VC terrorist tactics. Our experience was that the Kit Carson Scouts were fine soldiers, from humble origins, perhaps, but politically and militarily savvy. So long as we treated them well, we were repaid in kind. I even had one officer who wanted to adopt a scout so he could take him home to find a better life. There was nothing improper in this, but it could never happen—and never did, to the best of my knowledge. Without exception, those I released to go home for Tet returned immediately when the fighting started, although they had no way of knowing where we were without returning to LZ Ross for directions from the battalion that replaced us.

We didn't get much advance warning that we would be leaving LZ Ross, but no one was upset. Until we got to Ross, we had moved about once a week. Once careful plans were made to move the brigade, the battalions could respond with very little notice. We knew how many helicopters and trucks it would take, and when they arrived, we'd be ready. The movement plans ensured that the entire brigade could, ordinarily, transport all its forces from one spot to another in just a day or so. For the soldier, the rule was that if you couldn't fit it in your knapsack or carry it on your shoulder, you left it behind. By their nature, soldiers who move almost exclusively by air learn to travel light. CH-47 Chinooks would fly out the heavier necessities, but only the minimum required to support battle in case we fell into an unexpected fight when we arrived in the new AO (area of operations).

The first day we were to fly by helicopter from LZ Ross to Baldy, then continue north to Quang Tri by C-123 airplane. On the following day we were to proceed by helicopter to Camp Evans, north of Hue. At last, the 3d Brigade was returning to the control of the 1st Air Cavalry Division, our parent organization. The Americal Division was OK, but it never really appreciated how we operated under optimum conditions.

Lieutenant Colonel Sweet called his staff together to discuss the move the morning of January 24. There seemed to be no significant obstacles. Major Scudder, however, had been warned by the 3d Brigade XO (executive officer) that under no circumstances could we use any valuable truck space for ammunition as we usually did. Instead, we would be completely resupplied from new division stocks when we reached Camp Evans. "Don't ask for any more trucks," Scudder was told, "because there aren't any."

Scudder wasn't sure who was responsible for this directive, the Americal Division or the 1st Air Cavalry Division. Regardless of the order, he intended to take some of our ammunition with us, as we always did, hiding as many boxes as he could in the bed of each truck sent to help us move. Sweet concurred and told Scudder to come up with three basic loads—enough for several days of heavy combat. Only a madman would move through a combat zone in wartime without being able to defend himself. The order to move without ammo was absurd. "What crazy son of a bitch set up this deal?" I wondered.

On January 25 we started the move as planned. While most of us were busy boarding helicopters, Scudder quietly loaded the trucks according to plan, piling tents and supplies over the ammunition. He had to make some compromises, but the ammunition got loaded.

The next day we all married up at muddy Camp Evans, first the helicopters and then the trucks. We found, much to our surprise, that we had the only ammunition in the camp. There were no fresh stocks. Scudder's judgment was totally vindicated. The irony was that, without the ammunition we had smuggled into Camp Evans on trucks against orders, we could not have later been deployed toward Hue. Of course, Hue still hadn't been attacked at this point, but we couldn't even have defended ourselves at Evans without Scudder's foresight. Were we the only ones who knew there was a war going on? So it seemed.

In fact, we almost had to fight off an attack the night before at the Quang Tri airfield. We didn't realize it until we got there, but the airfield was a dangerous place to spend the night. The Marines who defended the field were nervous as they explained the problem to us, for even as we arrived, Marine planes were bombing enemy positions less than one mile from the airfield. The Marine briefing Sweet told him that it was not unusual for the enemy to make daylight attacks. He also told Sweet that there were no friendly troops between the enemy and the place allotted to us to spend the night. Sweet offered to move in closer to the Marines defending the airfield, but the Marine colonel commanding the airfield said that wouldn't be necessary. "Stay out of the action," he said. "It's our show, not yours."

Sweet looked at the area assigned to us and decided it didn't look safe, so he moved the battalion to the far end of the field out of sight of the Marine colonel. We got ready to repulse an attack, just in case. While we were digging in, a second battalion from the 1st Air Cavalry

Division arrived and began unloading nearby as the airfield commander directed. Sweet told the battalion commander, Lieutenant Colonel Herlihy Long, that he was moving into a dangerous place and advised him not to store any ammunition in the open, especially not near a building with a shiny tin roof the enemy had previously used as an aiming point.

"You command your battalion and I'll command mine," Long replied. The turf battle seemed to be contagious.

A few hours later, Long was killed when an NVA rocket scored a direct hit on the ammunition. There was also a ground attack, which we easily beat off—only three wounded. Even so, the daylight attacks were yet more evidence that the war was changing, based on what had to be a calculated NVA decision to pick up the tempo.

We were happy to leave Quang Tri for Camp Evans by helicopter the next morning at first light.

HUE'S BURNING

EACH WAR HAS HISTORICAL MOMENTS. IT'S GENERALLY agreed that Tet '68 and the Battle of Hue were the decisive moments of the war in Vietnam. An important portion of that battle—or campaign—was fought by our battalion. It was one of nine infantry battalions in the Army's 1st Air Cavalry Division. Despite the subsequent confusion, the chronology of the 2/12th's role is straightforward: after being moved a few miles south by helicopter from its new base camp at Camp Evans to an old French outpost north of Hue, the 2/12th Cav was ordered to execute a forced march to relieve allied forces defending the besieged city.

There were a few glitches before we got moving, none seemingly insurmountable, until we saw an NVA force in front of us blocking our way. When we called for artillery

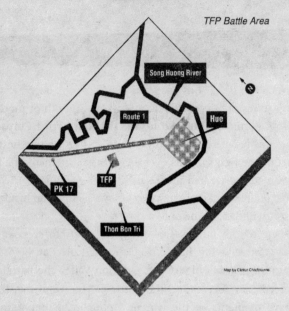

TFP Battle Area

support, nothing happened. Regardless, we were told to keep moving.

Those in command assumed the 2/12th Cav would face no serious risk until it reached Hue, maybe not even then, so preparations and plans that should have been well in place even before we left Camp Evans were never completed. Yet so brutal was the resistance, so meager the support, it took our battalion a month rather than a day to reach our objective. For part of that time, it was the Lost Battalion.

Those familiar with the major events of the 1968 Tet offensive will recall the scenes in Saigon: the U.S. Embassy being overrun, the streetside execution of a VC terrorist, the attacks around the city, and the strong points that were won back one by one. Less familiar is the attack on Hue, because there was almost no way to get news, especially TV coverage, in or out. It took only a few days to restore order in Saigon; it took a month or more before normalcy returned to Hue and northern I Corps. Cameras reached Hue finally, but only after the toughest part of the fighting was over. Even then, the media had access to the cleared areas outside the walls only. They were unable to capture up close what was going on inside the city until near the end of February.

One of the purposes of this account is to compare and contrast what happened to the 2/12th Cav before and after the fall of Hue. In Que Son Valley the battalion had three commanders—Ross, Gregory, and Sweet. Ross was like John the Baptist: he prepared us for the big event without participating in it himself. Gregory lost his life because he misjudged what was going on. He had qualities I didn't like, but they had little to do with his professional limitations. In a sense, Gregory really wasn't much different from most battalion commanders in the 1st Cav at the time. He followed the standard practice of commanding from a helicopter while the infantry companies of the battalion maneuvered separately toward their respective objectives, a practice Sweet instantly rejected.

In hindsight, the practice was based on arrogance— professional, cultural, and, yes, racial. The NVA could not possibly be our equal. The officer corps of the 1960s was trained to fight Russians. They envisioned massive tank and mechanized infantry battles. Force versus force. In Vietnam every American officer dreamed of the day when the little beggars would come out and fight, but they never did. Of course, when they did show their mettle in Hue, we were unprepared to cope with the challenge. Thinking of the enemy as "gooks" may seem foolish today, but that's how we thought of them. We believed there was something contemptible about an army that started a war and fought it with random terror, often against innocent civilians.

In this context, sending out companies to search for NVA or VC, preferably units but individuals if all else failed, was the only course of action we could understand. Occasionally there were bigger battles, but after the Ia Drang battle of 1965 when the NVA took on the 1st Cav for the first time with disastrous results, NVA commanders were understandably reluctant to meet the division's airmobile forces head-on. They made us come to them. The pattern was broken when they attacked LZ Ross with a regimental-size force. They were convinced that LZ Ross could be taken no other way. Only if LZ Ross fell would the United States be inclined to commit forces to the border areas, especially in I Corps. With U.S. forces drawn into the countryside, the NVA—working with what was left of the Viet Cong—could infiltrate the population centers. The cities would first be softened up with propaganda, then converted with a touch of terror.

If a city as important as Hue submitted to the Red Banner and if Saigon fell into Communist hands, the war would be won.

The will to continue the fight would evaporate in the United States, and even those people in South Vietnam who hadn't recognized the inevitable outcome would be forced to acknowledge the verdict.

We didn't think they would try to meet us head-on. And even if they tried, we believed we could stop them. During the several months that the 3d Brigade was attached to the American Division, 283,000 rounds of artillery were fired in support of brigade operations. A kill ratio of fourteen-to-one favored the brigade by a wide margin: 178 of our dead versus 2,500 of theirs. (Our figure is accurate. The NVA/NVC number is estimated, but probably not too far off.) Even with this abundant supply and firepower advantage, Campbell wasn't sure it was enough at all times. "At no time during the first two months of operation were our stocks up to desired standards," he recorded, noting that emergency airdrops of material were required on occasion.

Exit Gregory, enter Sweet. Sweet's first job had been to clean up the mess Gregory left behind. He did it quickly and at relatively little cost. Sweet recognized that the war had changed, but he had to assume it was a localized phenomenon. When he chucked the helicopter and took to the ground with the battalion, he did what he believed made sense at the moment. Maybe Gregory, if he had lived, would have reached the same conclusion, given enough time. The point is, Sweet's behavior was isolated to Que Son Valley, and the attack there was widely interpreted as a one-time event. Everyone else continued to operate on the basis of business as usual. The unrelenting attacks on the Marines at Khe Sanh were the only obvious exceptions.

When we got word that the battalion was going to be deployed northward from the Que Son Valley toward Hue to marry up with the rest of the 1st Air Cav Division, even Sweet had no reason to believe that the war had decisively changed, that we wouldn't return to the old drill of looking for the enemy one at a time. But there was one difference: Sweet was prepared to change, because he grasped the similarities between Que Son Valley and conventional warfare in Korea. Nonetheless, he wasn't prepared to push his views on anyone else.

The brigade move northward didn't go according to plan. Men and equipment just infiltrated toward their destinations as best they could. The move was horribly disorganized and resembled a migration of rodents far more than a precise military movement. Why? According to Colonel Campbell, "We did not expect enemy reaction. We expected a normal flow by both water and land. There was a critical shortage of wheeled vehicles. The trip took much longer than expected and the enemy interdicted the route with mines and dropping (blowing up) bridges." Some units even got lost during the five-day movement. "Many of the units expected to land close to Camp Evans (the new destination for both the brigade and division) actually ended up in Quang Tri for a considerable period of time," Campbell recorded.

This confusion tended to confirm Sweet's prediction that the war had changed, that it was about to become more than chasing suspects in black pajamas. I shared this view when it became apparent that what ordinarily would be a routine, well-planned, and precisely executed administrative move ended up being more like a march through a minefield. Campbell realized it, too, but not until after the fact. "It was an administrative move of the most basic type," he later told U.S. Army historians. "If we had to do it over again, we would move out in tactical formation insuring (the) tactical integrity of each battalion."

The operation got worse when we closed on Camp Evans north of Hue, just an empty spot in the middle of nowhere where a Marine battalion had encamped temporarily. We found there were no pre-positioned supplies waiting for us when we got there, which was counter to our expectations. Otherwise, we would have brought more supplies with us from LZ Ross. There was no gas for the few trucks we had or for our generators. There was no ammunition nor any fuel for the helicopters, which meant the brigade helicopters couldn't operate out of Evans for another four or five days, according to Campbell's account. "We were," he declared, "in no posture to meet a sizable enemy attack."

Major General Tolson was the division commander. "Initially," he recalled soon afterward in a June 1968 interview with Army historian Captain J. W. A. White-horne, "there were not great difficulties encountered in the movement, per se. The bulk of the troop movement was done by air . . . the difficulties in the actual move developed when the Tet offensive was initiated by the enemy near the end of January prior to our having completed the move. The scale of the offensive and the occupation of Hue right at the onset brought on many difficulties that existed during the month of February. But these were overcome and did not prevent us from taking a great part in the counteroffensive during the last part of January and all of February." I would argue that this assessment hides from the truth—that the 2/12th Cav impact on the battle of Hue was minimal at best.

Tolson acknowledges that the movement of the division north could have been better. "Of course the enemy operation not only affected our move north, as we were still far from being complete at the onset of the Tet offensive, particularly our support echelon," he recorded later. "It meant that during this phase, we found it very difficult to obtain logistics support and maintenance for our fighting units that were heavily engaged from the end of January on. During all this, we were still moving north and trying to get the maintenance and supply units installed."

The supply situation was indeed a tangled mess when the NVA struck with all its fury during the Hue attack and succeeded in accomplishing all its military objectives, including cutting most of our division off from its supply base before our supplies could be moved north.

Back to Tolson. "It took us a week to get [an artillery battalion] airlifted to Camp Evans because of the enemy situation in and around Hue and the bad weather which had started at the end of January. This move, which we normally could do in a few hours with hooks (cargo helicopters), took us over a week. As a matter of fact, we still didn't have all the artillery in then. It took four more days to get it into Camp Evans."

By this time, the 2/12th Cav, which had arrived at Camp Evans a few days before, was ordered to march toward Hue. Not only had we started the move before the artillery arrived, we were about to attack with no artillery whatsoever.

How did this happen? Why did it happen? What was done to limit the damage?

Who, if anyone, accepts responsibility? Why was Sweet later treated like a pariah rather than a hero for saving the battalion from certain destruction? What's missing from the official records and oral histories? Most of all, what are the lessons learned?

My purpose here is to answer as many questions as I can, guessing if I have to and if circumstances warrant. This is a risky business, because there'll always be somebody who'll wonder, "Why didn't he ask me? I knew the answer to that!" Colonel Norbert D. Grabowski, USA (Ret.), is one such person I almost missed.

During an accidental meeting in 1992 Grabowski told

me that he was the 1st Cav's transportation officer (TO) during Tet '68.

"So you're the sorry SOB who screwed up the division's move north from Bong Son to I Corps," I said bitterly. "I've been looking for you for a long time to find out why the move was so fucked up."

His reply stunned me: he agreed. As the TO, he tried to sell Tolson on the idea of putting together a division movement plan, since they had a plan locked in the safe for every other contingency. It was the middle of the summer of 1967, and Tolson shot him down with the assertion that the 1st Cav would stay in Bong Son forever, or so it seemed.

"We're not going to ever move this goddamn division," Tolson declared, putting an end to any ideas Grabowski had to draft a detailed and comprehensive movement plan. He realized there was no sense in drawing up a plan the Old Man would never look at, much less approve. Working on a draft contrary to the general's guidance could even be perceived as disloyal. The matter was dropped. Of course, when the division was ordered to move in January, the planning was far too hasty to yield results better than the disaster that occurred. That there was no fuel or ammo at Camp Evans was the least of the logistics nightmare.

Grabowski got word of the move one January morning from the acting G-4, who remembered the TO's earlier concern about the absence of planning for a division move.

"Well, your worst nightmare has just come true," he said. The division started moving out immediately, every and any way it could.

"There was no plan," Grabowski recalls. "We just pulled it out of our ass as we went along." After seven days with almost no sleep, he passed out.

CHAPTER 11

GETTING THE WORD
AT CAMP EVANS

DURING THE FIRST WEEK AT CAMP EVANS, WE HELPED to secure the base's perimeter while laboring to improve what we thought would be 2/12th Cav's new base camp for many months to come. Additional combat elements of the division arrived at Camp Evans with similar expectations. There soon was activity throughout the camp, which slowed down only when the winter monsoon started, forcing us to slough through ankle-deep mud after each rain shower. Evans itself was a dump— treeless, muddy, and just plain ugly. And still no new stocks of ammunition.

Helvey's Company A was taken off perimeter guard and ordered to patrol south of Camp Evans toward Hue. Company A found many signs of recent enemy activity, but did not see any actual soldiers.

Support elements of the division arrived about the same time to begin work on a new supply base at Phu Bai, another area formerly occupied by the Marines about five miles south of Hue. It was destined to become the Logistical Control Center, under the control of our Division Support Command (DISCOM). They stockpiled the supplies there that should have reached us but didn't.

Everyone was working too hard to notice what day Tet started. It began quietly in some places. With thunder in others.

"We woke up one bright day and got word that Hue was occupied, with the exception of the 1st ARVN [Army of the Republic of Vietnam] Division compound," Tolson recalled. "We got this word while I was in the morning briefing on 31 January." The 2/12 Cav had been at Camp Evans less than five days.

In fact, the attack began throughout Vietnam at 3:00 A.M., January 31. At the same time the NVA attacked Hue, they also hit Quang Tri, the place we'd just left. The attack on Quang Tri came as a complete surprise to everyone in the division. The day before a defector had told us that a major NVA offensive was about to start, but he was only an assistant platoon leader. News of that magnitude was considered important only if verified by a better source.

By the time I heard the story, portions of the 6th NVA Regiment, 12th Sapper Battalion, and members of the Hue City Municipal Unit had breached the defenses of

Hue and were inside the city. Apparently, some elements had infiltrated the city without being detected.

The 4th NVA Regiment cut Highway 1 south of Hue, timing their operation to coincide with the attack on the city. Their action prevented reinforcements or supplies at Phu Bai from reaching Evans or Hue. The only friendly elements north of Hue capable of reaching the city belonged to the 1st Air Cavalry Division. But when Route 1 was cut, the NVA successfully prevented General Tolson from bringing the full weight of his forces to bear on the counterattack. There was no way to supply the division, except by sea. They caught us by surprise. It was a brilliant tactical stroke.

The commander of the 1st ARVN Division headquartered in Hue was also surprised by the ground attack on the Citadel, believing such an attack was one of the things that could never happen. Rocket and mortar attacks? Yes, that was certainly possible, but not a ground assault, especially with sixteen battalions, the equivalent of two divisions. An ARVN after-action report candidly identified the failure to foresee a ground attack as a serious shortcoming of the government forces, observing that it was no wonder the 1st Air Cavalry Division was also caught by surprise.

Our 3d Brigade commander, far more likely to be kept informed of sensitive intelligence than I, heard the news of the attack about the same time I did. "The battle of Hue, as far as the brigade was concerned, started early on the morning of the 31st of January," Campbell said. "We had heard about and been alerted by the heavy attacks on Hue and Phu Bai and other places in the north. Our first light reconnaissance detected NVA flags in many of the surrounding towns and villages."

Tolson almost immediately instructed the 3d Brigade "to attack to the south, southeast from Evans, to destroy the enemy between Evans and Hue," according to Campbell's after-action account.

"The first day, we got in the 2/12th, they moved on out and in the process they had some thirty wounded and we still were a long way from Hue," he added. "The upshot of it was that it took us essentially 1 February to 24 February to accomplish our mission."

General Tolson, the division commander, was of course responsible for everything the division did or failed to do, the burden carried by all military commanders. But he alone cannot be blamed for being out-generaled by the NVA because his intelligence apparatus failed him. Still, the fact is that the NVA had better senior leadership on the field than we did. At least they made sure that their forces were supplied and supported. Tolson's problem was more than intelligence, however. When Sweet briefed Tolson and key members of his staff on Sweet's plans to move toward Hue to reinforce our troops, Tolson asked the division staff whether Sweet's plan could be supported with artillery, air, and logistics. Can we do it or can't we? When no one raised any objections, Tolson gave the order to go. He had no reason not to.

"Not a single man there said they couldn't support

us," Sweet recalled with some bitterness. "No one raised any objections." Since the plan seemed supportable, Tolson, said, "Okay, send the 2/12th to Hue."

A few days later, when we were surrounded, Sweet wondered why we were abandoned. "Earlier they all said, every one of them, that they would be able to support us. If there was going to be a problem, any problem, why didn't some asshole say something?"

Sweet doesn't mind my blaming Tolson for our situation, but he still feels the staff and major supporting commanders bear some responsibility for not telling the commanding general the truth. They knew they could never support us, but they kept their mouths shut.

A quiet man, Tolson never raised his voice above its customary drawl and was, ordinarily, a model of composure. He was an easy man to like. If he harbored anxiety or grudges, he never let it show in public. He was always a neat dresser, even during Tet. Sometimes I wondered if his aides didn't stay up all night pressing uniforms. He was also a placid man, which created the impression that he really wasn't energetic or inspired. Tolson was not a cowboy, a man hell-bent-for-leather. One of his brigade commanders compared Tolson to other generals he had worked for: "Tolson is the master tactician of them all. He takes chances but not too many." George Wilson of the *Washington Post* described the fifty-two-year-old general as coming across more like an old fishing buddy than a hard-charging commander.

In 2/12 Cav, we didn't anticipate the Tet attacks until

they happened. At every routine, boring, and uninformative briefing someone would say that we shouldn't relax our vigilance during the Tet cease-fire, but staff officers are supposed to talk like that, whether or not they are sincere. Even so, the artillery units were ordered to keep men on alert at the guns. Captain Bud Jeffries, Danny Redner's replacement as our artillery liaison officer, recalled being told that Division Artillery (DIVARTY) would answer any request for fire. Major Maury Cralle, the 2/12 Cavalry Battalion operations officer, was nervous. "I don't know what's happening," he warned Jeffries, "but something big is going on."

Later I learned from other sources allegedly close to sensitive intelligence that the United States knew about the Tet Offensive at least a week before it started, but neglected to take forceful measures to inform the troops. Once more I appreciate the importance of keeping a secret, but at what cost? One could argue that keeping this secret cost us the war. Maybe the intelligence community was just as surprised as everyone else, but better at covering its tracks.

The best I could ever find out was that the U.S. spooks at Phu Bai had eavesdropped on NVA radio conversations on January 30, the first day of Tet, and concluded that an attack on Hue was imminent. Security procedures didn't allow our guys to report this information directly to either the 1st ARVN Division inside the Citadel or the nearby MACV (Military Assistance Command, Vietnam) advisers headquartered just outside the walls, so they filed their reports with another spook team one rung higher at Da Nang. Ironically, by the time the sanitized report finally reached Hue, the attack was already under way. We had, apparently, learned little since the reporting fiasco associated with the attack on Pearl Harbor nearly three decades earlier.

12

FROM CAMP EVANS TO PK-17

EARLY ON THE MORNING OF FEBRUARY 2, ABOUT FOUR hundred of us (the foxhole strength of the battalion) boarded helicopters at Camp Evans and flew about ten miles south to the place called PK-17, a small camp surrounded by a minefield. It was originally a French Army outpost, but its few tin shacks had been converted into the headquarters of the 3d Regiment, 1st ARVN Division. (It stood at the post, literally a cement post adjacent to the roadway, marking the seventeenth kilometer from the center of Hue.)

For unknown reasons, about half of the helicopters that shuttled the battalion from Camp Evans landed in fields about one thousand yards from PK-17, a long way in a combat zone. Why they didn't land at the same place as the others remains a mystery. For nearly an hour there was gross confusion as the battalion assembled by foot before setting out together for the fort at PK-17. This misadventure was recalled several days later as the first sign that our luck had turned sour.

After assembling the battalion, it took another two hours or so to march around PK-17 and head toward Hue. We stopped for the afternoon within easy sight of PK-17, just within maximum range of the 155mm howitzers still supporting us from Camp Evans.

I expected to reach the walls of the city no later than the afternoon of the following day. General Tolson was already boasting, "When the first cavalryman hits the walls of Hue, the battle will be over." His biggest concern was setting the boundary between his division and the Marines, so we wouldn't fire on one another. Coordination meetings involving the Marines, Tolson, Ross, and Campbell resulted in agreement that we would march to Hue but not enter the city.

The orders from our brigade commander, Colonel Campbell, were clear and precise: "Move toward Hue, locate the enemy, fix his position and destroy him." This sounded brave and inspirational. It was also impossible.

We didn't know it then, but the weather, which became our biggest enemy, was changing by the minute. As soon as we marched past PK-17, the dark sky became even darker. Rain and wind followed. This weather dogged us for the rest of the month. The overall condition was described later in a division afteraction interview:

The day which started off overcast but balmy and comfortable soon became colder and wetter. This deterioration in the weather was to last for the next three weeks. The temperature dropped into the low fifties and sixties and emanated a penetrating chill. A misty drizzle began to fall, sometimes increasing to a drenching, cold rain, turning into a muddy fog. The clouds closed in and the ceiling fell to 300 feet at times, rarely exceeding 800 feet, and limited visibility to a minimum.

A heavy ground fog was particularly dense at night and would only diminish slightly during the day. Visibility was further limited by this, seldom extending beyond 500 feet. The dramatic change in weather caught the majority of the battalions unprepared and without adequate clothing.

It was Groundhog Day all right. And no shadow. The Air Force report had more detailed information:

Weather resulting from a moderately strong northeast monsoon affected the area of operations from 1–27 February. . . . Significant effects were: ceilings less than 1,500 feet more than 50 percent of the time (much of this was less than 500 feet); visibility less than or equal to three miles about 60 percent of the time, and less than five miles 85 percent of the time; measurable precipitation fell on 25 days with a trace recorded on one other; temperatures were 10 degrees below expected minimum. . . . Relating this abnormal weather to the global picture, it appears, from data available, *that the month of February was more severe than average in many parts of the northern hemisphere.*

General Tolson recalled that "the weather was so horrible at this time, the ceiling being 150–200 feet, and the enemy antiaircraft fire was so intense in and around the immediate vicinity of Hue, that it made it impractical and illogical to contemplate an air assault by any unit of the division in the close proximity of Hue. That is the reason why I decided to air-land at PK-17 and to advance the 3d Brigade toward Hue astride Highway 1."

If the weather was disastrous for us, it was ideal for the NVA. They couldn't have planned it better because it eliminated our advantage in firepower and combat support. They took a risk, but their eyes were open. That's more than I can say for our side.

I was really annoyed by the change in the weather, and it affected my disposition. I finally got on one soldier for whistling the tune "What a Day for a Daydream." He was a cheerful boy from Chicago with bushy red hair and brilliant freckles. He wanted to be a postman in civilian life.

Information about the enemy was nil. "Goddamn it, where's Spry?" I asked myself, knowing well enough that he had taken advantage of the Tet cease-fire to meet his wife, Nancy, in Hawaii. I didn't object to his R&R, but I missed his support. The brigade intelligence office didn't function very well in his absence. Tolson, when he was later asked about intelligence information, responded candidly: "We had very little intelligence at this point."

Although it was soon known that the enemy controlled large sections of Hue, Tolson believed that they had put everything into the attack. They might fire on us as we approached the walls of the city, but the way there should be clear. Tolson seemed to think that 2/12th Cav could reach Hue "astride Highway 1" with little or no difficulty. If he had been worried, he would have demanded a fire support plan to protect us in the event we met resistance.

Intelligence sources supplied only one piece of information: "Unconfirmed reports of enemy activity in the hamlet of Thon La Chu." Where the hell was that?

The NVA knew the answer, having selected Thon La Chu as the place to stockpile supplies and replacements for the Hue attack. For most of the battle the hamlet was also the headquarters of the "front" that commanded the fighting. We would call the "front" a battle group or task force, but the NVA adopted the Soviet usage. The front headquarters operated under the disguise of being the 6th NVA Regiment, although it wasn't a regiment at all, just a headquarters that could command and control the battle. The headquarters itself was protected by the 29th NVA Regiment of the 325C NVA Infantry Division.

Regimental forces, detecting our presence at PK-17, confidently reinforced their northern flank with ample forces from their two organic infantry battalions. We didn't know it, of course, but Thon La Chu was a hornets' nest and, next to Hue, the most dangerous neighborhood in the territory.

The lack of more specific information supported the conventional belief that there was little, if any, enemy activity between PK-17 and Hue. This belief provided the basis for the division's operating assumption: when the NVA saw us approaching, cutting off their supply route and blocking their withdrawal, they'd leave to avoid being trapped. They would see us and run. We were hot-shit Americans; they were cowards who only knew how to hit and run.

Sweet, far more skeptical, had no intention of marching the battalion down the center of Highway 1—it was too risky. He assumed that an enemy able to capture Hue was smart enough to protect his flanks, however light that protection might be. Besides, if the NVA had cut the southern routes to the city, why not the northern roads too? It wouldn't make sense to prevent reinforcements from reaching Hue from the south if there wasn't some kind of plan to counter the presence of the 1st Air Cavalry Division on the north. If we marched to Hue by the most direct route—along Highway 1—we were likely to run into an ambush, or at least booby traps. We had to assume that the highway was mined. The shoulders, of course, would also be unsafe.

So, rather than heading for Hue immediately, Sweet independently ordered the battalion to move far away from PK-17 to avoid being hit by stray rockets aimed at the Vietnamese fort, and dig in for the night. We would head toward Hue the next day by a circuitous western route through Thon La Chu, reaching the objective by evening, as ordered, if we were lucky. The route also offered concealment and cover. If we'd walked down Highway 1, there would be no hiding from anyone. This plan would also allow time for our supporting artillery, which we would need as we approached the city, to be displaced from Evans to PK-17.

Thon La Chu was selected at random. It was just one of a half-dozen checkpoints we might have picked to mark our route on the way to Hue.

We still had a problem, one that we knew a lot about. Our individual packs had not been moved forward from Evans. Never before had we spent a night without our packs. Packs are salvation. By the time we realized the scope of the problem, the weather had closed in. In bad weather, only a combat emergency justified taking the risks involved in flying our packs forward by helicopter. Scudder, back at Evans, pleaded with Lieutenant Colonel Ross to make an exception, which the G-3 turned down "with great anguish." The packs would have to wait until later.

When we left the packs at Camp Evans, we thought moving to PK-17 was a routine 2/12th Cav operation. We would only carry ammunition; the packs would follow a few hours later. It was normal for the 2/12th Cav to carry up to two hundred rounds of 5.56mm (M-16) ammunition per person, two or more fragmentation grenades, a block of C-4 plastique explosive, two canteens of water, maybe a poncho, and one C-ration meal. That's how we conducted an assault. Later the packs, carrying a poncho liner (a thin blanket), extra rations, socks, and so forth, would arrive by helicopter once the objective was secure, whether or not there had been an actual fight.

Left behind, then, were extra socks, sweaters, protective ponchos, and warm poncho liners. Grenades, mines, and shovels were left too. These materials were required to make our defensive positions secure. We could stand the physical discomfort for one night without risking much; taking chances with our security was another matter. As things turned out, the packs were not delivered for another week. Even then, they were rifled before we got them; a bottle of Hennessy cognac in Captain Helvey's pack was forever lost.

Small arms ammunition was one thing we were not short of because we carried plenty. The M-16 ammo was carried over the shoulder in belts or in cases attached to the wide pistol belt held up by suspenders. Each soldier carried several grenades and seventeen magazines for his rifle, with eighteen rounds per magazine. Twenty rounds in the magazine would jam it.

With the exception of the fact that almost no one got any sleep, the first night out of Evans passed without incident. But we were cold. Some warmth was possible if two men shared a one-man foxhole, hugging one another. It wasn't comfortable, but it helped. When the temperature falls into the low fifties, when you're soaking wet and not a single crevice of the body is dry, no one is going to be comfortable. Wind-chill makes the misery worse. If you ripped your uniform, you fixed it as best you could or went bare-ass naked.

One young trooper from Kentucky tried to solve his problem by making a shirt out of an empty rice sack, cutting holes for his head and arms. Finding a piece of charcoal, he decorated the shirt with a large letter S on the front. This makeshift effort inspired other soldiers to look at local materials. Some stuffed rice straw under their jackets, but newspapers were preferable, because they didn't itch. One soldier caught a chicken, which he stuffed live under his jacket. Kept him warm until he got hungry.

Food was not an immediate problem, because there were enough cans of combat rations to give everyone something to eat. It was a good practice to begin a day's march with a few cans, and most soldiers carried rations stuffed in a sock tied to their suspenders. The suspenders were needed to keep the ammo-laden pistol belt from chafing the hips.

It was a miserable, quiet night. No enemy contact. As it started to get dark, however, two NVA rockets were fired harmlessly at PK-17. Big deal! Over our radio we learned that helicopters from the 1st Squadron, 9th Cavalry had spotted some enemy near Hue and killed thirty-seven. This good news added zest to the evening gossip and helped us look forward to sorting things out the next day.

We still had no idea how bad things were in Hue,

so we were more curious than afraid. Two days before, during the first day of the occupation of Hue, the senior U.S. military adviser to the 1st ARVN Division told the Marines sent to relieve the city that the battle was well under control, and the only help he needed was to evacuate Americans to keep them from harm's way. The next day the U.S. advisory team at I Corps headquarters in Da Nang reported that all of the VC were being evicted from Hue, supporting an earlier statement from the corps commander that only a platoon of enemy soldiers had yet to be dislodged. General Earle Wheeler, chairman of the Joint Chiefs of Staff, even assured the Senate Armed Services Committee that the enemy had only "some troops" inside the Citadel and less than a battalion on the south side of the Perfume River where the MACV (Military Assistance Command, Vietnam) advisory compound was located. These and other examples downplaying the difficulties of clearing the city are recounted with great vigor and clarity in Don Oberdorfer's classic tale, *Tet!*

Up to this time it's hardly surprising that our battalion assumed that we would reach the walls of Hue just in time to help mop up. Under the circumstances, we'd need nothing more than small arms. Still, no one ever assumed we'd be asked to operate in any situation—foreseeable or not—without artillery fire.

Like everyone else, I dug a shallow foxhole to sleep in, just big enough for one. Being underground would keep me from being hit by a sniper, although it would obviously provide no protection at all from a direct hit by a mortar or a rocket. As I was getting ready to call it a day, Major Cralle stopped by with his enlisted radio-telephone operator (RTO). "Krohn, are you in this hole by yourself?" he asked. I said that I dug it and I was going to sleep in it. "In that case, share it with my RTO," he ordered. "But he's an enlisted man," I protested. "Do you think it's proper?" This soldier was twice my size, but I was tired enough and smart enough not to protest further. In the middle of the night I was awakened by his leg rubbing gently against my groin as he struggled in restless sleep. "This is absurd," I said to myself, rolling back on my other side. It was my only erotic experience of the campaign!

We were all glad to get started at 7:00 A.M. Since there were no packs—what food we had was eaten the night before—it was simply a question of the battalion commander ordering the direction and formation of the march toward Hue. He ordered a diamond formation, with Company A in the lead, B on the right, C on the left, and D trailing.

As we started to move on that cold, misty, miserable morning, the horizon was brightened by the fires still burning in Hue. Hue seemed like a long way off, although we knew it was no more than five or six miles. With the exception of a few hamlets, we had only flat, open rice paddies before us. It was easy to see in all directions. I looked around at the battalion and was struck by the sight: it was the first time I had ever seen us moving together in classic textbook formation.

One survivor was later reminded of the scene from the movie *The Longest Day,* where one moment the German forward observer saw nothing, but in the next instant, saw the entire invasion force where nothing had been before.

We moved quietly. No one shouted, and there was no reason to talk. The only noise was the wind and the sucking sound of boots in the black rice paddy mud. During one halt I asked a soldier nearby if he realized we might still technically be abiding by the Tet truce. Johnson had agreed to stop bombing the north for the duration of the holiday. The soldier grunted. He must have been from West Virginia or Mississippi, states that consistently produce the best, most uncomplaining soldiers. He confirmed my suspicion when I mentioned that Jane Fonda would be pleased. Well, what did he think of Jane?

"I wouldn't piss in her mouth if her stomach was on fire," he drawled.

13

DEAD IN OUR TRACKS

AFTER TRUDGING ALONG SOUTHWARD FOR ABOUT A MILE west of and parallel to Highway 1, the battalion entered the empty hamlet of Thon Que Chu, maybe ten to fifteen straw huts. Judging from the cooking fires still smoldering, it had been abandoned just a few minutes before. Our suspicions were confirmed when we got to the other side of the hamlet and saw civilians running away from us and into the woods to the west about three hundred yards farther on. It appeared on the map as Thon La Chu.

Following normal procedures, we requested a smoke round from our supporting artillery. In case we spotted enemy targets, we could then adjust high-explosive artillery rounds from wherever the smoke round fell. For the first time in anyone's memory, however, we were told

109

there wouldn't be any artillery support—not immediately, in any event. We had always taken artillery support for granted. Our artillery battery was still at Camp Evans. The inclination was not to take another step until our artillery moved forward, but there was no enemy in sight, so we kept moving. We hoped that the artillery would displace before we made enemy contact, and we assumed that the division commander was moving heaven and earth to ensure our support.

Later, the combat after-action report recorded the actual situation:

The battalion advanced with little incident, initially. Company A received a few sniper rounds at 8:50 A.M., which did no damage. However, it soon became evident that getting artillery support was going to be a problem. The battalion had displaced so suddenly that its normal supporting artillery battery (Battery C, 1st Battalion, 77th Artillery) was still in the process of moving into a firing position at PK-17 and was not yet ready to fire. The only other artillery support immediately available consisted of two 105mm guns from an ARVN unit at PK-17. These two pieces could fire on a grid square accuracy with no less than 1,000 yards—not very precise compared to U.S. standards of 50 yards—but could not adjust their fire as directed by our forward observers, because there were no interpreters available at PK-17. The entire day has to be characterized by a paucity of accurate tube artillery fire.

This report exaggerates. There was no artillery fire, not until late in the day, after we were surrounded. Although he had nothing to do with the problem, Captain Jeffries, our artillery liaison officer, had to absorb the entire battalion's unhappiness over not having artillery support. Jeffries himself was surprised and unhappy. The rest of us were bitter and disgusted. The system had failed us. No one above us had planned for trouble. Risk taking can be the result of either boldness or negligence. Poor planning is not boldness.

When Jeffries reached the 2/12th Cav at PK-17 the day before as Captain Redner's replacement, he was informed through artillery channels that Battery C was on its way forward from Evans. There might be a short delay getting clearance to move the battery south on the highway, but no serious delays were expected. It was normally a routine matter to sweep a road with military police vehicles before declaring it open. We did it every day. While we stayed in the vicinity of PK-17, there was nothing to worry about, because we were still within range of the division's heavier 155mm howitzer batteries at Camp Evans. We were at the far limit of their range, but they were sufficient.

While the rest of us worried about not having packs, Jeffries tested the 155mm support, requesting a smoke round. A few rounds were fired, but the distance from Evans to PK-17 was too great to enable him to adjust accurately. The rounds exploded closer to our perimeter than they were supposed to, so Jeffries decided not to push his luck, hoping we wouldn't need any artillery support that first night.

There is no record that the artillery battalion commander, Lieutenant Colonel James R. White, even knew what the tactical situation was, because White and his battalion command post were waiting to move north from the Bong Son area, where they were supporting the 2d Brigade headquarters. Battery C, 1/77th Artillery remained under the temporary control of the artillery battalion that was assigned to the 3d Brigade, the 1st Battalion, 21st Artillery, whose commander was Lieutenant Colonel James J. Coghlan, Jr. I know it's confusing to sort out this mixed-up command relationship, but the logic behind it is rather simple.

The ordinary organization of the 1st Air Cavalry Division called for the 2/12th Cav to be part of the 2d Brigade. The brigade's supporting artillery battalion was the 1/77th Artillery. Battery C, 1/77th Artillery was the 2/12th Cav's direct support artillery battery. For reasons unknown, but not uncommon, the 2/12th Cav was temporarily attached to the 3d Brigade when the 3d Brigade moved north to the Da Nang area to help beef up the Americal Division. When the 2/12th Cav moved, its direct support artillery battery was moved too so the infantry-artillery team would not be broken up. (Purists will point out that the team wasn't really attached to the 3d Brigade but rather placed under the brigade's operation control, or "op con." In Army parlance, the terms "assignment," "attachment," and "operational control" have legal meaning pertaining to support and personnel accountability issues, such as court-martial jurisdiction and fitness reports, but for the purposes of combat you take orders from the commander you're working for.)

So the issue of what Lieutenant Colonel White knew or didn't know, did or didn't do, is irrelevant, because during the Tet period the commander of Battery C, 1/77th Artillery worked for the commander of 1/21st Artillery, Lieutenant Colonel James J. Coghlan, Jr., a 1949 West Point graduate. Coghlan had his own story, little of which gibes with division accounts. He agreed that weather may have been part of the problem, and from the perspective of the division staff maybe it was safer to wait until the next day to airlift Battery C's six tubes from Camp Evans to PK-17. But the problem behind the problem was something entirely different.

From an administrative viewpoint, maybe it made sense to wait for better weather, Coghlan agreed. But the move from Evans to PK-17 should not have been an administrative move; it should have been a tactical movement. His argument is based on the fact that we were in a war zone, and should have religiously followed Army doctrine that calls for simultaneous displacement of artillery and infantry. In short, when you move one, you move both. The 1st Air Cavalry Division routinely violated this doctrine, normally so sacred that the artillery commander has the authority to displace with his companion infantry unit in order to maintain tactical integrity. The doctrine was established to cover situations like ours—so the infantry would never be left hanging.

If the artillery is self-propelled or towed by another vehicle, simultaneous displacement is normally not a problem, but in the 1st Cav the artillery batteries didn't have enough trucks to move their own tubes. Coghlan had only four two-and-a-half-ton trucks (deuce-and-a-halfs) in his entire battalion of eighteen 105mm howitzers. In an airmobile division, the 105s had to be moved by CH-47 medium cargo helicopters, or hooks, the only helicopter powerful enough to carry a gun and ammunition. The CH-47s were controlled by the division staff, who were understandably anxious to husband this precious, versatile resource.

When Campbell moved the 2/12th Cav administratively from Evans to PK-17, Coghlan vigorously protested to Major Bowman, the brigade operations officer responsible for writing the operations order that outlined what the brigade was going to do, and assigned responsibility to the various staff and commanders. The complaint was that the move should be tactical, not administrative, but at a minimum the tubes should displace with the infantry battalions, C-1/77th with us and C-1/21st with the 5/7th Cav.

"Bowman looked blank," Coghlan said, "like he didn't understand what I was talking about." Bowman confirmed that the infantry would move first, the artillery later, because that was the brigade plan. "I never got an explanation for that decision," Coghlan remembered. From then on he was not impressed with either Bowman or Campbell and made little effort to suppress his unhappiness.

When Colonel Richard "Pinky" Winfield, the division artillery commander, later visited Coghlan at PK-17, he asked Coghlan, "What's wrong down here?" In complete honesty—and in response to a direct question—Coghlan told him that "Colonel Campbell is incompetent and should be relieved." It may have been an honest expression on Coghlan's part, but Winfield thought it was insubordinate. "Pinky took it as a lack of ethics on my part," Coghlan recalled, "and told me it was my job to support the brigade commander whatever he was."

Coghlan faulted both Campbell and Bowman for not demanding a tactical move, and the division staff, by implication, for not insisting on it. And he still believes air mobility doctrine was seriously flawed because of the way it handled artillery movement, giving the brigade commander the helicopters to move troops but keeping artillery movement under division control. (By the time the division took part in the Cambodian invasion two years later, the flaw was discovered and fixed, according to Colonel Tony Pokorny, the division artillery's operations officer.)

When the fighting began as we moved toward Hue, Coghlan went to Bowman again and asked for the brigade's plans for the next day. Bowman replied, according to Coghlan, "We don't know, because we haven't heard from the battalions yet." A more aggressive, take-charge brigade commander would, of course, consider input from the battalions, but he wouldn't let the battalions make decisions that were his responsibility, thereby, in effect, relinquishing command. Coghlan suspected, but could not be sure, that Campbell's predecessor was relieved by Tolson a few months earlier for being too aggressive, a quality now needed.

So while the 2/12th Cav was moving the afternoon of February 2, our supporting artillery twiddled their thumbs unhappily in the middle of an open field waiting in vain for CH-47 helicopters to carry them to PK-17. They were ready and willing, but they were in the wrong place. When we moved out early the next day, Battery C was still waiting in the field for their pick-up. When the hooks finally arrived, we had long since left PK-17 and were already cut off and surrounded, leaving a red trail from PK-17 through Thon Que Chu to adjacent Thon La Chu.

Coghlan understands why Sweet and the rest of us are bitter about not having artillery support, and even why we blame the artillery community for the failure. "It was a damn tragedy, there's no doubt about it," he concurred.

Coghlan doesn't expect to be excused for the flaws in air mobility doctrine, especially when the flaws conflict with common sense, experience, and judgment. Maybe the division artillery commander didn't argue the case forcefully enough with the division commander, or maybe Tolson made the wrong call or the wrong compromise. During fights with the VC around Bong Son, the flaws would not be apparent, because we usually initiated the action and wouldn't start until we were lined up and ready. But the artillery fiasco during Tet provides an example of how the 1st Cav, except for Sweet, failed to recognize the changing nature of the war, and the price we paid for this failure.

Through the years, Coghlan took a lot of heat for a situation that was not entirely of his own making. Some have suggested that a more vigorous commander would have commandeered trucks and forced the artillery tubes just as close to Thon La Chu as he could drive, then fire point-blank into the NVA surrounding us. I think a better case can be made for using trucks if the entire operation was organized by the 3d Brigade commander, hell-bent on saving us regardless. Campbell was under no obligation to follow such a course. To have done so would have been risky—and might have aroused the wrath of Tolson and the division staff.

If Coghlan, Campbell, or Tolson had taken the risk, one—or all—of them might have become heroes.

CHAPTER 14

ATTACK NOW

WHEN WE RAN INTO THE EMPTY HAMLET AND SAW people fleeing, it was obvious there was enemy in the area. Hundreds of little paper North Vietnamese flags planted throughout the hamlet confirmed the enemy's presence. Nobody touched them for fear of booby traps. It wasn't the time to think of souvenirs.

The commander of Company A's lead platoon was the first to spot enemy movement in the treeline to our south. They were only two hundred yards away and didn't appear to be afraid. Following the division's standard operating procedure, we called for artillery support. Once again, Jeffries reported that our artillery battery still hadn't arrived at PK-17, but that division was sending us a couple of helicopters armed with rockets.

Sure enough, we could hear the whoop-whoop-whoop

of rotor blades coming in behind us, and we told the pilots to fire into the treeline where we saw the enemy. The pilots were apparently unfamiliar with the area and, in confusion, fired the rockets into the treeline where we were crouching. They killed one and wounded four. It was an unfortunate accident, but fratricide is one of those things that happen.

There was no point in asking for Air Force support: the weather was too poor for the kind of mission we needed. "I hope they're bombing the hell out of Hanoi," I thought aloud. There was no disagreement.

Sweet was agitated when he picked up the handset of his portable tactical radio (officially an Army-Navy Portable Radio Communications-25, or PRC-25, but unofficially and universally a "prick 25") and demanded to speak with Colonel Campbell, the brigade commander. Sweet told Campbell that we faced serious problems if we continued to attack from the southern treeline without artillery support. Sweet explained that we couldn't get the ARVN artillery at PK-17 to fire into the treeline because they had orders not to fire into "friendly" areas. The brigade commander told Sweet that he was under heavy pressure to keep the 2/12th Cav marching toward Hue without any more delays. "They want you to keep moving," Campbell said, and intimated he was powerless to change our mission. The order would be obeyed.

Sweet initially figured he could start moving toward Hue if the ARVN artillery battery at PK-17 would shoot supporting fire. Campbell assured Sweet the ARVNs would do their best. "Bullshit," Sweet replied. "That battery better support me. I can't make the attack without them."

In fact, the U.S. Army liaison officer attached to the ARVN artillery unit offered full services to Sweet. He was a crackerjack officer anxious to help. Major Mike Ferguson, now a retired brigadier general, lives in Pensacola, Florida.

Sweet begged Campbell one last time to ask the ARVNs for support, because we had proof we weren't attacking into a friendly area, the issue that seemed to concern them so much. Of course, the expectation all along had been that U.S. artillery would move into PK-17 long before we made contact. This, as it turned out, was a wrong assumption.

Campbell reported that the ARVNs were pulling out of PK-17 on orders from the ARVN general in Hue. They had been told to head east toward the South China Sea, then swing south and try to break through. "Shit," Sweet shouted. Now he knew there was no chance of any artillery support whatsoever. Campbell's calm assurances that help would soon be on the way just added fuel to the fire.

"You will attack now. Warmaster out!" Campbell ordered, ending the conversation. "Warmaster" was his radio call sign. Many of us were thereby ordered to certain death, and for no reason, it appeared. The probability of success for an unsupported unit of our size seemed small. The situation called for a combined task force capable of rolling over every cell of resistance blocking the path to Hue. Refusing the order was not a choice, however. Neither our culture nor our psyche could say no. We resigned ourselves to the order: "Come back with your shields or upon them."

There is no evidence in any available records that Tolson knew about our dilemma. Or that he didn't know, for that matter. Tolson himself was under pressure to get a battalion to the walls of Hue. Maybe he just kept his fingers crossed. Years later, I made a serious effort to find out just what Tolson knew. His answer was to turn his back and just walk away. "Just like he did then," I thought.

In sending the 2/12th Cav, Campbell perhaps felt he was executing explicit orders. He knew there was a problem with artillery, and probably assured himself that the division commander understood the nature of the difficulty. If he did this, what more could he do? But promises were not enough.

After the battle, Sweet complained bitterly to Campbell about the lack of fire support. Campbell counterattacked with a vigorous defense of the artillerymen who arrived later to support us. "They even fell asleep at their guns," he said, acknowledging they didn't have much ammo to fire, just some leftover smoke rounds. Sweet shot back "for all the good they did us, they could have shoved the guns up each other's asses."

• • •

WHAT SWEET DIDN'T KNOW WAS THE BEATING CAMPBELL took from Major General Tolson to air-assault more infantry next to the walls of Hue, even while the 2/12th Cav was getting ready to attack Thon La Chu. As Major Bowman later reported,

> During this period General Tolson exerted a great deal of pressure on Colonel Campbell to air-assault a large force into the rice paddies just southwest of the city. Campbell stoutly resisted this pressure on the grounds that artillery support was not adequate to the task. The enemy situation and location outside the city were vague at best, and intelligence reports showed many troops outside the city on all sides. We understood the tremendous pressure that was being exerted on Tolson to dash up to the city walls with his division's troops. Campbell, however, considered his assets carefully and felt that he had inadequate fire support and information to do the job. At the time, the ammunition stocks available to C Battery, 1/77th Artillery and the ARVN 105mm battery in PK-17 was less than 1,000 rounds. Our normal preparatory fires for an air assault were 350 rounds of 105mm per infantry company landing zone. Moreover, we had no medium or heavy artillery, and low aircraft availability, and a very vague situation.

Both Tolson and Campbell knew that Battery C was still en route from Camp Evans, but Tolson apparently lacked understanding of the ammunition shortages and appreciation of the situation in Hue. Campbell may have made a mistake ordering us to attack without artillery support, but he wasn't about to make the same decision a second time. If the 5/7th Cav, for example, had been air-assaulted to Hue, there would have been two battalions in roughly the same predicament. Campbell may not have been a terribly aggressive commander, but he was definitely not a "yes man."

AT THIS POINT IT DID NOT TAKE A GREAT BATTLE CAPTAIN to realize what was about to happen. There were an attacking force and a defending force separated by a field some two hundred yards wide, with nothing between them except a small cemetery . . . a few headstones. The defending force was well dug in, prepared for the attack. They had good positions with plenty of cover and excellent fields of fire for their small arms and automatic weapons. Their tactics were flawless. It was a force determined to stop the attackers before they could reach the hamlet behind them. The name of the hamlet was Thon La Chu.

The attacking force was also disciplined and determined. However, it was not a force accustomed to attacking with "cold steel." But it would do as it was ordered, even if it meant going "over the top." Unfortunately, there were only a few bayonets. Normally, they weren't much good in Vietnam, anyway. With all the firepower we had, especially artillery, who ever got close enough to use a bayonet? As a result, few soldiers carried them;

commandeers left the decision up to the individual rifle-man.

I was hiding behind a palm tree at the forward edge of the treeline. I couldn't help thinking about the trench warfare during World War I. Just before the order was given to charge, I checked again to make sure I chambered a round of ammunition in both my rifle and my pistol. I repressed an urge to empty my bladder, and clicked the weapons' safety catches off so they'd fire if I pulled the trigger. Despite the temperature, my hands were sweaty, and my glasses were beginning to fog.

"Move out," Sweet ordered.

Some four hundred of us got up to charge. A few never made it past the first step. By the time we got to the other side of the clearing, nine of us were dead and forty-eight wounded, cut down by accurately aimed interlocking fields of grazing fire. ("Grazing fire" is a military term for weapons fire that never rises in trajectory above the height of a man. Every shot has the efficient potential to kill or disable.) An estimated fifty additional soldiers received wounds that they deemed too slight to report; they did not want to interfere with the medics, who were busy treating far more serious cases.

Under the circumstances, I thought we had done rather well. The comparison with the Light Brigade didn't escape me. I was tired but unhurt, and I felt good about it. But the facts were uncomfortable to contemplate. Fifty-seven casualties after we started the attack, and we were stopped cold—we only got two hundred yards closer to Hue. I wasn't sure we had accomplished much. We made the NVA pay a price for stopping us, but not a high price: we killed only eight NVA (at best) and took four prisoners. We didn't know how many NVA wounded there were. We reported higher figures to brigade, based on wishful thinking that made us feel better, but privately we knew the enemy had scarcely been scratched. Regardless of their casualties, enough remained to fix us in place.

By the time we realized where everyone was, we knew that we weren't even in the center of the hamlet—we hadn't gotten much past the treeline at the edge of the built-up area when our forward momentum ground to a halt.

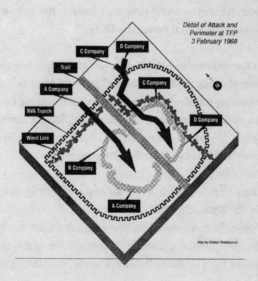

Detail of Attack and
Perimeter at TFP
3 February 1968

Map by Clinton Chadbourne

125

Our attack into Thon La Chu was not the American Army at its best. Certainly, it didn't have anything to do with air mobility, the 1st Air Cav Division's forte. The fact is, we were sent on a semi-suicide mission. There might be nothing wrong with this, if the decision were calculated. In our case, the decision was based on erroneous assumptions. Even so, the damage might have been controlled by rushing in forces to reinforce us, as Patton did when Bastogne was surrounded. For us, however, it was clear that we were on our own.

Individually we had done well. It was the system supporting us that had failed. The division's historians did their best to salvage something from the disaster.

After saying that air mobility is here to stay, they described Tet as the exception that proves the rule in an understatement that belies the facts:

> At the opposite end of the spectrum of mobility was the ground attack to relieve Hue. Using tactics more akin to breaching the Siegfried Line than to bold, dashing Cavalry charges, elements of the division attacked a strong, heavily bunkered enemy in weather that oftentimes precluded effective air and artillery support.

Weather may indeed impede air support, but is not normally an obstacle to artillery.

We no sooner arrived in Thon La Chu than someone asked the obvious question: "How are we goin' to get outa This Fuckin' Place?" After a while, we started using the expression TFP. It said it all. None of us knew the answer about how we were going to get out. We did agree on one thing, however—getting out would be harder than getting in.

When we attacked TFP, we had no idea how strong the enemy force was.

Originally, we expected resistance, because we saw enemy soldiers in the treeline before we attacked. We expected to overcome this resistance, because we believed in our superiority. We were anxious, for better or for worse, to get on with our real mission—Hue. One thing we never planned was what might happen if we ran into a force superior to ours. Obviously, we didn't know about Murphy's Law—if it's possible for things to go wrong, they will!

Just as soon as the battalion reached Thon La Chu, we spread out as much as we could and dug in a defensive perimeter. We had to get ready for a counterattack. Our strongest defense was to move into the treeline as far as we could get. The enemy anticipated our plans, and while we were digging in, they moved in behind us. We finished improving our defense just in time to realize that we were surrounded. That meant that we'd have to fight our way out. We did our best to show that we still had the firepower to exert our will by firing our M-16s at every visible target, but as the hours passed, it was obvious they were stronger than us.

TFP may best be compared to a darkened sand trap on a golf course in a Third World country tucked between a rifle range on one side and hand grenade pit on the other. Inside our perimeter were several hundred foxholes that must have looked like anthills from the air. The important point is that the foxholes marked the outer limits of the perimeter with no particular regard for the geography. As casualties mounted the perimeter shrunk and new foxholes were dug, almost before the enemy occupied the holes we were forced to abandon to keep our defenses tight. Any gap would invite sappers to sneak into our core, and no soldier could have driven off an attack from more than one direction at a time without our whole defense collapsing.

Inside our perimeter were shrubs and trees, so it was impossible to see the entire force from one position. It was dark enough during the monsoon season: the growth made it even darker and foreboding, as if it were under a witch-cast spell. There was never more than half-light, explaining why the attackers and defenders were so close. They had to be close to see each other.

The trees took a lot of hits in the trunks near ground level from small arms fire with little appreciable damage. Since no artillery was fired into the area until about 6:00 P.M., the upper branches stayed intact. However, this offered neither side any tactical advantage. Anyone attempting to climb for greater observation would have been an easy target for their riflemen or ours. It was important to keep eye-to-eye contact between each foxhole, so any shrubs in the way were removed as quickly as possible. Inside the perimeter, the shrubbery offered some protection to company commanders and their first sergeants who moved from hole to hole throughout the day to keep up morale and ensure that ammunition was evenly distributed. A maze of old paths confused everyone.

The shrubs were only about waist high, about the size of blueberry bushes.

With the exception of the coconut-bearing palm trees, the only possible use of any of the vegetation was to provide a wind screen for the nearby village. The ground itself was nearly flat and sandy with almost no topsoil, so digging foxholes required relatively little effort. The holes were dug where we stopped, without reference to the map or our mission. There was one stone hut in Company A's sector, about twelve feet square. Helvey made it his command post.

It was either noisy or quiet. We either whispered or shouted.

Later I was asked why the NVA didn't simply overwhelm us immediately, getting rid of us once and for all. At any moment they were close enough to charge us and could have, literally, wiped us out. Why didn't they? The answer is, the NVA commander was not a fool, and his mission was to defend the command post running the Hue occupation, not destroy us and—in the process— most of his own force. At this point, we had shoulder-to-shoulder defenses with interlocking fields of grazing fire. Anyone coming at us on the run would be cut down, almost from the moment he stood up to begin the assault.

It would have cost the NVA perhaps one thousand casualties to take us, allowing a three-to-one advantage to our side. Replacements for one thousand soldiers would have had to come from North Vietnam or from forces drawn from units holding Hue, neither an acceptable alternative. When the NVA commanding the forces surrounding us decided it was enough to check us in place and forgo suicide attacks against us, he was accomplishing his mission at the least cost. Destroying the 2/12th Cav was not his mission; protecting the headquarters of forces storming and holding Hue was. The NVA commander accomplished his mission perfectly when we attacked his dug-in defenses. Reversing roles would be to surrender his superior position, giving us a chance to do to the NVA what they did to us.

"In the Que Son Valley," Helvey remembered, "we fought the 2d NVA Division in several knock-down, drag-out fights. So we knew what we were getting into. We reacted the way we should have reacted at Thon La Chu, but at Thon La Chu we were outnumbered and outgunned."

Sergeant Chris Jensen agreed. "We tried to put out lots of fire, but whenever we poured out the bullets, they poured them right back at us. I couldn't believe a firefight could be this bad. They said there was probably an NVA battalion in there. Well, if they said the whole North Vietnamese Army was in there, I'd believe it."

Snipers from Company A who were positioned just a few feet in front of the unit's main defensive line nearly burned up their rifles shooting enemy soldiers no more than twenty yards away. "We used to see firepower demonstrations at Fort Benning," one survivor recalls, "but I never expected to see it for real."

When we realized that the NVA weren't going to counterattack immediately, we called for helicopters to evacuate the wounded. As they removed the dead and dying, I thought a lot about the day's activities. No doubt about it, we had taken it on the chin. The 1st Cav Division G-3 journal noted that the division that day had fourteen KIA and eighty-one WIA. Nine KIA and forty-eight WIA were from the 2/12th Cav. This couldn't be forgiven or forgotten.

As I sorted things out in my mind, some images were stronger than others. I watched the body of one medic being loaded on the medevac (medical evacuation) helicopter. We had spoken earlier before the attack, and he told me he was from Sacramento, California. He said his family was in the grocery business. His name was Lau. We broke off our conversation about the best way to prepare beef with ginger when the attack started but promised each other to pick it up later. He was literate, cultivated, and cheerful, like many other soldiers I met in Vietnam. He was one of the soldiers killed in the attack, shot while trying to reach another soldier hit in the head by sniper fire. With complete disregard for his own life, Lau had crawled from safety to reach the fallen soldier, who was probably already dead. Lau got no more than a few feet before he was cut down by sniper fire. No one ordered the young medic to risk his life—he did it on his own.

Lau was too good, too gentle, to be in such a place, Helvey recalled. "He was the best of what a human being should be. He reminds me of what Jesus Christ must have been like. He was too fine a person to be exposed to the terrible shit we were putting him through."

CHAPTER 15

SCUDDER, A MIRACLE MAN

AFTER THE MEDEVACS ARRIVED AND DEPARTED, A FEW supply helicopters started coming in, bringing us fresh supplies of combat rations and small arms ammunition. We had run out of both. One of the supply ships also brought Major Scudder. Although he could only stay for a few moments before returning to Camp Evans on the last ship out, he thought it necessary to appraise our situation firsthand. He wanted to hear from us directly what our priorities were, regardless of the risk to himself. It was an act typical of Scudder.

In wartime, many acts of heroism are performed on the battlefield; some are recognized and awarded and some are not. That's how life is. The work performed behind the battle lines is rarely recognized and almost never rewarded, although the efforts performed there are often of heroic proportions. Scudder is one such unsung hero.

Scudder did not deploy with maneuver units of the battalion on the march toward Hue. He stayed behind at Camp Evans to ensure that the combat elements of the battalion received the support needed to sustain themselves in battle: food, ammunition, replacements, and so forth. Normally, arranging for supplies is not a very exciting job for a former company commander.

During routine times, the executive officer does little more than monitor the work of the battalion staff operating in the rear area, ensuring from time to time that food and clothing reach the forward operating units; that the battalion's administrative functions proceed as they're supposed to, so that people leave and depart as scheduled with the proper rank and decorations; and that there is a battalion representative at all the brigade staff meetings, however irrelevant to the needs of his own organization. Normally, this is very prosaic work. But Tet was not a normal time. Established systems that were functional in the past suddenly ground to an abrupt halt. Few officers knew what to do.

Scudder, like Helvey, was a dazzling wartime officer, whose body chemistry thrived in war. When the Tet Offensive caused the division's support mechanism to collapse, Scudder seized the responsibility for taking care of his unit and shouldered the battalion's support burden. Without him, we wouldn't have made it.

When we pleaded for ammunition through routine

sources, we were told that there was none available, that the division's stocks hadn't arrived yet, regardless of what the conditions were at TFP. Scudder instinctively grasped that without ammunition the battalion would die, and sensed that he was the only one who could save it. He was right. We might have made it through half the night, until one outpost after another ran out of ammunition. We would have tried to distribute the grenades fairly, but they wouldn't have lasted long either. First one position would be overrun, then another, until the few remaining soldiers fell from wounds or exhaustion. What was left of the battalion would have to surrender.

With the hours before dark ticking off and the weather nearly unflyable already, Scudder saw that complaining wouldn't do any good. Even if he won the argument, the battalion was about to die unless ammunition could be moved forward immediately. Not in five hours or tomorrow, but IMMEDIATELY. With no one to turn to, Scudder took on the challenge alone.

Scudder searched high and low until he found what he was looking for: grenades and small arms ammunition piled up at the ordnance disposal site to be destroyed when the experts got around to it. The munitions had been left by the Marines and declared unserviceable. There were probably too many duds in the discarded lots to justify using the ammunition in combat. Scudder snatched the stuff before the experts could stop him and got it on the next helicopter out. It must have made the purists nervous as hell, but it saved the life of the battalion.

It may sound frivolous to make a big deal over socks, but later we needed dry socks to prevent trench foot and immersion foot—painful diseases that can incapacitate soldiers. Scudder scrounged some old socks somewhere, but they needed to be laundered. At least they needed to be dried. Scudder went to the division laundry for help. He was told that there was no gasoline to run the dryer, but if he would furnish the gas, they'd dry whatever he brought in until the gas ran out.

A West Point graduate and normally an officer inclined to follow the book, Scudder set out to find gas so we could get dry socks. The fuel came from the commanding general's personal kitchen or mess—Scudder didn't ask for it, he stole it. It was only sufficient to operate the dryer for an hour, barely enough time to dry 250 pairs of Army-issue socks. It was also the only change of socks the battalion received during the entire month of February, and even then it was not enough to go around.

Scudder decided he needed a landing pad in the battalion area at Camp Evans so he could get materials to the field faster by not having to move everything twice. It was muddy at Evans, and the helicopters bogged down in mud. At the time, road graders and other engineer equipment were tied up building an air strip to handle Air Force cargo planes. Scudder knew that soldiers are susceptible to liquor, although he didn't drink himself. With bribes of whiskey, offers of new boots, and vulgar intimidation when it seemed to be effective, Scudder "borrowed" some of the men and equipment from the airfield long enough to get a helicopter pad built.

During our second day at TFP, so many helicopters had been shot down trying to reach us that we had trouble getting our wounded out. When no one responded to our requests for medevacs, we turned to Scudder for help. He looked around Evans until he found three crews who volunteered to go in one more time to evacuate the non-walking wounded. He didn't try to smooth-talk the pilots into the mission, because he was asking them to risk their lives. The teenage aviators liked the sound of Scudder's voice and thrived on excitement.

The pilots cranked up their helicopters and flew the mission. Scudder's not even sure that they checked with their own commander. But they got the wounded out, just like they said they would. All three helicopters were so badly damaged by enemy gunfire, however, that they either crash-landed or had to be salvaged as junk. The wounded made it to the division hospital, and most survived. Those who did survive have the pilots and the surgeons to thank, of course. They can also thank Bill Scudder.

When a lieutenant colonel said he wouldn't let Scudder fly ammunition to us on a medevac going after the wounded (against the Geneva Convention!), Bill pulled his .45 and put it against the man's forehead. The order to fly the ammo out was given. Bill today denies this story, perhaps out of embarrassment. But it was widely told at the time. Anyway, I believe it. And so does Helvey.

Before he left TFP, Sweet gave Scudder an order, perhaps the last order he would give anyone: "Get to General Tolson and tell him if we don't get artillery support soon, this battalion will be completely lost. It will cease to exist."

As Scudder's helicopter lifted off, we fired the last rounds from our 81mm mortar to help suppress enemy fire. We had only carried a few rounds into TFP with us, and the mortar was the only indirect weapon we had to support us. We needed more ammunition. Major Maury S. Cralle, the operations officer, radioed back to PK-17 and Evans for resupply, but the results were discouraging. I was sitting with Sweet when Cralle gave him the bad news. "There's no more 81mm mortar ammunition. That's it."

Scudder's helicopter landed at PK-17, because that is where Tolson had flown when he heard we had run into trouble. Ignoring the presence of Colonel Campbell and his operations officer, Major Don Bowman, Scudder walked straight to the general and delivered the message Sweet had given him.

Tolson acknowledged that the 2/12th was in serious trouble. But he assured Scudder that the long-awaited artillery had already arrived at PK-17, and the ammunition was not far behind.

"It's not here yet," he said, "but we can do it—maybe within an hour." His prediction was correct. Within an hour the 2/12th Cav, decisively engaged at TFP and fighting for its life, heard the beautiful sounds of incoming artillery rounds rallying to its support. It was the first we'd heard in nine hours.

Lieutenant Colonel Ross was next to Tolson when Scudder confronted him. Ross shared Tolson's deep concern. He still felt close to the battalion he had commanded until just two months earlier. Ross knew that the battalion couldn't survive without artillery support, but he didn't know how to get it any faster than waiting for the delivery Tolson had promised. "You can't get blood from a turnip," Ross explained later.

No one knew how much longer the 2/12th Cav could hold out, even with artillery support. If the battalion went under, it would have been a disaster for the division and the American armed forces in Vietnam. With the end in sight, the division's chief of staff, Colonel George Putnam, alerted Ross to be prepared to take over command of the 3d Brigade from Campbell, whose stock had fallen considerably during the past few days.

Whatever errors in judgment contributed to TFP, there was little that anyone could do now that Campbell was not doing, and the switch was never made.

There is no doubt that Campbell had made some mistakes. It was Ross's opinion, for example, that Campbell had been too cautious. He thought that Campbell was not getting good advice from his S-3, Major Bowman. "I was goddamn mad at Don Bowman at PK-17," Ross declared. Ross, on the other hand, has not discussed the things that might have been done by division. One thing was moving artillery to PK-17 by road. A few vehicles might have been blown up, but so what?

When ordinary systems collapse, extraordinary people are called upon to do extraordinary things. Scudder, so far as I know, was the only person to risk his career and reputation for a higher calling. The rest let us gut it out.

Conventional wisdom has it that it's lonely being in command. No one was lonelier than Dick Sweet at TFP. His plea for help was acknowledged, but that's all. That's a heavy load to carry, and you carry it forever.

So much happened on February 3 from the time we left PK-17 until we were surrounded, it's not surprising that the official division record doesn't contain much. We know that Sweet sent Scudder to talk with Tolson directly about our predicament the afternoon of the third, but it is far from clear how much the division staff knew. Based on a close reading of the division G-3 journal, some of our artillery problems can be reconstructed, however. Late in the afternoon of February 2, about one hour after the 2/12th Cav arrived at PK-17, Colonel Campbell asked Lieutenant Colonel Ross, the division G-3, for permission to refuel the CH-47 helicopters transporting our artillery from Evans to PK-17 from JP-4 fuel stocks at Camp Evans. The request was turned down, and the helicopters were told to refuel far north at Dong Ha, because the available "fuel at Evans is for emergency only." About three hours after that, Ross did permit ARA (aerial rocket artillery) helicopters to refuel at Hue-Phu Bai, helicopters that would be required, presumably, to escort the CH-47s to Dong Ha, or from Evans to PK-17, after they picked up the artillery pieces.

On February 3 the division G-3 journal doesn't mention our not having sufficient artillery support for the attack. It does record our morning contact with the NVA defending Thon La Chu, an estimated two companies, with the observation that the 2/12th Cav was "presently engaging the area with artillery." That was only the several rounds fired by the ARVN, before they suddenly and inexplicably stopped firing, to displace closer to Hue.

At 11:20 A.M., according to the G-3 journal, Ross was informed that we had been surrounded at Thon La Chu and he ordered the battalion's "direct support artillery battery to move from Evans to contact area movement ASAP." Ironically (and wrongly) III MAF (Marine Amphibious Force) relayed information to the 1st Cav that the "VC were beginning to leave the city of Hue."

The G-3 journal has twenty separate entries of helicopters being shot down or shot at that day, including one CH-47 medium-lift Chinook that was trying to carry a load of 105mm artillery ammunition from Phu Bai to PK-17. A late afternoon entry confirms that ammunition that left Camp Evans by truck at 4:50 P.M. arrived at PK-17 at 5:45 P.M. My hunch is that the drivers sweated blood the entire trip and drove like hell, for their sakes as much as ours. The trip was apparently without incident, but imagine the drivers' shock to find PK-17 under mortar fire as they pulled in. One hit on the ammo in the back of a truck would have spread destruction to the others, a disaster for everyone concerned. Fortunately, that didn't happen, but it's a fairly safe bet that the possibility was on everyone's mind.

I tried to figure out later just how many helicopters sent to our aid were shot down that day, but the data just wasn't there. The problem is, it's virtually impossible to make a precise count, because of the reporting procedures. The reports note the unit and type of helicopter being shot at, and usually the location, but not the mission they were flying. A single extract from the G-3 journal for February 3 is illustrative:

> 2030 hours. From 11th Aviation Group. Company B, 228th Aviation Battalion, at map coordinates YD914168, CH-47, altitude 20 feet, 110 knots, received 30 rounds automatic weapons fire, 1 hit, not flyable. 1320 hours, B Co, 228th Avn Bn, at YD971113, CH-47A, 25 feet, 80 knots, received 60 rounds automatic weapons fire, 2 hits, not flyable, returned fire, 2 enemy killed.

The journal was signed by Major Phil Pons, our former S-3 who had moved to division headquarters as an assistant operations officer under Lieutenant Colonel Ross.

CHAPTER 16

CORDITE STINKS

EVERYONE WHO MADE THE DASH ACROSS THE SLAUGH-ter ground to Thon La Chu remembers the trip his own way. Lieutenant John J. Lewis of Company A remembered it as "the first time I had actually seen the enemy with weapons in hand . . . the first time I've seen them in combat." Sergeant Chris Jensen III, who had been in Vietnam nearly a year, "couldn't believe a firefight could be this bad. After a while, I was just praying that the ARA choppers would come back and that artillery would open up. Just drop something on them, drop anything." Praying didn't help. The support wasn't there.

After we established an all-around perimeter defense, the fighting continued without letup, and at least one NVA sniper succeeded in breaking through our thin, pale line. He made the mistake, however, of crawling into the area held by the men of Company A, who could stalk just as well as the sniper.

"When we were almost up to him, the sniper stood up and tossed a satchel charge at one of our men, then he dived back into his hole," recalled Specialist 4 David D. Dentinger. Dentinger realized something had to be done, so he dropped a grenade in the hole. A few seconds later the sniper was dead.

Specialist 4 Frank J. O'Reilly, Helvey's RTO and one of the most likable young men in the battalion, missed his pack. It had been left behind with the others. "We didn't have any water or purification tablets, and the river water was too muddy to drink," he remembered. "We were eating sugar cane, bananas, and onions. The same cigarette might be smoked by twenty people."

The company was under fire throughout the night and the next day. Lieutenant Lewis recalled never being out of enemy crossfire. "Finally we had about one man each in our foxholes who wasn't wounded, and there was a good chance we'd be overrun. We had to get out."

I remember the race into Thon La Chu, especially the strange sounds that still resonate in my eardrums—the rifle shots going past my head exploding like firecrackers, and the flatulent-like noises, like a horse farting, from our machine guns returning the fire. There wasn't much talking because there wasn't much to say, just calls for "medic, medic" from those who didn't make it across the field without injury.

Occasionally everything went quiet, save for the

crackling static of the radios. Then the firing would start up again, loud and obscene. The muddy fields fought back with an unpleasant oozing noise as men rushed toward the woodline by the most direct route, rarely looking down to measure the land. We fired our M-16s as we ran, but the shots were unaimed and couldn't have done much good. Although we were as beautifully conditioned as jungle animals, we panted loudly when we finally reached the treeline. The field was only two hundred yards or so across, but it took every bit of energy I had to sprint from one side to the other. Stress contributed to the exhaustion as much as the exertion, and when I finally reached safety, I gasped for air as if I'd just won a ten-mile race in the Hue Olympics. It was a fool's paradise, because the NVA resumed firing as soon as they got their defenses reorganized to accommodate our new positions.

If I thought much about dying, I don't remember. About the only defense mechanism that really works in a jam like TFP is not thinking, at least about the future. Anyone who thinks too hard in this situation is in for real trouble. As a bachelor, I had no family to worry about. When I left home to go to college, I walked out the door for good. In fact, few of us were married. Still, Sweet was married. And Maury Cralle remembered that he was very conscious that he had a wife and five little girls back in the States. But I suspect they tried hard not to think about the future.

Enough was happening—I worried only about the

here and now. Was my rifle clean enough? Should I fire a burst to check it? Was it safe to crawl from my foxhole so I could take a leak near the bushes? What if I had to have a bowel movement? Would I have enough courage to squat by the tree as I just saw someone else do? Should I update my intelligence estimate? The answer to the last one was easy. I should. We were surrounded and I didn't have the slightest idea if they would attack us with an all-out assault or if they would just leave us hanging.

My sense is that shell shock is caused more from thinking too much than from the cacophony of combat. There was either a lot of noise or total silence. When our perimeter was being probed, the racket was deafening, both from incoming fire and our shooting back. War movies replicate the sounds fairly well, however implausible the plot or unrealistic the dialogue. But I have yet to see a movie about which I could say, "Yes, that's what it was like." They're always too heavy on the action scenes and too light on the waiting. Others carry political messages, usually too obtuse to take seriously.

The only smell was cordite—or what I think cordite smells like. If we stank, we all stank equally. There was some burning scrub, but everything was too wet to burn well, adding to the caustic bouquet.

If I couldn't look into the future, I spent a fair amount of time thinking about the past, searching for some experiences that prepared me to handle where I was at TFP. What came to mind was some wilderness canoe tripping I had done in northern Ontario. Anyone who has ever capsized during a storm and finally made it to shore with no dry clothes or bedding and no way of starting a fire for days will appreciate our condition at TFP.

Sweet was quick to understand. I was slower. It took me about twenty years to grasp the idea that the system that worked so well in Que Son collapsed in Hue. Up until then I thought the two battles were similar because of the horror of battle. I did not realize how they differed. In the first battle, the leader failed but the system worked. In the second, the leadership was sublime, it was the system that failed. I recognize that systems work because men make them work, but even so, in the Que Son Valley the supporting systems operated nearly to perfection. As we moved toward Hue, however, very little support came through conventional channels the way it should. And some support arrived only very late in the day.

Years later, when I started talking to others about this paradox, word got out about the track I was taking. I was surprised—and should not have been—by the number of telephone calls I got directly and through others imploring me not to write this account.

CHAPTER 17

ARTILLERY FIASCO

WHEN THE AMMUNITION FINALLY REACHED OUR ARTIL-
lery battery at six that evening at PK-17, Jeffries called
for fire missions. He was sitting in a foxhole a few feet
from mine near the center of our perimeter. He was told
that only five hundred rounds had been brought in with
the battery. Additional ammo was supposed to be given
to us immediately, but was inexplicably delayed until
next morning. But five hundred rounds were a lot better
than nothing. "They were the best five hundred rounds I
have ever fired," Jeffries remembers.

Sweet and I agreed. We might not survive for another
twenty-four hours, but at least we would make it through
the night. It wasn't glorious, but we made it. As we fought
off attacks, we heard that PK-17 was being rocketed. Battery C even took some hits. We knew that the NVA had

Captain Charles A. Krohn, Saigon, February 1968.
(Author's Collection)

Lieutenant Colonel M. Collier Ross, left, and Command Sergeant Major Freeman near Landing Zone (LZ) Ross. They are sitting in a UH-1 "Huey" helicopter. (Courtesy Dane Maddox)

Daniel Z. Henkin, assistant secretary of defense for public affairs, presenting the Silver Star decoration to Captain Charles A. Krohn at the Pentagon, 1968. (Department of Defense)

Captain William I. Scudder. He asked the author to mention the company mascot puppy, Little Kling. (Courtesy William I. Scudder)

A 2d Battalion, 12th Cavalry soldier on patrol in the Que Son Valley, October 1967, near LZ Ross. Note the M-79 grenade launcher. (U.S. Army)

Brigadier General Richard S. Sweet. The author last visited his gravesite at Arlington National Cemetery on Memorial Day 2007. (U.S. Army)

A captured North Vietnamese Army (NVA) photo believed to have been taken before the attack on LZ Ross. Civilians are probably members of the political cadre attached to the 2d NVA Division. (Courtesy A. Earle Spry)

A captured photo showing an NVA column believed to be moving toward attack on LZ Ross in Que Son Valley, December 1967. (Courtesy A. Earle Spry)

U.S. and South Vietnamese officers examine a model of Hue used by the North Vietnamese to plan their attack during Tet '68. The model was discovered after the attack in an assembly area near the city. (Courtesy A. Earle Spry)

Captain Dane Maddox stands next to a captured NVA 82-mm mortar at LZ Ross, January 1968. He fired illumination rounds whenever he needed to find the latrine at night. (Courtesy Dane Maddox)

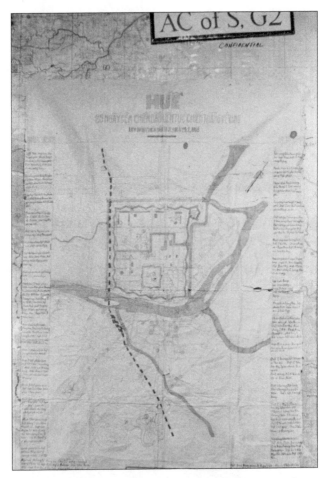

A captured NVA map showing their attack plans for the city of Hue. Notes around the border record an after-action report from the viewpoint of the NVA forces. (Courtesy A. Earle Spry)

A 105-mm howitzer of C Battery, 1st Battalion, 77th Artillery taken during a lull in the Battle of Hue, February 1968, at PK-17. Despite the mess in the vicinity, the tube itself is spotless, ready for action. (Courtesy Dane Maddox)

Two unidentified, exhausted soldiers from the 2d Battalion, 12th Cavalry taken just after the battalion escaped encirclement. (Courtesy Robert L. Helvey)

Private First Class Hector L. Camacho, the 2d Battalion, 12th Cavalry's best scout, during the Tet '68 Offensive. (Courtesy Robert L. Helvey)

Captain Robert L. Helvey, left, and Sergeant First Class Sherman Anglin just after escape from TFP during Tet '68. Note the athletic jersey under Helvey's fatigue jacket showing the number "6." (Courtesy Robert L. Helvey)

Major A. Earle Spry, intelligence officer of the 1st Cavalry Division's 3d Brigade near the Que Son Valley, November 1967. (Courtesy A. Earle Spry)

Captain Bud Jeffries, artillery liaison officer to 2d Battalion, 12th Cavalry at Camp Evans, just prior to the Battle of Tet. Jeffries preferred to wash his uniform himself. An open-air latrine is in the background. (Courtesy Lewis I. Jeffries)

OFFICE OF THE COMMANDING GENERAL

_____ 19___

Memo to : _____

<u>MISSION</u>

(1) SEAL OFF CITY ON
WEST + NORTH WITH
RIGHT FLANK BASED ON
SONG HUONG.
(2) DESTROY ENEMY FORCES
ATTEMPTING TO EITHER
REINFORCE OR ESCAPE
FROM HUE CITY.

JOHN J. TOLSON
Major General, USA
Commanding

This is the order handed to Colonel Campbell (dictated by Major General Tolson to his staff at LZ Evans) that resulted in the 2d Battalion, 12th Cavalry being ordered to attack toward Hue. (Courtesy Hubert S. Campbell)

An unnamed Kit Carson Scout, center, with other members of Company B, 2d Battalion, 12th Cavalry, at LZ Ross, standing in front of the battalion chapel. Lieutenant Roger Kehrier is at left, Captain Phil Pons at right. The man to the far right is unidentified. (Courtesy Phil Pons)

Captain Charles A. Krohn, right, talks with his interpreter, Sergeant Phung, at LZ Ross. The third soldier is unidentified. The author assumes Phung perished after the NVA conquest in 1975. (Author's Collection)

Colonel Hubert S. Campbell. (Courtesy Hubert S. Campbell)

A view of PK-17 during the Battle of Hue. Note the bottle of hot sauce in the foreground used to make combat rations more palatable. The rafters in the building behind are needed to carry the weight of sandbags, the only protection against incoming NVA rockets. (Courtesy Dane Maddox)

Lieutenant Colonel Charles A. Krohn being promoted by Major General James B. Vaught at Fort Stewart, Georgia, 1979. Mrs. Krohn assists Vaught. Vaught later commanded the operation to rescue Americans held hostage in Iran (Desert One). Author provided public affairs support during post-operations activities. (U.S. Army)

1st Cavalry Division Commanders, Post-Tet Conference, March 1968. 1st row: Col Winfield, DivArty; Col Gude, 22th Avn Gp; Col Stansberry, Spt Cmd; Col Putnam, CofS; BG Irby, ADC; MG Tolson, CG; BG Davis, ADC; Col Rattan, 1st Bde; Col McDonough, 2nd Bde; Col Campbell, 3rd Bde. 2nd row: LtC Davis, 15 Med; LtC Dubia, 1-8 Cav; LtC French, 1-12 Cav; LtC Robinson, 2-7 Cav; LtC Brown, 327 Avn; LtC Speedman, 2-8 Cav; LtC Sweet, 2-12 Cav; LtC Stannard, designee, 1st Bde; LtC Emerson, 15 Spt Bn; LtC Tyson, 2-20 ARA; LtC Dixon, 228 Avn; LtC Vaught, 5-7 Cav; LtC Wasiak, 1-7 Cav. 3rd row: LtC Love, 2-5 Cav; LtC White, 1-77 FA; LtC Gentry, 13 Sig; LtC Creed, 27 Maint; LtC Townsley, 8 Engr; LtC Diller, 1-9 Cav; LtC Runkle, 1-5 Cav; LtC Klobe, 1-30 FA; LtC Boykin, 2-19FA; LtC Metz, 229 Avn; LtC Coghlan, 1-21 FA. (U.S. Army)

Under the dirt in the foreground is the mortar pit where the 2d Battalion, 12th Cavalry hastily buried eleven soldiers on 4 February 1968, before escaping encirclement later that night. The soldiers' bodies were recovered later by the 5th Battalion, 7th Cavalry. (Courtesy James A. Cervera)

Another view of the mortar pit, including a school and children on left. (Courtesy James A. Cervera)

This picture was taken in 2000 by Jim Cervera, who searched for and found the mortar pit where his brother and ten other soldiers were hastily buried the night of 4 February 1968 when the 2d Battalion, 12th Cavalry escaped encirclement at TFP. The battalion found refuge atop the mountain in the distance. The power lines in the foreground are recent. (Courtesy James A. Cervera)

their range, because PK-17 had taken a direct rocket hit earlier in the afternoon. It killed one and wounded seven.

Not a single round of the five hundred was wasted or expended needlessly. Targets were zeroed in close to the east and west sides of our perimeter only, however, partly to save ammunition, and partly for safety's sake.

Army doctrine calls for massed artillery fires to support both offensive and defensive operations. If we had one thing going for us in Vietnam, it was all the artillery we wanted and then some. It was everywhere, and normally no mission was too small for fire. We had so much artillery that we used to dream up missions just to keep the guns hot. The supply was inexhaustible. Just how generous the 1st Air Cav was with firepower can be gleaned from a single example recorded in the division newspaper, *Cavalair*, in an article bylined by Specialist 5 Don Graham, one of the paper's reporters. It has to do with an episode that found four 2/12th Cav soldiers pinned down by a single sniper in the Que Son Valley near LZ Ross: "Protected by the rice paddy dike," Graham reported, "the U.S. soldiers watched three air strikes, helicopter rocket runs, and more than one thousand rounds of artillery pour down on the enemy positions."

The four cavalrymen took advantage of the spectacular firepower demonstration to crawl back from the dike. Safely, they rejoined their unit just twenty-five yards away. It probably cost the U.S. taxpayers several hundred thousand dollars to deliver the ordnance on the target, but who can argue it was not worth it?

When our attack into TFP was staged without any artillery, the idea was so improbable that we couldn't fully grasp the significance until after we were surrounded.

Here's how it should have happened: First, we should have used the artillery to screen our attack by firing smoke rounds into the woods, obscuring the enemy's vision. Later, as we mounted the attack and started to move across the open field, we would have requested high explosive artillery shells to be fired into NVA positions, making them keep their heads down. The smoke would have continued until we reached the far side of the field. Then, after we reached the woodline, we would have adjusted the artillery fire around our perimeter, keeping the enemy at bay with accurate barrages—surrounding ourselves, in effect, with a wall of steel.

This is economy of force in action—using artillery instead of men to do the job. It's part of our national strategy and has been for a long time—ever since we determined that we were rich enough to substitute vast amounts of matériel for manpower. Few tire of repeating the theme. Even a recent Library of Congress report notes the obvious: "Massed firepower consistently takes precedence over massed manpower to help compensate for U.S. quantitative inferiority. Aerial bombardment and artillery barrages reduce enemy resistance and friendly casualties." This policy statement was as accurate in 1968 as it is in 2008. With a little more command attention and perhaps a little more patience, we could have proven the rule rather than the exception. We could have validated the wisdom of our nation's rational, long-standing doctrine.

The 105mm artillery pieces of Battery C could have provided this support, if they were positioned within range. The tubes will fire a projectile more than six miles with an accuracy of plus or minus fifty yards.

Captain Dane Maddox, commander of Battery C, understood how much we needed his support, because his battery and our battalion were teammates. We each felt uncomfortable without the other. Separation affected our moods. Maddox later declared that he felt more a part of the 2/12th Cav than his parent artillery battalion. "It was that close a relationship," he said. He knew we should have displaced from Evans to PK-17 simultaneously. In fact, Maddox was alerted to move on February 1, about the same time we were. As it was, we moved on February 2, according to plan. When it came time to commit heavy lift helicopters to move the artillery, however, the decision was that the weather was too bad and the helicopters too precious to risk moving forward until the following day.

On February 3, two of the 105mm guns were finally flown into PK-17, but virtually no ammunition—only forty rounds each—accompanied the guns. Maddox arrived with the two guns, leaving his executive officer with four guns remaining at Evans.

The CH-47 helicopters did not take the guns directly to PK-17, however, because they were afraid that PK-17, regularly under mortar and rocket attack, was too dangerous to approach with so lucrative a target. Therefore they dropped the tubes about three hundred yards away from the fort and departed before they could be fired on by enemy gunners, who required several minutes to adjust their aiming mechanisms for that new distance and direction. This delay was fine for the helicopters, but it left Maddox with two useless guns and their crews out in the open. The guns were not self-propelled.

There were two ways to get the guns ready to fire: walk to the fort at PK-17 and ask the Vietnamese commander for a couple of trucks, or haul the guns in by hand. The tubes were still sitting in the field when we attacked TFP. Later they were dragged into firing positions by the crews.

The other four tubes didn't arrive until the next day, and might not have arrived at all except for the resourcefulness of Maddox's executive officer, who got tired of waiting for helicopters and moved the tubes himself by borrowed truck. Another good man! "I don't know if the division even knew he had moved those tubes," Maddox said later.

Tubes are no good without ammunition, of course, and the five hundred rounds Maddox got on February 3 were soon expended. Fortunately, trucks carrying ammunition began arriving at PK-17 on February 4, rolling into the old fort about the same time as the convoy led by Maddox's executive officer arrived. The ammo was probably carried from ships by helicopter to the trucks, one or two pallets at a time.

This is the time for throwing darts. Let's review the mistakes, the would-have-beens. Let's Monday-morning-quarterback. Helicopters that dropped the first two tubes on February 2 should have gone back right away for more ammunition. Even if the pilots didn't want to land at the fort, they could have dropped sling loads where they left the tubes. Maddox could have used the trucks at the fort to pick up the ammunition. Perhaps fifty casualties would have been prevented, and it might have kept us from being surrounded.

If it was too risky for helicopters, it would have been worth the risk to run an ammunition convoy down the road from Evans to PK-17. With a battalion about to be annihilated, why not take a chance? As it turned out, this road stayed open throughout the entire Tet campaign.

During the time we were surrounded at TFP, artillery support was not the unlimited supply we were accustomed to at LZ Ross. We had to watch every round, because we didn't know how good the supply was or how long it would last. When we were offered fire support from the Navy, we took it.

The problem with naval gunfire is that it cannot be adjusted close to friendly positions, which is what is needed in close combat. There are two reasons: first, naval gunfire has to be readjusted each time the ship reverses course, which is time-consuming; second, and more important, the trajectory of naval gunfire is so flat that it's dangerous to position friendly forces on what is called the gun-to-target line. Slight changes at sea or ammunition variations can cause the high explosive rounds to fall too far or too close.

Still, naval gunfire is better than no fire at all, and we took all we could get and were thankful for it. The second night at TFP we emptied the cruiser *Northhampton* of its remaining arsenal of 1,140 rounds. That was a lot of shooting for the crew of the *Northhampton*. "The Navy didn't believe at that time that anyone could have that sort of fire mission for them," Ross recalled. But it is unlikely that we were telling the Navy how bad it was onshore. Being surrounded was not the kind of thing the 1st Cav would advertise.

It was nip and tuck at TFP, but Sweet was in control and kept calm. The only time he got excited was when he noticed Major Cralle crawling around, firing his M-16 rifle to see if it would work. "Goddamn it, Maury," Sweet yelled, "get back in the foxhole." Cralle didn't think this was very funny, but it broke the tension. (Cralle picked up the nickname "Ladykiller" after he shot a woman firing a concealed pistol at Sweet later in the Tet campaign—she missed Sweet but hit his radio operator.)

There was a lot of activity at TFP that afternoon, and each time a helicopter arrived or departed, we'd fire all the weapons we had into suspected enemy positions, hoping to divert their attention away from our only means of support—aerial resupply.

Most of our effort was spent digging foxholes. Soldiers like to dig fancy foxholes with overhead cover, shelves, and grenade sumps; then, in case any enemy grenade should fall into the hole, it rolls into the sump and explodes harmlessly. When you're short of shovels, there's no time to dig anything except a basic position, then pass the shovel to the other soldiers waiting for it.

Holes are dug in priority. First priority was the positions where we emplaced crew-served weapons—mortars and machine guns. Last priority would have been the latrine, but we weren't immediately worried about field sanitation. Besides, no one would dare stand up to empty his bladder. You did what you had to do the best way you knew how. Army field sanitation doctrine doesn't cover this contingency. Major Cralle solved his problem by peeing in a C-ration can, which he cautiously emptied over the side of his foxhole. At six feet two inches, he would have been an easy target otherwise.

We could have used camouflage materials. If we had had them, we would have hung the ponchos over our foxholes to keep out the rain. But the few ponchos we had with us were used for litters to carry and shelter the wounded. Exhaustion was also starting to catch up with us. Soldiers directly on the edge of the irregular perimeter tried to take turns sleeping, but there were too many interruptions to make sound sleep possible. Nor was the atmosphere conducive to relaxation. There wasn't time for small talk, and nobody was in a mood to read, even if they had a paperback.

Those inclined to pray did so: the time had never been more propitious. It was clear to everyone that we were surrounded by a stronger enemy that could take us anytime they made up their mind to. Still, we were so close to death—it was all around us—there was no inclination to panic.

With death so near, one might think that there would be turmoil and confusion, even anger or fear. Yet this wasn't the case at all. During the pauses between gunfire bursts, soldiers concentrated on what they were doing. I dug a foxhole for myself and a radio operator who had a wounded hand and wasn't able to hold a shovel. From time to time, I'd crawl over to Sweet's makeshift head-quarters—a three-man foxhole—to see what I could do to help. I tried to figure out what the enemy was doing, searching with my binoculars as best I could. Sweet carried a terrible burden. The least I could do was stay out of his way.

There was a certain uniqueness to our situation, not unlike the fate of pioneers crossing the western fron-tier. We operated in a closed world, a world in which the only thing that mattered was what happened to us. We shared the same risks regardless of rank, age, or race. The chain of command reflected an appropri-ate distribution of responsibility, so we worked hard to make it work. But the only people respected (except for the wounded, of course) were those who contributed something.

In addition to the weather and the NVA, we saw a third enemy: the 1st Air Cavalry Division with everyone in fetal lock. Yet our trust for one another was complete.

No unit in any army had our cohesion. We were the greatest battalion ever.

In Saigon, newsmen were being told that Hue would be cleared in short order, that it was "just a matter of time." Maybe "in the next day or so," one briefer predicted. If he knew about us, he didn't let on.

CHAPTER 18

TAKE A BREAK,
DEATH WILL WAIT

DURING THE FIRST NIGHT OF OUR ENCIRCLEMENT WE reported to brigade that our perimeter was shaken by the explosion of two enemy rockets. As it turned out, that wasn't true. They weren't enemy rockets—they were errant projectiles from our own supporting artillery battery. What happened is that one of our artillery observers was so tired that he adjusted the artillery in the wrong direction. Instead of adjusting the fires two hundred yards forward or right, he called for changes that brought the shells two hundred to the rear or left, whatever the case was.

Considering the universal exhaustion, it was not an unforgivable error, but I was annoyed when one or two rounds landed ten feet from my foxhole. Fortunately, I was trying to sleep at the time, and was not injured by any flying shell fragments. Nor was anyone else. Still, the concussion stunned me, and for a time I was unconscious. When I recovered and became alert enough to realize that I hadn't been wounded, I was glad the NVA didn't get me. When I discovered that I was almost killed by friendly fire, however, my mood changed.

I protested to whoever informed me about the mishap that I wanted the name of the artillery observer responsible. If he were accident-prone, I thought his latest error should be reported as a matter of record.

"I won't tell you his name, because you really don't want to know," my informant said. "He's a fine officer, and he's done an outstanding job for the battalion. He's probably saved your life plenty of times. It would be a black mark on his record if you reported him. Do you really think that'd be something to be proud of?" I agreed to drop the matter, and even apologized for making a fuss, although I had some lingering doubts.

"I just had the hell scared out of me," I said, trying to put the best face on it I could, "so if there are going to be any more mistakes, let's make them on the enemy's side of the line, not ours." To the best of my knowledge, this was the last and only adjustment error recorded at TFP.

The more senior people at TFP took it upon themselves to help the younger soldiers see our situation in perspective, and spent as much time as they could going cheerfully from foxhole to foxhole. No one was more effective in this role than our command sergeant major, Richard C. Halperin.

Before he was named the senior enlisted man in the battalion, the command sergeant major, Halperin had been the first sergeant of Company A. I was glad he was picked for the battalion job, because he always stayed busy doing something useful. During Tet he never left Sweet's side except to take care of some pressing matter, keeping Sweet informed about the state of morale.

Halperin looked the part of a sergeant major: he was thirty-six years old—just two years younger than Sweet—and he had nearly twenty years of Army service, having joined in 1950 to fight in Korea. He and Sweet were our only two veterans of the Korean War. Halperin didn't have anything against the Brooklyn Hebrew Orphanage, where he was raised, but when the North Koreans crossed the 38th parallel, he was caught up in patriotic sentiment and joined the Army along with some of his friends.

"Kate Smith was a big thing in those days, and I wanted to be a part of what was going on. I really liked the way the uniforms looked, too," Halperin recalled.

Halperin was the father of five, but he was as devoted to the battalion and the Army as he was to his family. He was a master at teaching the ropes of the profession to our fresh lieutenants without embarrassing them, and I think a lot of our sergeants got their ideas from him. "Lieutenant, we can do it that way if you want to, but I think that . . . ," he would say, diplomatically heading off a greenhorn mistake.

During the march toward Hue, Halperin was still

suffering from psychological wounds over the death of a lieutenant killed in the Que Son Valley. Halperin had been breaking the officer in to the battalion's way of doing things when he was killed by a sniper.

"When I first saw him, he looked so young, I didn't know whether to burp him or salute him." He watched over the lieutenant like a protective father, chewing him out one hot, sunny day for risking a sunburn by taking off his fatigue jacket. "Platoon leaders are supposed to set the example."

On the day the lieutenant was killed, Halperin's platoon was leading the company. The sniper killed the point man first, then shot the squad leader who moved forward to investigate. Despite Halperin's warning, the young platoon leader charged forward recklessly toward the sniper, who fired another shot that killed him instantly.

"I was so angry that he let himself be killed that way that I just couldn't touch him afterward," remembered Halperin, who had let others carry the body away.

Later, Halperin took a shine to Helvey. If it hadn't been for Halperin, Captain Helvey might never had been given command of Company A back at LZ Ross. He might instead have spent the rest of his tour as commander of headquarters and headquarters company, a caretaker job.

Halperin couldn't help but notice that few soldiers of Company A liked Helvey's predecessor. Halperin didn't like him either, and reported to the battalion commander that if Captain S_____ wasn't relieved, someone would kill him, maybe even Halperin. The battalion commander asked his advice about a replacement, and the old sergeant suggested Helvey.

Young soldiers respect the age and experience of sergeants like Halperin.

Their affection may not be obvious to outsiders, but it does not pass unrequited, especially in combat. Despite his outward gruffness, for example, Halperin always attended wounded soldiers himself. Teenage soldiers often reacted to being wounded in a predictable way. "Take a look, Sergeant. Did I get it down there?" Halperin would assure them that their manhood was still intact, which seemed to make everyone feel better.

"The 2/12th Cav could do anything better than anybody," Halperin recalled later. "The bond of the battalion was closer than any other unit in the United States Army. Yet, it wasn't the leadership—it was everyone." Truly we were a team.

Halperin died a few years ago while working at Fort Meade, Maryland, as a civilian, apparently of a heart attack.

CHAPTER 19

DAY TWO:
HELL'S LAST CIRCLE

OUR SECOND DAY AT TFP, MADE WORSE BY THE NIGHT that passed, began dark and dirty. At 3:00 A.M., four enemy mortar rounds slammed into our perimeter. The damage was slight, but it put us on edge so that further sleep was out of the question: mortars could be a prelude to a ground attack. A few minutes after we were shaken by the mortars, several of our trip flares went off in no-man's-land, which heightened our fears that we were being probed. If the sappers found any soft spot in our defenses, that's where they would concentrate forces for the main attack. To show the NVA we were tight, we had to fire at every suspected movement. Maybe our demonstration of vigilance would make them think twice about hitting us before daybreak.

If we had had a reserve force in our battalion, we

might have been able to rotate some of our soldiers so that a few could sleep while others watched. But there was no reserve force, except for the command group—Lieutenant Colonel Sweet, Command Sergeant Major Halperin, Major Cralle, a couple of radio operators, and me. If we were penetrated, the command group was the only force we could commit to a counterattack without pulling forces from another side of our perimeter. Because we were surrounded, this would be out of the question. But if we counterattacked with the command group, we would have lost all command and control, all contact with the outside world. It would have ended up every man for himself, and within a few minutes the fight would have been over. The specter of defeat provided an incentive to stay awake.

The weather helped us keep our eyes open, perhaps the only favorable thing that can be said about it. Even as it was, it was hard to stay totally alert. We were beginning to reach the limits of endurance, and no one was sure how much longer he could hang on.

Afterward, Helvey's radio operator, Specialist 4 O'Reilly—the soldier who carried his PRC-25—recalled this night with loathing. Any one of us could have said the same thing: "The night was cold and miserable. And without packs, ponchos, and poncho liners, we froze. We had gotten less than six hours' sleep in the past forty-eight hours. We didn't have water and the river water was too muddy to drink."

At first light, lacking any kind of guidance, we started

to talk about what to do next: stay at TFP or continue to move toward Hue, provided we got some help breaking out of the encirclement. The discussion was broken off abruptly at 8:11 A.M. when the remnants of 2/12th Cav were attacked on all sides. They must have been fresh soldiers, at least a battalion strong. They assaulted without warning.

The attack was supported with a mortar barrage. Over two hundred shells landed inside our perimeter. One exploded ten yards from my foxhole, killing four soldiers who were trying to get our mortar into action. We fought back with small arms fire in "a mad minute that lasted ten minutes."

It never got to the hand-to-hand stage, but when the NVA withdrew, most of our ammunition and energy were expended. The casualty report was also depressing: we had eleven more killed and fifty-one wounded. We could see eight dead enemy soldiers just beyond our perimeter, and we must have wounded many more. We did take one prisoner. We thought that we had killed more NVA than we could see, but that was beside the point. They still had plenty of fresh soldiers and lots of ammunition. We weren't getting any reinforcements and very little resupply. Physically, we were failing fast.

We had too many wounded to treat at one time, and some medics were among the casualties. We doubted that helicopters could reach us now to help with the problem. Reinforcement by land wasn't any more promising. It was time to take inventory, while we still had radio contact with the brigade: Company B's second platoon was all but lost, and the other three companies were down to less than half strength. Company A, which started at 140 men and bore the brunt of the battle, was reduced to fewer than 50. In all, we had only 200 soldiers able to carry on the fight.

Out of necessity, we stopped thinking about continuing toward Hue. We had too few men, too many wounded, very little ammunition, and no way to evacuate the dead. We didn't have enough strength to carry the wounded. Leaving them behind was not an option.

Could we escape? We thought the enemy force surrounding us was weakest on our northwest corner, near the field we had crossed into TFP the day before. Still, they had every escape route covered by carefully laid automatic weapons fire, so there was no hope of returning to PK-17 via this route. We might have been able to find a way through, if we could have studied the enemy positions, but it was too dangerous to snoop. Anyone standing near, or crawling close, to the perimeter was shot or grenaded. If the enemy had attacked again, he might have succeeded in overrunning us. They didn't seem to have a problem with replacements: when one was killed, other NVA soldiers dragged the body away and a fresh man took his place.

We tried to take advantage of every bit of protection we could find, which wasn't much. No one had to be reminded to keep his helmet on. Black Hats, or Pathfinders, soon realized that their black baseball caps were giving them no protection from small arms fire and mortar fragments. They recognized the foolishness of wearing caps, a right they had traditionally demanded. Their argument was that steel helmets interfered with their ability to guide helicopters into small landing zones, like jungle clearings. I always thought this was a peculiar argument in wartime, so I felt vindicated as I watched the Pathfinders remove the helmets from the dead and place them on their own heads. I thought their decisions settled the argument once and for all.

We did manage to grab three more prisoners. We sent them to brigade on one of the few helicopters to land at TFP, but I can't find any record of their completing the trip. The helicopter must have been one of many shot down.

I recall Captain Helvey "informally" interrogating one of the prisoners for combat information of immediate value. Helvey's knife never actually touched the soldier's throat, but the technique was effective enough to do the trick. Unfortunately for us, but to the delight of the POW, the evacuation helicopter arrived just before the "moment of truth." It's just as well. Skilled interrogators at brigade and division knew how to elicit the same information using more professional means.

About forty yards from our perimeter, facing Company C, was an old stone house, its roof blown away. It may have been a chapel of sorts at one time, but the NVA had installed a mortar there. At first we thought the mortar fire was coming from within our own perimeter, so close was the thumping sound from the mortar rounds being dropped into the tube-like barrel. But when the rounds landed, we knew they weren't ours and looked for the source of the mischief. The mortar had to be destroyed, whatever it took. It was too deadly and too accurate.

The stone house was too close to fire on with our artillery, and too far for us to reach in a ground attack. Even if the attack succeeded, it would have extended our perimeter beyond our ability to defend it; and if we attacked it and withdrew, the NVA would only reoccupy it afterward. The question was really moot, because we didn't have the moral or physical strength left to attack. We tried firing our weapons at the building—the lead slugs knocked out little chips, but couldn't penetrate the stone. The mortar fire against us continued.

At our wits' end, we thought of trying hand grenades, but the range was too far, about forty yards. The only hope was to throw a grenade through the open roof, a small target at that distance, considering the trajectory of a grenade. It would have taken a miracle to pull it off, and none of us wanted to try.

While we were debating what to do next, a soldier nearby looked out of his foxhole and saw what had to be done. No one asked him his opinion, so he didn't offer it. Instead, he just stood up in his foxhole and tore the pin from a grenade. He spit a stream of tobacco juice toward the target, then effortlessly lobbed the grenade toward the building. It fell right through the roof and exploded. Until that moment, nobody knew that Private

First Class Daniel T. Bolsky was a professional pitcher in civilian life. The NVA never set up another mortar in the building, which was fortunate for us, because we weren't sure Bolsky could perform the miracle twice.

At mid-morning we received word over the radio that a lone helicopter was headed our way in a one-time attempt to bring ammunition we urgently needed. Maybe it could carry out some of the wounded, but not all. This sounded like good news to us, but it forced Sweet into making the saddest decision any commander can make: "Classify the wounded."

Since there was only room to evacuate those who had a good chance of survival, the senior medic had to decide which of his patients had the best chance. Those who might die on the way to the hospital would have to be left behind. Those who were classified likely to live would be evacuated first.

The medic did not like to play God, but he knew his duty and made the selection. Many of those not selected were fully conscious of what was happening, yet none complained. When the helicopter arrived, took on its human cargo, and ascended, there were many wet eyes and heavy hearts. The enemy fired on the helicopter, but the good bird never wavered.

At 11:20 A.M. the enemy mounted another full-scale attack from all directions against us with rifles and grenades. Thanks to the resupply of ammunition, we were able to stop the rush to penetrate our defenses, but it took an hour before things became quiet again. Our lack of energy was showing more than ever. We decided we were too weak to hold the existing perimeter, so Sweet gave the order to close it up tighter. It seems that every time we lost a soldier to enemy fire, the perimeter became that much too large.

In addition to the dead, who still had not been evacuated, we had some thirty-eight seriously wounded remaining. The slightly wounded were not even counted as casualties. Another helicopter arrived without much warning at 1:45 P.M., and a dozen more wounded were literally thrown aboard, while the helicopter hovered a few inches above the ground. We thought it was surely the last attempt to reach us, as the enemy fire and poor weather put the pilots and crews in a situation every bit as precarious as our own.

There were still about fifteen wounded soldiers, almost all conscious, who did not make it out on the last bird. Their fate was apparently sealed, and there was nothing more we could do for them except to make their last moments as comfortable as we could. It was a shabby, disheartening prospect. Some friends stayed near their wounded comrades, holding hands. Two wounded soldiers held one another's hand so they wouldn't die alone.

Then, just as darkness and fog were closing in, we heard the whoop-whoop-whoop of a helicopter's rotors overhead. It was diving toward the center of our perimeter, pulling up just as it reached the ground. It took perhaps twenty seconds to pack the fifteen remaining wounded aboard the helicopter, far beyond the maximum authorized load limit of eight or nine. Then it left as quickly as it had come, dodging a hail of enemy fire as it flew off. Still lying on the ground side by side, like life-size manikins in some grotesque toy shop, were eleven soldiers who were already dead or too close to death to warrant evacuation. Those who died quickly spared us the agony of sharing their prolonged misfortune, a consideration for which I was somehow grateful.

Those dying by inches from horrible sucking chest wounds seemed the most unfortunate, although I couldn't tell if they were conscious or not. Their soiled fatigue jackets had been torn open by the medics, and I could see and hear the blood rhythmically oozing and gurgling about their youthful chests, collecting in the hollow parts in crimson-black pools. When the punctured lungs finally filled, the sloshing noise would end abruptly, and the soldier's friends would carry him away for a private burial in our mass grave. No Viking warrior was ever bid farewell with greater dignity.

One soldier, as messy as the rest, with cropped blond hair but eyes too glassy to let me see the color, made me think how lucky I was not to be lying next to him, sharing his hopeless situation. Yet I felt tremendous compassion. His stare seemed to ask the question: "What have I done to deserve this?" "You did nothing wrong," I thought to myself, trying to hold in my emotions. "Your misery and suffering can be traced to a tragic drama composed by distant, indifferent hands. You did your duty and will be remembered by those you never let down." He was a very handsome boy. I'm sure he left a dozen sweethearts in tears when he announced he was leaving home to join the Army.

It would have been good for morale to evacuate the dead, but there were good reasons why we couldn't. The normal practice was to evacuate the wounded in medevacs as soon as we could, and the dead in cargo helicopters after the daily supply missions were completed. Medevac helicopters were identified with a red cross on a white field, and were not normally used to carry anything but wounded soldiers. In desperate circumstances, however, exceptions were made.

Afterward, Sweet told me a story about the last helicopter out of TFP. It was an episode of consummate cowardliness, and Sweet was the only witness. Just as the helicopter was lifting off, an unharmed soldier hurled himself on top of the injured soldiers. He had been apparently waiting for an opportunity to escape with the wounded, although he wasn't wounded himself. The pilot was jolted by the shifting load, but managed to correct the helicopter's balance and continued his climb and successful departure. Subsequent disciplinary action was averted when the soldier was sent back to Detroit on emergency leave to attend his mother's funeral. He deserted, rather than return to Vietnam. We were still involved in the Hue campaign, so we couldn't court-martial the soldier or prevent him from returning to Detroit.

Although I sympathize with soldiers suffering from battle fatigue, it's my experience that those who are truly suffering are more likely to become helplessly withdrawn than to seek escape at the expense of their friends. I found that out a few days after we had escaped from the trauma of TFP when our battalion-size patrol came under enemy fire.

A soldier near me, who was carrying a mortar tube, was hit on the forehead with a shell fragment. The blood from the wound flowed freely over his eyes. The soldier thought he had been blinded. Throwing his mortar aside, he ran into the woods in panic, his arms akimbo and his body jerking frantically as he moved toward the enemy positions. I rushed after him and grabbed him by the hand. He was crying like a baby, but finally calmed down. "I'm blind, I'm blind," he sobbed. With my free hand, I wiped the blood from his face. I saw a nasty gash on his forehead, but his eyes were all right. I instructed him to count to ten, then open his eyes. The trick worked, and he recovered his composure immediately. He confessed his embarrassment over the trouble he had caused me, and I thought he might start crying again. So, with my hand in his, I led him back to where the mortar lay.

When he spotted the tube, he released my hand and picked it up. "I guess we may be needing this," he said. He slung the tube over his shoulder, and started to rejoin his squad. "I think you're right," I replied. But I wasn't sure he heard me.

CHAPTER 20

SAVING THE LIVING, LEAVING THE DEAD

WHEN THE LAST LOAD OF WOUNDED WAS LIFTED OUT OF TFP, Sweet had time to think about our next most pressing priority—moving the battalion to a safer and more defensible location. Sweet's freedom of action was limited to what the brigade and division commanders would agree to, but neither was in much of a position to ignore any reasonable suggestions. In fact, if there were any good ideas being talked about at higher headquarters, we never heard about them, so why not take the initiative? Anyway, we knew more about our problems than anyone else.

Sweet shouted at me to move over to his foxhole. When I got there, he didn't tell me at first what was on his mind, but he gradually worked around to it, thinking as he talked. "Charlie, I've been thinking that we must get out of here. As I see it, we've got three choices. First, of course, we could stay here and wait for the 5/7th Cav or some other battalion to break through and relieve us. Second, we could try to renew our attack through Thon La Chu. Third, we could try to make a break for it, possibly to the high ground southwest of here. You're the S-2; what do you think?"

"I think it's about time somebody started thinking," I said, relieved that we might not have to stay at TFP much longer.

We talked about the pros and cons of each choice. If we stayed much longer at TFP, we might be overrun anytime. Neither of us thought this would be good for us or help our country.

The safest thing to do, we thought, would be to retrace our steps to PK-17, but that seemed kind of cowardly. We still had hopes of accomplishing our original mission of relieving the defenders of Hue. If we crawled back to our brigade, it would leave those in Hue in a situation as bad as our own at TFP. We put ourselves in their shoes and wondered what it would be like to hear the news that the battalion that was supposed to relieve you chickened out.

The idea of moving to the high ground to the southwest sounded attractive. It would put us closer to Hue. There were risks too: would we be able to break through our encirclement and move deeper into enemy-held terrain without putting ourselves in greater jeopardy than we already were? There was good high ground to the southwest, but what if the enemy already occupied it in order to control the infiltration routes into Hue?

It wasn't one of his original ideas, but Sweet also toyed with the thought of moving the battalion to a settlement about one and a half miles to our east. It was surrounded by rice paddies and would be easy to secure. He called brigade and asked them to check it out by air. A forward air controller was dispatched to look the place over, but when he got within range, the NVA started firing at him with 37mm antiaircraft guns. He got close enough to spot an NVA battalion defending the area, which was reported to us, and we scratched that proposal from our slate.

Sweet spoke with some other members of his staff to measure their reaction to his proposals. I think he hoped that if he could put off making a recommendation for a few hours, brigade staffers would be working up proposals of their own with the weight of the division behind them. But we couldn't wait forever.

When we didn't hear anything by 4:00 P.M., Sweet reached Campbell by radio and presented our proposals. It took a few minutes to complete the conversation because we had to use a fairly complex code book to encrypt the message to keep it secure. Even encrypted, the message was brief:

If we continue our present mission and attack toward Hue via Thon La Chu, we'll be cut down. If we defend our present position, we'll be nickel-and-dimed to pieces. If we are exfiltrated to gain a more defensible position, we can flank the enemy stronghold and disrupt him. I recommend we do it.

Campbell was next to his radio operator when the encrypted message arrived. He told Sweet to wait. A few minutes later, Campbell returned to his radio and told Sweet he accepted his recommendation to leave TFP after it got dark. He also said that he couldn't be responsible if the plan didn't work, because after we escaped we'd be on our own. Big deal!

So long as we had permission to leave, who cared who was responsible?

Approval of the plan was all we wanted. The good news was like a jolt of electricity to a patient in cardiac arrest, and was the biggest boost to morale we had had since leaving Camp Evans. I learned later that General Tolson was asked to decide himself whether we could make the move. Based on our request and the recommendations of Lieutenant Colonel Ross, the operations officer, and Colonel George W. Putnam, Jr., the division chief of staff, the general consented.

How do you break out of an encirclement without letting the encircling force know or guess what you're doing? First, you recognize that maybe it can't be done if the enemy is alert, observant, or lucky. Second, you hope you can deceive the enemy into believing what you want him to believe. And third, you recognize that if you fail, you're probably going to be in a worse position than when you started.

I can think of no military maneuver more difficult than breaking contact with an enemy surrounding you so that he won't be inclined to pursue. When opposing forces are separated by no more than fifty yards, there's no sure and simple way to keep your preparation quiet. Once the enemy detects what's going on, he's not likely to sit still.

What are the problems of preparations? For one thing, what do you do with eleven dead soldiers who were not evacuated? How do you dispose of the small mountain of excess equipment that once belonged to the dead and wounded? If the exfiltration is detected, should the wounded be left behind, so the rest can get away to fight another day?

What about the exfiltration route? It means crossing several streams. Are these streams too swollen from the recent rains to be forded? Are there bridges? Booby traps? What do you do if the enemy is waiting for you at the next position you intend to occupy? Do you fight or look for another position?

Where will the artillery support come from? How much? Will resupply be possible in the new position? Reinforcements? Will the mission be changed? What's the weather going to be? What's the status of friendly units?

The list of questions goes on for as long as you want it to. Sooner or later, you have to be satisfied with what you already know. Some risks can be reduced, but there's no way to be confident that everything's been planned for.

There were less than four hours from the time we got approval to move to the time we intended to leave. Sweet called in the commanders and staff to let them know the plans. We crowded into and around his foxhole. Sweet did not say getting out would be easy. He did not say he was sure we would make it, because we all knew it could end up in disaster. What he did say—and we agreed with—was, "It is better to go down fighting than die trapped in a cage like an animal."

That's not a bad statement from the lieutenant colonel commanding a battalion of infantry in the United States Army. Our uniforms didn't look like much, we hadn't washed or shaved in days, and we smelled horrible. But we were thinking and acting like soldiers.

The time set for breakout was 8:00 P.M., just after it got dark. Sweet selected the time because he figured that the NVA soldiers would be getting ready for the night ahead and would be less likely to notice our departure. He hoped they'd expect us not to try to leave until after midnight; with luck, leaving soon after sunset would catch them by surprise.

Night moves are not for amateurs, even lucky ones. So it was fortunate that Sweet had rehearsed night movement when he took command of the battalion back at LZ Ross. We had some experience to fall back on. We knew, for example, that under the best conditions there are bound to be command and control problems. Land navigation is never easy at night, especially when you're under radio silence. Illumination is helpful, but there wasn't any moon. Given the problems, the best thing to do was to make sure all the commanders understood what the plan was, and that they would pass as much information as they could to their soldiers in the time available. We were fortunate that Sweet used to teach night tactics back at the Fort Benning Infantry School.

There was no way to reconnoiter the route, because so many contingencies had to be considered at all levels of planning—from battalion to squad. The route was to be southwest through inundated rice paddies. All paths were avoided where our movement might be suspected, because if we were detected too soon, the whole plan would fail.

About 6:00 P.M. small groups of soldiers started collecting their things to get ready for the move. Because of the enemy's ability to observe our movement before twilight, this was a critical phase. A clever enemy, sensing what we were about to do, wouldn't interfere with our preparations. He'd wait and ambush us as we tried to escape, cutting us down in the open where there was no place to hide. In fact, it would be much easier to destroy us trying to get out than it would be to attack us while we were in fortified positions.

We tried hard to give the appearance that nothing unusual was going on. While we were getting ready to get out, we still had to be ready to fight off an attack. Commanders had their hands full doing many things at once; the self-discipline of individual soldiers counted for a great deal.

There was a problem with the excess equipment: radios, mortars, machine guns, and rifles that we had no use for and couldn't carry with us. We didn't want the equipment to fall into enemy hands, but we couldn't destroy it before we left without tipping our hand. The problem was solved by the team of engineers accompanying us. They assured Sweet they could time demolitions to blow the equipment after we left—sufficiently long after we left to discourage the enemy from pursuing us, assuming they weren't already. This meant that if our departure was noticed before the equipment was blown up, the enemy could take possession.

Out of the enemy's sight, some soldiers rigged up dummies, which they placed in their foxholes after dark. They weren't likely to deceive anyone for very long, but it might give us an extra few minutes to escape before we were noticed. A lot can happen in a few minutes.

Soldiers were told that there'd be no smoking or joking when we got ready to leave. O'Reilly's reaction was typical. "The word had gone out just before we left that there would be no smoking. That we didn't have to worry about, because no one had any cigarettes."

Orders were also given that no one would fire back at a sniper, because he'd only be firing at suspected movements. If we fired back, we'd simply confirm his suspicions, alerting the entire enemy force. If one of our soldiers got wounded, we'd carry him away in a makeshift litter fashioned from ponchos. We couldn't plan for more than a few wounded; the question of leaving them was never addressed.

There were still the eleven bodies to deal with. We knew who ten of them were, but one had been with the battalion such a short time that no one knew his name. Often, in haste to attend them, the medics cut away clothing that held the only clue to the identification of casualties. Sometimes papers in billfolds were lost in combat or not carried at all. The only thing we could do was to leave the bodies at TFP. Carrying them out was too risky, because it would take four soldiers to carry each body: we did not have forty-four soldiers to spare for this task. Carrying the dead out would also weaken our already tired force, adding to the confusion as the porters shifted their loads among themselves. We all agreed with Sweet that under the circumstances, our obligations to the living exceeded our debts to the dead. It wasn't a perfect decision, but it was the best we could do.

We buried the dead in a shallow grave—the abandoned mortar pit—hoping the bodies would not stay there too long before they were recovered. Unfortunately, they weren't recovered until seventeen days later, when the 5/7th Cav finally reoccupied our old positions on February 22. We didn't think the recovery would take that long, but there was a lot we didn't know, such as the size of the force opposing us at TFP or their reason for being there. The 5/7th Cav didn't get into TFP easily: it took four U.S. battalions to force the enemy out.

We learned later that there was considerable unhappiness over our leaving the dead behind. Some former members of the division haven't forgiven us yet. Perhaps some of the next of kin feel the same way. The most grief was caused by the soldier we couldn't identify. I understand the problems we caused whoever had the job of figuring out who he was: it must have been a nightmare. I'm glad I wasn't the officer who had to tell his next of kin that he was dead, then try to answer the questions about why it took so long after he was killed to make the notification. I would have done the job, but I wouldn't have liked it.

We made the right decision leaving the dead behind. We never doubted we'd recover the bodies later, when conditions permitted, and we expected to be given the recovery mission ourselves. Having led a team that found the bodies of our battalion staff killed just a month earlier in Que Son Valley, I considered myself an authority on the subject. The only fear we had was that the NVA would dig up the bodies and mutilate them out of vengeance. We did our best to prevent this by placing a note over the bloated rise of earth that covered the bodies declaring in Vietnamese, on our honor, that the mound contained only the bodies of eleven soldiers and no paraphernalia of war. They apparently saw our note and believed it. Call it professional respect.

When it came time to recover the bodies, we were intentionally not selected.

Campbell apparently believed that we had gone

through enough already and that our soldiers didn't have to be further depressed by digging up the bodies of their friends.

However bad the night of February 3–4 was for us, there's no entry in the division journal that even suggests that they knew we were surrounded or in any serious trouble. An 8:00 A.M. entry on February 4 reports information from 3d Brigade that the 2/12th Cav was "under heavy ground attack from three sides." A few minutes later, according to the journal, another ARA helicopter sent to help us was shot down by enemy gunfire.

Just before noon, the G-3 was notified by 3d Brigade that the first elements from the 5/7th Cav started to arrive by helicopter at PK-17. Several of the companies were immediately deployed to help defend the perimeter. By 4:30 P.M. the entire battalion was in place under the command of Lieutenant Colonel James Vaught. Tolson notified his G-3 to be prepared the next morning to move two infantry companies from another battalion at Evans to PK-17, freeing up the entire 5/7th to maneuver toward us "if needed."

Nothing else about the 2/12th Cav appears in the journal until 6:30 P.M., when Major Bowman reported to division that our battalion planned to move from Thon La Chu at 8:00 P.M. toward more defensible terrain to the west. This is followed by a delayed entry that noted the 2/12th Cav was under heavy attack from three sides at 4:00 P.M., possibly a regimental-size force. Delayed entries are not uncommon, because it's hard to take the time to report battles when it takes so much effort just to manage the battle and coordinate the artillery fires and other support. This doesn't mean, necessarily, that those who need to know aren't being kept informed of vital information they need in order to do their jobs. It just means that specific records can't be easily put on paper until the fog of battle clears enough to make reasonable assessments. The delayed report included information about our casualties: twelve U.S. KIA and thirty WIA. Through intelligence channels I reported an estimated one hundred enemy KIA, obviously weighted on the high side.

CHAPTER 21

LEAVING TFP: OUR ONLY HOPE

DEPARTURE PREPARATION WAS COMPLETE BY 7:00 P.M. When the signal was given, soldiers started moving quietly from their foxholes to assembly points nearer the middle of the perimeter. They formed in two lines to save space, reducing the length of the column by half. Normally a column would be dispersed to reduce the likelihood of mass casualties, but in night moves the first aim is to keep people from getting lost. Companies A and D, which were on the south side of the perimeter, left their positions first. Companies B and C, on the north, protected the moving column.

Sweet ordered all the radios turned off except the artillery radio. He didn't want anyone calling off the escape for fear we couldn't do it. "Some Nervous Nellie may try to stop us. If they don't like what we're doing, fuck 'em."

Company A was again picked to lead, and Helvey selected the lead platoon because it was the best at night operations. Others rotated the dirty jobs on an equitable basis; Helvey never did. The platoon sergeant had worked with Helvey for a long time, and they got along well. His name was Clifford Lowe, a Ranger School graduate. Lowe was due to rotate back to the States soon, but he never shied away from his duty. He had been wounded in Que Son Valley.

"His loud sigh made everyone laugh," Helvey recalls, when Lowe learned he was not being picked to lead us out of TFP. "It was certainly heard by the North Vietnamese a few yards away."

Once we drew the conclusion that the enemy strength was weakest to our north, Sweet made the decision to move first in that direction. We believed we detected a small gap in their northern positions, maybe seventy-five yards wide. We hoped it was wide enough for us to slip through in total darkness without being caught. About forty hours had elapsed since we first made contact with the NVA early in the morning the day before. We knew instinctively we were too ragged around the edges to do our best, but we had to try.

Our column moved slowly northward back toward PK-17 without incident. The first checkpoint was the graveyard we had fought through two days earlier. We figured if we could get the entire column past this point, we stood half a chance of making the move successfully.

After the cemetery, we swung southwest, PK-17 to our

back. The next checkpoint was a stream, about 350 yards farther on. It took maybe an hour to reach it, one slow step at a time. No evidence so far that the NVA knew we had left TFP! Hopes were rising, and the column started to move a little faster. Then . . .

A sharp metallic clang to our left flank from the woods: it was a machine gun bolt slamming shut to the firing position. We froze in our tracks, waiting for the gunner to squeeze off the first burst. I pictured the gunner alerting the regimental commander that he saw us trying to slip away to freedom. In a moment everyone would be given the word to fire. . . .

A million thoughts now, all of them bad. This was it. We waited for the avalanche to fall, frozen in place. Eternity lasted maybe twenty seconds, but nothing happened. The NVA machine gunner had a sloppy finger. The column began to move again as if nothing had happened, the only sound the boots sucking up mud as we each took one calculated step after another.

We were only four hundred yards away from TFP, according to official records, when movement became increasingly difficult as the battalion approached the river. The ground became more and more boggy and soon the entire battalion was squelching in mud and water. A suitable fording site was found and the troops began crossing the river.

The river was about twenty feet wide and varied in depth from four to five feet, with a bottom of spongy mud and steep banks. The men crossed in pairs, assisting each other up to the banks. It took two hours for the entire column to cross.

Whoever wrote this portion of the after-action report knew what he was talking about, except for one point: the river was deeper than five feet. I had to throw my head back so I could breathe without drowning. The extra few inches made the difference.

After we crossed the river, it was obvious that our casualties from the fighting the day before were far worse than we realized. Some soldiers, who probably should have been medevaced earlier, hid their wounds from the sergeants and officers so they wouldn't have to leave. But as we put more and more distance between our column and TFP, the wounds couldn't be hidden any longer:

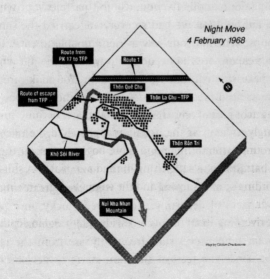

Night Move
4 February 1968

Route from PK 17 to TFP

Route 1

Route of escape from TFP

Thôn Quê Chu

Thôn La Chu –TFP

Thôn Bổn Trì

Khê Sôi River

Núi Nha Nhan Mountain

there was no way the injured could stop the limping. It was a ragtag combat formation. The walking wounded didn't slow us down, however, because our pace was slow to begin with. If someone wasn't able to walk without assistance, there was always a buddy willing to help lighten the load. Many soldiers had to walk with their arms around one another to maintain their balance. Their rifles would be passed to someone else to help distribute the burden. At one point, I was carrying three rifles and a couple of pistol belts of ammunition.

"The thing that impressed me," Sweet said, "was not their professional skills, although they had that. It's what they did for each other."

Soldiers shared whatever food they had, helped bandage one another's wounds, and parceled out what little ammunition we had so everyone carried the same amount. When anyone saw a friend unable to carry his own weapon, or who needed help walking, he did what was necessary without second thought. You took care of those in need first, then yourself. It was the extra power that is not part of any organizational chart.

At 9:00 P.M. we received a radio message that we weren't to attempt the night move—that it was too dangerous. "Stay put." Right! Too little, too late.

The risks of returning to TFP were even greater than the dangers of departing. Having been lucky once, we weren't going to try it twice. This incident demonstrates how far higher-level staff frequently are from the real world. Once the tactical situation starts to develop on the ground, staff work is overtaken by events. Instead of leading the battle, higher-level commanders have no choice but to follow the action and pray for the best. It would have been more honest to say, "OK, guys, you're on your own."

We got wet fording the river, but it didn't make any difference; after four days and nights without sleep, we were too tired to notice the cold. After the crossing, the wind helped dry our clothing, now mostly rags. The evaporation made it seem colder. Who cared? I lost my map in the river crossing, but there was nothing I could do about it. It must have floated away when I was holding my rifle and binoculars over my head as I waded through. The map had no compromising information on it, but losing it was unprofessional. I also felt the disadvantage of being slightly less than five feet eight inches. "Short guys don't have to dig deep foxholes, but tall guys can wade deeper streams."

As we completed the river crossing, the equipment which had been left behind for detonation exploded in a huge ball of fire. And shortly thereafter, persons at the rear of the column saw trip flares around the perimeter go off. Some claimed they heard small arms fire. Our ploy had worked. We were going to make it after all. There was no way they could chase us now without paying a high price—they'd have to attack us across open fields, just as we assaulted them at TFP.

Our artillery, which had been silent so far, now went into action. Before we left TFP, Jeffries arranged for all available guns to fire on TFP at the same time, when he gave the command. Now he gave it. A few moments later, we could hear the 105s fire from PK-17. Within seconds, hundreds of rounds of high explosives crashed into TFP, adding, we hoped, to the enemy's confusion and casualty count. Some white phosphorus smoke rounds were also fired into TFP so that the light from the exploding shells would not silhouette our moving column, while hopefully ruining the enemy's night vision until we cleared out. The scene looked like something from the underworld, but there wasn't enough time to watch. Mysteries enough lay ahead.

It was good to hear the artillery again, and our calls for support were answered promptly and accurately from that point, just like they used to be. The division's situation report for the day confirms suspicions that support was good: seven thousand rounds were fired, mostly in support of 2/12th Cav. This is a lot of ammunition, when you take into account that the division's daily average for the entire period of the Battle of Hue (February 2–26) was about 2,200. Artillery fired on February 4 marks a kind of high water mark. It saved the Lost Battalion.

Staff Sergeant Henry J. Paschal, from Seattle, was behind Private First Class Hector L. Camacho. It was Paschal's job to tie a knot in a shoestring for every hundred yards we walked. This helped keep us on course, because we still couldn't see more than a few yards in any direction. Ranger Lowe was behind Paschal, more or less running the operation.

Looking back, Paschal later said, "When I was an instructor at Fort Ord, I taught a land navigation course. We had a night course there, and when we made the move everything started coming back to me. The only thing I can say is that I was scared and everyone else was scared. I prayed before we left that we'd make it all right, and I prayed the whole move."

Camacho, of Mayaguez, Puerto Rico, didn't have any trouble finding the river, but it wasn't so easy locating a shallow crossing site. "I wouldn't have worried if I'd been alone. I could have made it. But I had to find a place the whole battalion could go. That was my big problem all night. That, and I had to make sure everyone could keep up with me."

On his first attempt to find a shallow crossing, Camacho ventured into the water about five yards and walked off a drop-off. "He was out so far we couldn't see him," said Platoon Sergeant Sherman T. Anglin, from Goleta, California. "Finally, we heard him splashing toward us and knew he was swimming back in." Camacho was a fearless one-of-a-kind soldier with natural scouting abilities. He was uniquely qualified to lead Company A and the battalion out of hell. He was the ultimate point man.

A point man is the soldier who precedes a unit as it advances to make contact with the enemy, normally moving alone about twenty to fifty yards in front of the main column. Although there are other soldiers protecting the column's flanks, the vanguard is the most dangerous position—the least desirable duty to be assigned in combat.

There is always the danger of being the first to trip the wire of a booby trap or to walk into an ambush.

It is only an unusually stalwart soldier who can perform this duty well, concentrating all of his mental and physical energies to ensure that those who follow tread a safe path. Because of the dangers, most company commanders impartially rotate their soldiers in the point position. The precise selection is normally delegated to the platoon leaders, platoon sergeants, or squad leaders.

It was different in Company A. Camacho pleaded to perform point habitually, and Helvey acceded to his request after Mousie went back to the States. Helvey knew of no one who could outperform Camacho. He also knew that it was a matter of time until Camacho became a casualty. Camacho must have known this too, as did everyone else in Company A.

Yet, for the several months that Camacho was the permanent point man, he served his company and his country with distinction, defeating several enemy ambushes. So extraordinary was his ability, it is difficult to think of him without reference to the occult. The peculiar thing is that Camacho was always smiling.

Like other point men, Camacho was not asked to make moral judgments.

His sole job was to protect the column, which meant he had to fire on any suspicious movement. One cannot survive even the first enemy encounter without an instinctive ability to react instantly to a threat, however slight. Any movement must be attacked with the understanding that it's more important to be safe than sorry. A point man doesn't have time to hesitate, consult, or reflect.

Simply put, a contemplative point man is a contradiction. Such a person could not survive. Battlefield poets and Hollywood types do not pull point. Camacho had all the ingredients of a good point: he was young, uncomplicated, and a dead shot. He and men like him cannot be recruited or selected by the Army—any army—they can only be found on a battlefield after they decide for themselves to step forward.

CHAPTER 22

HUGGING JEFF

JUST AS CARS PULLING AWAY FROM A TRAFFIC LIGHT don't all move at the same time, so were there spurts and pauses in our column's movement out of TFP. Sometimes we walked at a normal rate, while at other times we had to wait for a few minutes until the trailing column caught up with itself. All in silence, all in darkness.

Whenever we halted, some of the exhausted soldiers would fall asleep on their feet, waking up just in time to correct their balance. It was a nightmarish feeling. One soldier accidentally squeezed the trigger on his M-79 grenade launcher—something resembling a shotgun— and the small grenade projectile slammed into the mud at his feet. The projectile, a little larger than a golf ball, has an arming device inside it to prevent the round from becoming lethal until it has traveled several yards. This safety device kept it from exploding, but the noise was deafening. Fortunately it didn't draw enemy fire. It was the only careless accident we had during our exodus.

We walked, waded, and waited throughout the night, expecting Armageddon at every muddy turn. By midnight we had passed Thon La Chu, moving parallel to another almost-anonymous hamlet, Thon Bon Tri.

We knew Thon Bon Tri wasn't abandoned, because we could see signal lights flashing in the treeline. This may have been part of "some enemy guide system to aid infiltrating NVA and VC forces . . . or a recognition signal which, when unanswered (by us), the guide prudently did not investigate," we noted in our after-action report. Later we learned that this otherwise undistinguished hamlet, like Thon La Chu, was an NVA supply center and route into Hue.

As we continued farther south, we trudged within two and a half miles of Hue and found our path dangerously illuminated by powerful air-dropped flares floating over the city. The Air Force, always ready to please, responded to our urgent request to discontinue their mission for the rest of the night, presumably with the concurrence of Hue's defenders.

At first light on February 5, we climbed a hill we thought was safe, just to make an assessment of where we were. We also wanted to get out of the rice paddies. The hill was covered with rocks the size of outhouses. There was no evidence of the enemy. We were still wet and hungry, but everyone had made it safely so far. We enjoyed the first opportunity to bask in the glory of our success, the wounded celebrating most of all. It was a wonderful and glorious feeling. No language can describe our ineffable emotions—it was joy akin to a religious experience.

It was drizzling, and there was no sun. But our safety signified that the flood was receding; it was only a matter of time until life would begin afresh. It was a rite of purification. We had been chosen to survive. We were alive and safe; nothing else mattered. Those of us who had spent the past thirty-six hours at TFP had looked forward to only one thing: escape—the escape we had just pulled off. We didn't feel we had helped to write a chapter in military history, nor did we think beyond the immediate and urgent problems related to our individual and collective survival.

After the sensation of floating wore off, we had to think again of what was happening in the world around us. We had no idea what the overall tactical situation was, especially in Hue, but it was bound to affect us. We had to start thinking again about how we fit into the big picture. We were still in deep trouble, like miners in a tunnel that had just collapsed. We could hold on for a while longer, but if help didn't reach us soon, we'd be in trouble. We had a few hours, however, to rest before doing anything.

Stretched out behind a rock, half awake and half asleep, I had a sense of awe, a feeling of pleasure I've never had before or since. The horror drifted away, and I could dream about the details of our disaster selectively. I was glad we hadn't taken any more casualties. Sweet said he would make the decision about what to do with more wounded soldiers only if he had to. We could all hold our heads high; I'm not sure we could have if we had to leave wounded behind.

We were suddenly shaken from our euphoria when we spotted a small group of enemy soldiers scampering toward us from the woods on the other side of the nearest rice paddy. They were about seven hundred yards away, but I saw through my binoculars that they were setting up a mortar. We were within range. We couldn't take them under fire, because we didn't have any weapon that could reach that far. Damn!

We all started firing from our positions on the side of the hill, although it didn't do any good. I went through two magazines of M-16 ammunition before I came to my senses. There was nothing we could do to quiet the mortars, and there was nowhere we could run. Was this going to be TFP all over again? When the first round landed in the midst of Company D, it killed an officer and wounded fifteen soldiers, including every member of the company's artillery liaison party. They paid the price of poor dispersion.

Fortunately, while the rest of us fired our rifles without effect, Jeffries was calling for artillery support. Just when we thought there was no way to silence the mortar, the first round landed right on top of the NVA crew. Direct hits like that are rare, and we couldn't help cheering. It was like a scene from an old Western.

Later that night Jeffries and I found shelter together on a cot in an old ARVN hut. The only way to keep warm was to hug each other as we rested on our sides. Sleep came quickly. As I drifted off, I thought how fortunate it was that Jeffries was with us and what a fine friend he was to me and to our battalion.

I wasn't the only one who recognized a debt to Jeffries. After the battle, Sweet recommended him for a Silver Star for bravery in action during the Tet campaign. The citation only records acts of valor on February 4, but he behaved gallantly throughout the entire period.

> When his unit became heavily engaged with a numerically superior enemy force and was forced to withdraw to a more defensible position, Captain Jeffries remained to call in and adjust artillery fire on the hostile emplacements. Continuously exposing himself to intense enemy fire, Captain Jeffries moved from position to position to control the artillery fire that neutralized several enemy emplacements.

The first hill was not our final destination for that day. We sought the higher ground to the south that would be more difficult to attack with mortar fire. We could see an ARVN outpost at the crest of the hill. It looked abandoned, but after a moment of observation, I saw a few soldiers come cautiously out of hiding to the edge of their perimeter to study us like curious animals. We exchanged signals to prove that we were Americans. They motioned for us to join them. The ARVNs were glad to see us, of course, because our presence assured their own safety. There was only a squad of soldiers left to defend the outpost, no match for the NVA should they decide to attack. The ARVNs didn't have much to offer us, but they let us move into their huts and gave us what little food they could spare. I don't know what was in the pot, but it was warm and well seasoned. It was the first meal I had in almost four days.

Some of the younger soldiers were still hungry, so they convinced their company commanders to send reconnaissance parties into the abandoned village at the base of the hill. Company A's first "reconnaissance" party returned with a string of six live ducks.

Meanwhile in faraway Saigon, reporters were dished out more stories of allied successes. As for the Battle of Hue, it was all over except for "small pockets" of enemy resistance. When the so-called small pockets refused to go away during the next few days, the briefers found other things to talk about. The more enterprising reporters had reached Hue themselves and were sending back on-the-spot accounts of the fight still raging on the other side of the walled city. (In fact, the NVA flag flew over the Citadel until February 24, dominating the horizon far longer than anyone, including the NVA, anticipated.)

We stayed at the ARVN outpost for the next four days, drying out and filling up. We were in no apparent danger, and the little huts seemed luxurious. A short time after our arrival, the system started working again, and we were resupplied with food and ammunition.

We were even visited by General Tolson. His helicopter was fired on when he arrived, and again when he departed, by enemy entrenched on the far side of the village below us, but there was nothing we could do to prevent it. For a few minutes he walked around, talking to soldiers, commending them for their valor, and trying to measure the state of morale. It was a nice gesture, more appreciated, I think, by the officers who knew Tolson than by the younger, violent men who didn't recognize him as their division commander. His starched uniform and smooth face offered a striking contrast to our rags and beards. Some soldiers got up and saluted. Some didn't.

After he left, other ships came in bringing athletic jerseys Scudder had scrounged. He couldn't find clean uniforms to send us, but the sweats were warm. Those who were fortunate enough to get one looked like refugees—warm refugees.

Helvey donned a jersey with the number six stenciled on the front. It is visible under his fatigue jacket in a photograph taken at the time. Six is the number normally reserved in the Army for commanders. It is customarily used to mark the commander's jeep, and it is used in radio conversation, such as "Let me speak to the six."

Tolson didn't come back to visit the battalion again for another couple of days. The soldiers still didn't recognize him, and he felt slighted. He'd try to talk to them, but they kept on digging their foxholes without looking up. "They won't stop digging for me," he complained to Sweet inside a small hut near the site. Even as they talked, soldiers who needed overhead cover for their foxholes ripped the roof off the hut, which expedited the general's departure.

At that point the strength of the battalion was down to 191 officers and men. Those who survived valued their own safety more than the general's conversation.

Our new position had considerable tactical value, because it overlooked the main infiltration and exfiltration routes to and from Hue. So long as we were on the hill, the NVA couldn't move in daylight without being spotted or risking being fired on. The NVA still held Hue, but they were being challenged. Psychologically their campaign had failed, because there was no national uprising; but they were not about to surrender Hue until they were forced out.

The NVA could still move by us under cover of darkness, but even this was made more difficult when we received a Quad 50—four .50 caliber machine guns mounted together. We'd fire it every time we heard movement in the valley, and if it didn't hurt anyone, it must have frightened the hell out of everyone who heard its terrible, distinctive roar. The weapon was still a useful part of our inventory, although it dated from World War II, when it was used for antiaircraft protection.

It was Sweet's opinion later that he made a serious error not moving a company or two back into the valley to block the major routes by day and night. It would have been an ideal spot for night ambushes, and a good idea to build blocking positions in the valley. Nonetheless, I don't recall discussing the matter at the time. I suppose an even better suggestion would have been to bring in another battalion to do the job. Sweet had to be concerned how 191 men could withstand a multi-battalion attack from the NVA forces still in the area.

We couldn't wait on the hill forever, so on February 8 we sent two companies on a search-and-destroy mission into the village below—the one where we found the ducks. Company D uncovered more evidence of the enemy's presence in the form of spare weapons parts, two gas pumps, several helmets, and some ammunition. They destroyed everything, leaving intact about two tons of milled rice, which must have been left behind by village civilians.

They also found an old man hiding in a hole. According to the official report the man, "although afraid and in poor health, gave information concerning NVA movements." The two companies continued searching until 2:45 P.M., when they returned to the hilltop. They reported finding $155 in Shanghai currency, printed in 1930. I have no idea what happened to the money.

The NVA still held TFP. To support another attempt to dislodge them, we were ordered to leave the hill on the morning of February 9 and attack through the woods to our north. The 5/7th Cav was going to attack southward. This seemed reasonable.

We bade adieu to our Vietnamese hosts before sunrise

and descended into the woods below. I was surprised that the ARVNs didn't follow our column, but perhaps they felt safer staying put than joining us in the contested flatlands. Walking into the village and through the woods was happily uneventful, but as we approached a river running through the woods (in fact, the same river where I had lost my map four days earlier), we came under heavy sniper fire from the northeast side of the river. The fire halted our advance.

Every time we tried to move, a sniper would shoot. They rarely missed. Sweet called Helvey forward and told him to get rid of the problem. Helvey said he would try to flank the area where the sniper fire was coming from, which he identified on the far side of a bridge about one hundred yards to our north. Helvey pointed out that it would take a little time to move into position to attack the snipers, because he had to cross the river downstream to the south, behind us, to make sure the snipers didn't see him coming.

Instead of taking his company, Helvey asked for three volunteers to go with him: he thought four men were enough to do the job. Camacho was the first to step forward. The only thing the rest of us had to do was to fire at the snipers once in a while so they wouldn't suspect what Helvey was up to.

We didn't see anything of Helvey's team for about thirty minutes. Then we watched them emerge on the opposite side of the river, moving north in leaps and bounds. Helvey spotted the snipers in a large foxhole near the bridge, and deployed his team around them in a box-like formation.

It was really beautiful to watch Helvey's boys in action. They took turns firing at the snipers, and as one fired the other three inched closer to the foxhole. Each time a sniper rose to fire, he saw a different sight. They must have been petrified as the end approached. Finally, Helvey got up and just walked to the hole and dropped in a grenade. He killed all five. I was impressed with Helvey's courage and asked him where he learned the trick.

"Well, I'll tell you, Charlie," he drawled, "I grew up in West Virginia and my dad used to take me squirrel hunting. We never missed a season. Those squirrels are mighty clever, but my dad and me . . . well, we're not so dumb, either." Helvey could afford to talk that way. First, we were good friends. Second, he had been selected as my successor. My tour was nearly over.

While we were talking, my Vietnamese interpreter walked up to me and dropped a dud M-79 round in my hand. The effect was the same as if he had handed me a time bomb, liable to explode at any second. Apparently the interpreter didn't realize the danger; he must have thought he had captured something belonging to the enemy. If he knew the danger, he never would have touched it. Nobody's that dumb.

There was no easy way of telling how long ago it had been fired or why it didn't explode on impact. I had to assume it was armed and deadly. Holding my hand flat and more or less steady, I shouted for everyone to get the hell out of the way. I didn't know exactly what to do. At first, I considered throwing the dud as far as I could, but I wasn't sure what the jar of tossing it might do. Perhaps I should have given it back to the interpreter. Instead, I bent down and let it roll off my hand into the grass. Then I ran. The dud didn't explode. Unfortunately, I didn't have any way to celebrate my deliverance: there wasn't a drop of whiskey in the battalion. I couldn't help shaking. After a while, it stopped.

I was still upset when I heard the report that Camacho had been shot. The foot wound wasn't serious, but he had to be evacuated. Before the helicopter arrived to take him away, he had a request: would someone carry him over to the bodies of the five snipers he'd helped kill? My last recollection of Camacho is seeing the smile on his face as two buddies lifted him Indian-style toward the bridge where the bodies were piled.

CHAPTER 23

HELVEY'S RAIDERS

AFTER HELVEY GOT RID OF THE SNIPERS, WE PUSHED northward through the hamlet without meeting any further resistance. We didn't see any sign of life. Apparently he had killed the only soldiers left behind to delay us.

When we got to the northern edge of the wooded area, we came to a rice paddy with another wooded area. Beyond it, to our north, was the hamlet of Thon La Chu and the NVA front headquarters. We remembered the night a week earlier, and paused. We knew the enemy that surrounded us then was still there. And so were eleven bodies.

Cautiously this time, Sweet sent a company to scout the woods on the other side. Before the company could enter the woods, however, all hell broke loose. The company became decisively engaged. They couldn't move forward and they couldn't move back. One lieutenant was killed immediately and another ten soldiers were wounded before we could withdraw the unit to safety.

It appeared that we'd have some serious trouble reaching our objective, so Sweet decided to wait until the next day before making another try. In the meantime we would wait where we were until dark, then try to probe them again to get a feel for the size of the force we were up against.

The hamlet had been evacuated before we got there, but it was otherwise intact. Near the center of the hamlet was a clean, whitewashed maternity clinic similar to many facilities built with U.S. aid. I noticed that our soldiers had removed the clinic's door to use as a foxhole cover. I knew that the enemy had recently occupied the area—witness the snipers—but they hadn't touched the clinic. Why did we have to destroy it?

I brought the matter to Sweet's attention. "It's funny," I said. "We build the clinics to win the hearts and minds of the people. The NVA comes in and doesn't touch them, even though they were built by Americans. We come in, and within five minutes start tearing them down." The door was returned to its hinges—a little worse for wear perhaps, but nothing a carpenter couldn't easily repair.

We couldn't wait in the hamlet forever, because our orders required us to move north. We needed to know if the woods in front of us were heavily defended. If the defenses were heavy, more than our battalion would be needed to break through. We had learned that lesson.

Once again Sweet turned to Helvey for help, asking, "Let me know what's in there." His request meant patrolling behind enemy lines on the dark and rainy night of February 11, 1968.

Helvey accepted the mission without complaint, then returned to his company to ask for volunteers. It wasn't necessary to ask. Almost everyone wanted to go. At this point, Helvey was the world's most popular man. He selected Lieutenant Michael Ackerman, O'Reilly—Helvey's radio operator—and ten others, for a party of thirteen.

While Helvey was checking out his men, Chaplain (Captain) Dan Clem came to visit Company A and asked Helvey if he might offer a prayer for those about to undertake the dangerous mission. Helvey thought it was a good idea. "We were psyching up the troops and I thought the chaplain's words might do some good, but—instead of saying something inspirational—he asked God to be with the boys who were going to die." Helvey liked Clem, but his prayer was too much. He spoke to Sweet about it and asked him to keep Clem away from his company.

When it came time to move out, Helvey and his team were ready for behind-the-lines reconnaissance. It wasn't the kind of operation that conventional infantry often performs, but it's one of those things that have to be done once in a while. Helvey's team was ideally suited for the mission. They were all pros, and they had worked with each other long enough to react instinctively to each other's needs.

The night protected their movement with rain and

mist, and Helvey's starlight scope let him see through the night weather to ensure they didn't walk into an ambush. Nothing happened until they got halfway across the clearing, when they found the body of one of our soldiers killed that afternoon. The white skin looked weird against the wet, soiled uniform. Helvey paused long enough to notice that the fallen soldier had died of a chest wound and that his jacket had been removed, possibly by a medic. Later, Helvey would bring the body back to our lines.

From a rendezvous point near the body, Helvey's team made two trips behind enemy lines. They found the enemy in positions along two treelines. If the battalion were to attack, "we could get inside the first treeline and still have another one to penetrate."

Helvey's company discovered the second treeline on their second try. That's when they were spotted. Specialist 4 Michael Oberg was standing by a tree when an NVA soldier walked up to answer a call of nature. Thinking that Oberg was another NVA soldier, he started a conversation. Since Oberg didn't know a word of Vietnamese, he did the only sensible thing—he shot him.

Specialist 4 David Dentinger killed another NVA soldier who was unable to fire his own AK-47 rifle because Dentinger was standing on it.

Helvey didn't pull out until all men were accounted for. There were no casualties, which pleased Helvey. Just as they began crawling back, an enemy recoilless rifle round struck a little building they had used for cover a few moments before.

Sweet was glad to have Helvey and his team with us. They had accomplished their mission perfectly. We now knew it would be suicidal for the battalion to attack. The thirteen volunteers saved the 2/12th Cav from potential destruction.

We told brigade that the enemy was too well dug in for us to dislodge them with a single battalion. Their bunkers were built too solidly for our machine gun fire or artillery fire to penetrate. Based on our information, the brigade called off the attack. We were told to go back to the ARVN mountaintop outpost. For safety's sake, we stayed put until dawn.

When we got back to our old position, just after first light, we realized what an expensive trip it had been. There were two dead and fourteen wounded. We thought another soldier had been killed. We reported him as KIA to brigade, saying we couldn't recover his body until later. Much to our delight and surprise, Private First Class Lewis Williams showed up unharmed the next day.

He had a fascinating story to tell. Apparently he had been knocked out during the first attempt to scout the treeline the afternoon before. As he was coming to, he heard Vietnamese voices, and played dead. He acted well enough to fool the NVA soldiers, who removed his wristwatch, billfold, and rifle. Afraid to move until it got dark, he lay in the paddy, motionless. When night came, he low-crawled back to our position. He didn't make his presence known to us until it was light enough for us to see him; otherwise he might have been fired upon by his own buddies. Soldiers learn to be careful in combat.

One of the reasons Helvey's raid was successful is that he used the starlight scope to good advantage. It magnifies available light and makes it possible to see at night. While it cannot pierce fog or smoke, it's a vast improvement over binoculars or the naked eye.

When the expensive scope was first introduced, we had a hard time getting soldiers to use it. They were afraid they'd have to pay for it if it got lost, and it's easy to lose things in the jungle. But they were even more afraid that the scope caused blindness. This rumor was based on the flash seen in the scope when it was aimed at an artillery burst. The flash did cause temporary night blindness, but the condition was only temporary. The soldiers assumed the worst and didn't want to take a chance. It's hard to bury folk wisdom, and combat breeds a lot of tales.

Sometimes folk wisdom isn't wrong, as in the case of the M-16 rifle. The first model was lousy, except for the slotted flash suppressor, which we used to twist wire from cartons of C-rations. Helvey tells the story of a fight he got into near LZ Ross. Of the twenty soldiers trying to fire on the enemy, only ten had rifles that would work. His act of defiance was to throw his own jammed and worthless rifle into a rice paddy, where it may be even now. He was not worried about the enemy finding the rifle later and using it against us. "Why would they do a thing like that? They wouldn't bother, because they had a better weapon—the AK-47."

The Army soon fixed the problem and came out with a much better version—the M-16A1. Regrettably, they got rid of the one feature everyone liked when they redesigned the flash suppressor. We had to find alternative ways to open C-rations. We were instructed to put only eighteen rounds in the twenty-round magazine, which was a nuisance then and apparently still is now.

The AK-47 was an excellent weapon, and some of our soldiers took to using it despite Army policy against it. Later we found out the reason for the policy. Helvey had a lieutenant who fancied an AK-47 but had to give it up. "Lieutenant Jensen was always in the front of the fighting, and he created too much confusion. No one knew for sure if they were firing at the enemy or at Jensen."

The same day that Helvey led the patrol behind enemy lines, the 5/7th Cav attacked TFP from the north. Colonel Vaught reported what happened. "Once we started to attack, everything went all right. Charlie Company to our right smacked into an NVA company moving north to bolster defenses against our main attack. Our men were chewing them up pretty well. They spotted several NVA dead floating down the river, but then we started taking almost four casualties a minute and began to withdraw."

It was the third time the 5/7th Cav had aborted an attack against TFP.

The weather improved later in the day and the Air Force came in with sixteen tons of bombs and five tons of napalm: they all landed on target in the center of TFP. It was the first time we had seen the Air Force since Tet began.

On February 21, four battalions, three on the north and one on the south, attacked TFP for the last time. On February 22 the enemy abandoned the area and TFP was declared "clear." Some of the soldiers who recovered our hastily buried dead were from the 101st Airborne Division. One of the paratroopers, Staff Sergeant Joe R. Hooper, of Zillah, Washington, mistakenly told a reporter from *Stars & Stripes* that they had been buried alive. Corpses deteriorate quickly in that climate, so it's easy to understand how he made the mistake. Hooper was awarded the Medal of Honor for his exploits on February 21 when he killed twenty-two NVA soldiers.

The day the enemy lost its hold on TFP, they started withdrawing forces from Hue. I can imagine their dejection at being close to success, then watching it slip away. Militarily, they lost the Battle of Hue. As the NVA withdrew forces from Hue, they assembled in the mountains to our west and pumped themselves up with propaganda. We captured one report which boasted of "twenty-five days and nights of continuous fighting for the wonder victory of Hue, January 31 to February 25."

I recognize that it's sometimes difficult to separate victory from defeat at a strategic level, and I appreciate how they won strategically. But as an infantryman, one-on-one the 2/12th beat the NVA on the ground. But what a price the NVA paid—or should have paid—in the eyes of the world. In one hamlet near Hue, we found the bodies of fifteen women and children.

"They had all been shot at close range," reported Lieutenant Colonel Zane Finkelstein, the division's top lawyer, who investigated the atrocity. "Some of the children had their skulls crushed by rifle butts. They had been herded into trenches and killed." Who knows the reason for this brutality? And forty years later, who remembers or cares? But everyone remembers My Lai.

The pictures of TFP taken immediately after Tet do little justice to the way it looked while we were there. Bulldozers brought in to establish a new firebase for an artillery unit flattened the hamlet. While we were there, the tall palm trees were unmolested, and the surrounding rice fields had none of the ugly waterfilled craters that distinguished the area afterward.

Perhaps the now-industrious villagers have restored the little community to the way it was before the war interrupted their tranquility. In that climate, vegetation grows fast. Perhaps no evidence of chaos or mayhem is left. Perhaps the rectangular gardens are filled once more with flowers. Our foxholes are gone, of course. But I suspect some scars denoting our presence will remain for a long time. I simply cannot believe that time could obliterate every trace of what happened there.

CHAPTER 24

TFP

WHAT DID WE RUN INTO WHEN WE HIT TFP? AND WHY was the enemy trying so hard to evict us, since the big battle was in Hue? TFP didn't mean anything to us, that's for sure. What did it mean to the NVA?

We found out later that the NVA was controlling the Battle of Hue from TFP, and that we had stumbled into their headquarters. Our fight was with the security forces protecting the headquarters, obviously a crack outfit. The force consisted of a regiment with the equivalent of three battalions. Our encounter at TFP threatened to upset their plans to take Hue more than if we had reached the city itself. This is the best case I can make for our having done any good.

Ordinarily, an enemy regiment would be attacked with a force no less than a division, the accepted wisdom being that the attacking force needs a three-to-one advantage to ensure success. Consequently, our force was perhaps one-ninth the force needed to do the job properly. No wonder we were stopped cold!

It may not have been practical to send the entire 1st Air Cavalry Division to reinforce us, but the assistance of a few battalions from the several available would have been appreciated. Why, then, was no help forthcoming?

There's no clear answer, and those who know haven't said. Available documents shed some light, however. Apparently the original plan was to reinforce us with the 5/7th Cav. At least one report stated that the 5/7th Cav was airlifted from Evans to PK-17 the day we were surrounded, and "made preparations to move into the contact area on the following day." Instead of reaching PK-17 on February 3, however, the 5/7th Cav didn't arrive until February 4. By that time, we were encircled and planning to get out. It was too late for help.

The 5/7th Cav was commanded by Lieutenant Colonel James B. Vaught, who was brought in to replace Lieutenant Colonel Long after he was killed at Quang Tri. (Vaught later became the overall commander of the unsuccessful raid to free Americans held hostage in Iran.)

What was the rest of the division doing? Not much, is the frank answer. The 1st Brigade, in Quang Tri with four battalions, represented the preponderance of the division's assets. Tolson had been earlier ordered to defend the city, which was expected to be the prime target, if the NVA decided to stage a Tet offensive. Tolson later explained:

> The only mission I had at that point [before Tet] was to be prepared to move into Base Area 101 and 114 and to defend Quang Tri city from the south and southwest.

Indeed, Quang Tri was attacked at 3:00 A.M. on January 31—the same time Hue was attacked—but the Battle of Quang Tri was over by noon the next day. The division had only one soldier killed during light fighting. The battle was over, in fact, by the time the 2/12th Cav left Camp Evans for PK-17. Surely some of those forces could have assisted us.

The 2d Brigade was still south in II Corps, waiting to deploy northward into I Corps, when the Tet Offensive forced a change in plans. However, the 2d Brigade of the 101st Airborne Division was attached to the 1st Air Cavalry Division and had two battalions in cavalry country. One was with our 1st Brigade at Quang Tri, and the other was at LZ El Paso south of Hue awaiting transportation to Camp Evans when the NVA struck. They would have made the move, "but the weather was still not permitting this."

What about the three battalions assigned to Campbell's 3d Brigade? The 2/12th Cav was one; the 5/7th Cav was another. A third was retained at Camp Evans for base defense. As Tolson said afterward, "The bulk of my helicopters, approaching two hundred, were already laagered there, and this meant that I had to be certain that Camp Evans was secure."

Tolson, one of the fathers of air mobility, was perhaps too enamored of the idea of flying to recognize its limitations. Maybe the commander of the 1st Air Cavalry Division had no choice, having indoctrinated himself in the tactics he preached to others.

The airmobile aspects of the 1st Air Cavalry Division resulted from its having approximately 450 helicopters, mostly UH-1 (Huey) models.

Myths developed that helicopters made the division different, that it could do things other divisions couldn't. This was, at best, only partially true. During the Battle of Hue, for example, when we moved from a guerrilla to a conventional war, large-scale use of helicopters was out of the question. Those who recognized this changing aspect of the division's predicament were exceptions. Lots of helicopters and many dreams went down in flames together. (Since Vietnam, helicopter and weapon technology have come a long way, ensuring the usefulness of helicopters in modern warfare, as witnessed by their ability to destroy targets during Desert Storm. During Vietnam, however, there was no way unarmored Hueys could fly through machine gun fire without risking catastrophic consequences.)

The myths resulted from our early days in Vietnam, when we were undisputed kings of the air. With abundant support, the 1st Air Cavalry was more potent than other divisions. The story went: the Cav could orient on the enemy rather than the terrain. We could chase the enemy wherever he was, without worrying about roads or the lack of them.

During Tet, the concept of air mobility had a coronary. Fate picked Sweet to pull the plug.

The 5/7th Cav made some effort to help us, after they flew into PK-17 on February 4, the second day of our encirclement. We received a radio call from the battalion, letting us know that they had occupied blocking positions on high ground to our north. "Drive 'em into us, and we'll blow 'em away." We were incredulous. Hadn't Vaught been told what our situation was? Did anyone really think it was within our power to drive anyone anywhere? Then we started to laugh: it took our minds off classifying the wounded.

On the morning of February 5—after we left TFP—the 5/7th Cav moved from its blocking positions and headed toward TFP. On February 7, the battalion made contact with the force that had surrounded us. The 5/7th avoided encirclement, but things didn't go very well. "Progress was halted by the stubborn resistance of the enemy. Artillery and ARA [aerial rocket artillery, or helicopters armed with rockets] were called in on a well-fortified enemy. . . ."

The 5/7th Cav tried to attack again on February 8, "but they were halted by heavy volumes of enemy automatic weapons and mortar fire." TFP was attacked several more times, but it wasn't breached until February 27. And when TFP was taken, it was only a matter of a few days until the NVA pulled out of Hue. Perhaps the NVA withdrew from Thon La Chu because it made no sense to stay there once the decision was made to abandon Hue. My hunch is that our force at TFP helped the NVA make the obvious decision, but we were not the sole cause.

Although the weather played a part throughout the Hue campaign, the real problem the division had during this period stemmed from a shortage of supplies. Much to his credit, Tolson did not try to hide the problem. Still, his admission didn't alter the facts.

> I'd like to point out that our supply situation obviously was very nip and tuck. I had the 1st Brigade very heavily engaged near Quang Tri and now the 3d Brigade even more heavily engaged near Hue. We could have used some more combat troops, and I was asked on one occasion by General Westmoreland on February 17 if I could use some more. My response to this question was that I could only handle but two more battalions because of the logistical problems.
>
> In other words, we were at the point where if you added more troops, then you had the problem of supplying more troops, and the supply setup at this time was very tenuous.

The Marines were not able to open the road from Da Nang north, so division supplies had to come in over the beach at Cua Viet east of Dong Ha. They would then be brought to Camp Evans by truck in daily convoys led by the division's provost marshal. Small amounts were flown in directly from ships offshore by large CH-54 cargo helicopters (flying cranes). The cargo was carried in bus-like pods, which had been used earlier in a ground configuration to house elements of the division head-quarters.

So serious was the shortage of gasoline during Tet that military policemen were sent on scouting missions at Camp Evans to empty the fuel from mess hall stoves so there would be sufficient quantities to operate the generators powering the division radios. Tolson had no choice, and ate cold food like everyone else. His cooks might have tried to hide the general's gas—and might have succeeded—if Scudder hadn't stolen it to dry our socks. In fact, the general's mess was on half rations during Tet. "I think the whole division was on half rations too," Ross recalled.

Life in the division headquarters became a little more difficult after the NVA rocketed Camp Evans to destroy parked helicopters. One rocket hit an ammo dump, setting it ablaze. "Ammo was exploding everywhere," one survivor recalled. "One stray round even penetrated the CONEX container that held the beer and wine used in the general's mess. We all went out to look at it later, thinking it was really funny." A number of helicopters were also destroyed. Since there wasn't any fuel, they weren't doing much good anyway.

The exploding ammo apparently unnerved Major General Tolson, who, according to one eyewitness account, rushed into the TOC (tactical operations center) in a state of great agitation. Dirt that had been piled over the ceiling beams to protect the TOC's occupants against a direct hit fell through the cracks, adding to the surreal atmosphere. Tolson was shouting, but no one could understand what he was trying to say. Everything seemed to be running together. When Lieutenant Colonel Ross overheard the commotion from his small private office in the rear of the TOC, he walked over to Tolson and grasped his arm in a friendly way. Without sacrificing any decorum, Ross led Tolson back to his office. A few minutes later, Tolson emerged as if nothing had happened. Ross deserved a lot of credit for his handling of this difficult situation.

Ross remembers how a young corporal helped keep the division alive after the decision was made to parachute ammunition into Evans. "He would tell them when to punch it out of the airplane, and the next thing you saw was a parachute coming through the clouds." Trucks on the drop zone would take the ammunition directly to the artillery firing positions.

Ross agrees that the supply problem cannot be laid solely on the weather.

"Even if the weather was okay, supply problems would have existed. The solutions would have been easier, however."

Whatever the case, the NVA took advantage of the weather, and the weather favored their strategy. If the division had had more supplies to start with, the 2/12th

Cav might have reached Hue sooner and blunted the edge of the NVA's psychological victory.

The final official word on the supply situation came from Tolson, when he looked back on the problems the division faced moving northward:

> The only major areas which presented significant problems for an intra-theater move were pre-positioned supplies and maintenance support. Of specific concern were the pre-positioning of aviation fuel and artillery ammunition. Pre-positioned supplies were established for the 1st Air Cavalry Division in the I Corps Tactical Zone; however, the supplies were not physically located at the sites where the division was located. As a result, when the enemy severed the [roads] external to the 1st Air Cav Division's area of operations during the Tet Offensive, certain items of supply became critical to the using units.
>
> In the future, pre-positioned supplies should be co-located well in advance at the site where the using units will be stationed.

Another way of looking at this is to recall that if the division had stayed in the place near Phu Bai originally designated by III Marine Amphibious Force Commander, Lieutenant General Robert E. Cushman, the 1st Air Cavalry Division would *not* have been separated from its supply base. It was Tolson's moving his headquarters to Camp Evans—albeit with Cushman's acquiescence—that was the cause of the separation. (Whether the supplies originally earmarked for the 1st Cav would have been sufficient, given the later tempo of the combat, is a matter I have not looked into. There is some evidence that the Marines weren't managing the supply situation as well as General Westmoreland wanted, perhaps explaining why, on February 12, he established a provisional MACV-Forward headquarters presence in Phu Bai under command of General Creighton Abrams. This is not to be confused with the MACV advisers' compound just outside the walls of Hue. Phu Bai is about five miles from the Hue city walls.)

In sum, Tolson said that military units should not be separated from the material needed to wage war. It's a pity he didn't learn that lesson before Tet. Sweet and Scudder could have taught him.

CHAPTER 25

HEROES NOT FORGOTTEN

APART FROM THE AMERICAN CASUALTIES, WE HAD LOSSES among our Vietnamese interpreters and Kit Carson Scouts.

Just after we were surrounded at TFP, Wild Card's scout, Ba, was hit and evacuated to PK-17. Scudder was alerted and waited to meet the medevac chopper. In fact, he met all medevacs. Ba had been assigned to Company C while Scudder was still commander, about four months earlier. Scudder was very suspicious of all Vietnamese, based in part on his father's being held POW by the Japanese for three years during World War II. Scudder's father was part of MacArthur's staff left behind under the command of General Wainwright when MacArthur was evacuated to Australia. After the war Scudder heard his father's stories of horror about captivity in Manchuria.

When Ba first arrived at C Company, Scudder was

nervous. He knew the scouts were former VC, and he wasn't sure how sincere Ba's conversion was. So no rifle for Ba. Scudder didn't want to be assassinated, and his boyhood background added fuel to the fire of suspicion. He watched Ba like a hawk.

Later Scudder came to like Ba, and promoted him as the "best scout in the battalion." When it came time to arm Ba with an M-16 like all the other scouts and interpreters, Scudder arranged a major ceremony, a rite of passage, as he later described it. The vote was unanimous.

So, after the scout was wounded, "I met Ba at the aid station," Scudder recounts. "He was cold but still alive, so I tucked him in a blanket, the way you do a baby."

It was the practice to ensure that every wounded soldier was labeled before putting him on another medevac that carried the WIAs to hospital ships offshore. In Ba's case, Scudder completed three labels identifying him as a scout under his personal protection. He hoped this would ensure Ba got the same treatment as Americans, proving Scudder himself had been converted.

One label went on the wrist, another on the lapel, and the third on the ankle of the fast-fading Vietnamese. Ba went out on the next available helicopter right behind Scudder's prayers. The next day Scudder learned that the helicopter had a mishap at sea and all aboard were lost before reaching the hospital ship. Even today Scudder has no idea if Ba's family ever learned what happened.

• • •

WHILE WE WERE SURROUNDED AND CLINGING TO LIFE, helicopter pilots routinely risked and gave their lives to reach us with any supplies they could get their hands on, often while gunships from Bravo Troop, 1/9th Cav flew protective cover. During one of these typical death-defying missions near Hue in early February, one Bravo Troop pilot, Lieutenant William Babcock, was shot down and held briefly by the NVA.

A few minutes after a forced landing in an unsecured field, he found himself and his damaged helicopter surrounded by an enemy force.

"These guys were all VC and they were well equipped, all carrying an AK-47 or larger. They started walking toward us [Babcock and his door gunner] across the field, away from the chopper," Babcock said, still uncertain if any friendly forces heard his earlier frantic radio call for help. In fact, four helicopters listened to his SOS and started an urgent search. The two-hundred-foot ceiling made the job almost impossible. Finally, another B Trooper, Warrant Officer Thomas Maehrlein, spotted Babcock's downed, burning helicopter through the fog and went in for a closer look before attempting a rescue. About fifty enemy soldiers in two groups were spotted hiding behind a nearby hill, so Maehrlein's door gunner opened fire with his M-60 machine gun. Neither Maehrlein nor his door gunner recognized two Americans in one of the groups until they fell flat on the ground, while the enemy soldiers fled for the woods. "It's lucky we didn't shoot them," Maehrlein recalled.

Maehrlein landed his helicopter, and a moment later Babcock and his door gunner scrambled aboard, leaving ten enemy bodies behind. Babcock was proud of his fellow troopers; "It's good to be with Bravo," he bragged. "They come after you no matter what."

Not every pilot was as lucky as Babcock and his crewmate. Dozens were killed or wounded trying to help us, and they had as much to do with saving us as anyone else. About six thousand helicopter crewmen were killed during the war, and my hunch is that most were teenagers.

During the approximate period of this story, the 1st Air Cav Division lost 119 helicopters. Most carried a crew of four.

CHAPTER 26

AFTER THE BATTLE IS OVER

WHEN HELVEY TOOK MY PLACE AS THE BATTALION intelligence officer, there wasn't any reason for me to stay in the field. As I left the hilltop, Sweet was alerted to move the battalion toward Hue again, which meant it was unlikely I'd see any of my friends again before going home. I said good-bye and returned to Camp Evans. I had a week to rest. I was ready for it.

There was still fighting going on in Hue, and the city itself was hard to recognize by this time, thanks to the bombing that began on February 7. It may have been effective, but it wasn't decisive in the final analysis. What forced the NVA and VC from inside the Citadel was fourteen infantry battalions, including four Marine battalions fighting house-to-house. By February 13 there was more rubble than houses in most sections of the city. The southern side of the section in the vicinity of the MACV advisers' compound was cleared by February 13, but inside was another story. Countless unburied, putrifying corpses made the smell of the place, as well as its visual appearance, ugly. The 1st Air Cavalry Division had finally pulled itself together. They approached the city walls in organized combat formations.

I slept for about twenty-four hours—the first real rest I'd had in weeks. It felt good to be clean again and back on a regular schedule. With no personal affairs to wind up, I decided it would be a good idea to write up a recommendation for Sweet's Distinguished Service Cross, the nation's second-highest award. After that, I put together some narrative for an award for the battalion—a Presidential Unit Citation, which is the highest possible unit award. In both cases, I wanted to do the writing myself.

Writing the recommendation for Sweet's award was easy: all of the facts were fresh in my mind, and there was no problem finding people to write corroborating statements. The words came easy to everyone. I didn't sign the recommendation myself, because it would carry more weight to have the signature of the brigade or division commander. It was enough that the words were mine.

I felt strongly about the quality of Sweet's leadership and admired the way he led us out of TFP. Perhaps we could have made it without him, but I doubt it. He never cracked when the pressure got heavy, and his personal example inspired the rest of us to keep going.

The DSC is a high award, but he deserved it. The only person who disagreed, apparently, was a Marine colonel sitting on the awards board at the III MAF (Marine Amphibious Force) headquarters. He couldn't understand why an Army officer should get the DSC—just behind the Medal of Honor in order of precedence—for the Battle of Hue, which he probably considered a Marine show. What did the Army have to do with Hue? They weren't even there! On the other hand, neither was the Marine. General Creighton Abrams and Cushman's deputy, Army Lieutenant General Richard G. Stilwell, heard about the dispute and gave orders to stop the bickering. Word of the matter leaked back to Sweet after the award.

What none of us knew then was that when Abrams heard of the Battle of Hue and our encirclement, he moved from Saigon to Phu Bai. He even visited the fort at PK-17 on February 16.

A couple of months later, he returned to visit the 1st Air Cavalry Division, and Campbell introduced Abrams to Sweet. "What battalion do you command?" Abrams asked. "The 2/12th Cav, sir." "And how old are you?" "Thirty-eight, sir." "Did you make any mistakes during Tet?" "Yes, sir. I made several. Leaving the packs behind was the critical one." This was a mistake, but not Sweet's.

"I'm told you inflicted horrendous casualties—about three thousand. Well now, you go back and tell your soldiers I watched every move they made. No American unit has ever acquitted itself better in combat. Tell them I said that." He also asked if Sweet suffered emotionally from the casualties.

"I just find a private place and let everything go," Sweet acknowledged. "I do the same thing," Abrams replied.

The senior general in Vietnam was William Westmoreland. He didn't visit us after Tet, but he did send a congratulatory message to Tolson and commanders of other units involved in the offensive.

IT WAS NOT UNTIL MANY YEARS LATER THAT I LEARNED that our encirclement had been monitored in the Pentagon by the Joint Chiefs of Staff in a room still called The Tank.

A friend of Sweet's was present in The Tank. He was also being transferred to Vietnam in a few days. As soon as he got to Vietnam, he reached Sweet with a private message: "You must never talk about what happened . . . ever. . . . It's apparent there was a massive command fuck-up." Sweet took the advice. The idea was that too many heads would roll, including many innocent ones, if the world learned the real story of the Lost Battalion.

I suspect, but cannot prove, that the Presidential Unit Citation was sent to the White House because Sweet kept his word.

Only after I had nearly completed this account did Sweet seek release from his vow of silence from the senior officer he'd given it to, and Sweet's recollections became an important part of my narrative. What made him change his mind? In part it was my description of our being cut loose. Sweet felt there was nothing to be gained by keeping mum. Besides, he had held his frustrations close to his chest for too long at great personal cost. It wasn't Vietnam Syndrome, but a General Abrams–like variant.

The symptoms include sleepwalking. Lieutenant Colonel Ross noticed Sweet's problem when they shared a tent while Sweet was preparing to take over the G-3 job from Ross, several months after Tet. Later it got worse, reaching a climax when Sweet, as a brigadier general in the mid-1970s, went to sleep on the third floor of Fort Bragg's VIP quarters, only to awaken without explanation in the basement coal bin.

My own lay observation is that much later in life he also showed signs of melancholia, particularly when thinking about the events at Thon La Chu, and a day didn't pass without some reflections on those horrible hours. His remorse isn't self-serving, so far as I can tell, and experiences of this nature happen often to others, including Bob Helvey and me. Still, tears come easier to him than to either of us, perhaps a reflection of the burden of command and the responsibilities he shouldered for so long almost single-handed. Who can blame him for trying to fight back? Time has affected him in other ways. Nearly twenty-five years later, in an interview with a reporter, he referred to Bob Helvey and his select volunteer team that acted as the battalion vanguard between Thon La Chu and Hue as his "goon squad." In context,

I don't think he consciously used this expression as a degrading term—which it certainly is—but he wouldn't have used it at all if he was thinking with the same clarity with which he handled the battalion when he was the commander.

Sweet's Distinguished Service Cross was presented to him at Camp Evans on October 18, 1968. General Andrew J. Goodpaster, deputy commander of the U.S. Army Military Assistance Command, Vietnam (MACV), presented the award with appropriate remarks.

"Speaking on behalf of the entire command in Vietnam, we honor and salute this performance and the unit of which it was a part."

There wasn't much more to say. Regrettably, only about thirty soldiers who served during Tet were still assigned to the 2/12th Cav. The rest had either rotated home or to other jobs or had been evacuated as casualties. Goodpaster asked that the tape recorders be shut down after the formal citation was read so he could speak to Sweet privately. "I know how you feel," he said. "So many casualties that you feel unworthy and embarrassed. The real reason we are here is that when your country needed you badly you were not found wanting."

After the ceremony, Sweet recorded some of his sentiments on a tape that he mailed to his wife, who was living in Springfield, Virginia. After expressing his gratitude to everyone, he finished with a comment about that night march out of TFP: "We were sure it would work. . . . I found out later nobody else was."

After I left for the States, Helvey returned to PK-17, taking my place as the battalion's intelligence officer. The Battle of Hue was still going on. Helvey liked gathering information firsthand, so when he heard of another ARVN compound bypassed by the NVA on their march to Hue, he flew in to find out if they knew what was going on in the city.

The ARVN told him that when the attack started, members of the Viet Cong infrastructure in the neighboring village came out of hiding, carrying clipboards with the names of those to be eliminated. Afterward the VC joined their NVA counterparts in the Hue attack. When the NVA started to lose their hold on Hue, the VC returned to the village while the NVA headed toward Laos. The VC must have forgotten that their cover was blown, and they were rounded up by the ARVN unit Helvey visited. Helvey was familiar with the compound from his first tour in Vietnam and made no effort to rush back to PK-17. He still had friends there who remembered his appetite for beer and duck.

When the Tet offensive was over, both sides needed time to lick their wounds. The wounds of the 2/12th Cav were wide and deep. Starting with Company C's first contact in the Que Son Valley on January 2 through the day after Company A made its daring behind-the-lines raid, the battalion had taken 311 casualties: 60 killed and 251 wounded. Sixty percent of the assigned strength of the battalion.

Estimated enemy killed were 634, but that is an estimate that I helped falsify. For all practical purposes, only the first 281 from Que Son were based on a reliable body count.

None of us liked counting bodies, but we were forced to do it. Someone was keeping statistics, and there was no other way to satisfy their demand for data. It was easier to fake than to count.

Throughout the Tet period, replacements were needed badly by the 2/12th Cav. We really didn't start to regain authorized unit strength until after the Hue campaign, because there weren't many replacements coming into the division, and it would have been hard to get the few who did arrive forward while the fighting was going on.

The division's personnel officer even reported that "during the Hue Campaign, 1–26 February, maneuver battalion strength became a critical factor as unprogrammed losses were heavy." *Unprogrammed losses?* He also wryly observed that it was difficult to move post exchange merchandise from Da Nang to Camp Evans, and this "service was severely handicapped by transportation available." Ammunition presumably had a higher priority than candy bars and Rolexes. The precise reaction of the PX officer is not recorded, however.

There were problems identifying the remains of soldiers killed in action, "caused by poor communications and lack of follow-up by unit personnel responsible for reporting. The wearing of identification cards and marking of boots was stressed as essential to the system."

It's hard to disagree, of course. But if the personnel

officer had tried to find out why we didn't have time to identify and report every KIA, he might have been less anxious to blame us for screwing up his reporting system.

Another footnote to this story is that those outside of the battalion never got wind of the expression "TFP." Official records refer to the area as "Ti Ti Woods," a kind of pidgin Vietnamese meaning "small." I suppose TFP was an expression we used only among ourselves.

We also learned afterward how the NVA were able to fortify TFP so strongly.

It seems they took possession of American materials that were stored there, earmarked for pacification programs in the area. One report was that Thon La Chu was supposed to be a demonstration village or hamlet—I use the expressions interchangeably. Because of its status, extra allocations of building supplies were made available, and the NVA simply diverted some to their own use, even though they didn't have the permission of Robert Komer, the pacification czar.

We in the 2/12th Cav believed that our situation at TFP was avoidable. Yet Americans stranded in Hue were as bad off. They were so short of food, for example, that they had to take it away from Vietnamese refugees at gunpoint. If our suffering took off some of the pressure, it helps make our own deprivations and sacrifices more meaningful.

No one knows for certain how many civilians were executed by the NVA—those who now claim Ho Chi

Minh City as their capital—but nearly 2,800 bodies were recovered in mass graves near the fields of execution. In one grave near the city, the skulls and bones of 438 men and boys were found.

It is a little comforting to know that the mass executions in Hue might have been more genocidal had we not shown up when we did. So long as we threatened the attackers from the rear, they didn't have time to kill everybody.

When the Army writes its official history of the Hue massacre, these are the statistics that will be recorded, based on documents in Army archives:

Number of civilians killed in the vicinity of Hue: 3,800
Number of civilians confirmed massacred: 2,786
Number of civilians discovered in mass graves: 2,226
Number of non-Vietnamese civilians murdered: 16

I was fortunate to interview Lieutenant Colonel Melvin W. Russell, who was in Hue during the attack. Then a twenty-nine-year-old Army captain, Russell was an adviser to the 1st ARVN Division headquartered in Hue. The stories he told me and the photographs he took left no doubt in my mind why Hue was considered the most beautiful city in South Vietnam. It was a charming city of tranquility, culture, and commerce.

His photographs capture the loveliness of old buildings and the dignity of its 140,000 inhabitants. There was unmistakable serenity in these pre-Tet snapshots, taken by Russell as he wandered about the city exploring marketplaces and discovering new vistas in the ancient capital, its castles and shrines. His post-Tet photos of Hue show the city looking like those horrible scenes that reached us from Europe after World War II drew to a close. The impact of Hue's destruction was stunning: less than 20 percent of the city was undamaged, according to estimates at the time.

It is also interesting how Helvey came to be selected as my replacement, when he was so obviously qualified as a company commander, a job he loved. When Scudder confirmed that I was due to leave for the States, he sought out Sweet for a private discussion. "Helvey's time is running out," Scudder explained. "If you don't replace him soon, he'll be dead." Sweet agreed.

Helvey missed Company A, where he was a folk hero, but remembered a story he had been told a long time before Vietnam by an old sergeant with a lot of wartime experience. "Life in combat is like a roll of toilet paper. The more you use, the less you got left."

Colonel Campbell reflected on the Tet period years later, contrasting it to experiences during World War II and the Korean War. Compared to them, "it was a cake-walk." He pointed out that his regiment in New Guinea took more casualties in one month than the 3d Brigade lost in the entire time he was in command.

COLONEL CAMPBELL IS CAUGHT IN THE MIDDLE OF THIS story, something of a buffer between an angry Sweet and an avuncular Tolson. Overall, this does Campbell an injustice, because he was more than a cipher, a lot more. Campbell's caution, however, which worked so well for him during the Que Son battle, had the opposite effect in the Hue campaign.

When the fight began in the Que Son Valley, Campbell was slow to commit massive numbers of helicopters for relief operations. This is not what the NVA expected.

Based on their understanding of how Campbell's predecessor operated, the NVA set up helicopter-killing zones deep in the Que Son Valley—machine gun positions near the peaks of several mountains overlooking the valley through which our helicopters would ordinarily fly in the course of a relief operation. When the NVA pulled away from LZ Ross, they expected massive numbers of helicopters to be sent into the pursuit. Campbell's cautious nature kept the helicopters grounded until the situation on the ground was better understood, stopping an inevitable slaughter. We lost a few helicopters, including Gregory's, but far fewer than we would have lost otherwise.

"If Colonel Campbell hadn't been in command, we'd have done exactly what the NVA expected us to do," one brigade staff officer surmised later, "and the results would have been horrible."

The map captured from the NVA recon party indicates exactly where they planned to emplace their heavy machine guns. This portion of the plan was undoubtedly executed with the same precision as the rest of the planning.

Campbell was the same cautious commander when the 3d Brigade was in the Hue area, but by then caution was a liability. During the Hue campaign there was widespread belief that Campbell was far too cautious, even for Tolson. Tolson's browbeating apparently got to Campbell, and he became much more subdued than he was in the Que Son.

Campbell recorded this friction in his diary on February 12: "General T[olson] PO'd on my use of 2/12th." To his credit, Colonel Campbell gave me his diary, maps, and other papers to use in this book without restriction.

CHAPTER 27

FORGOTTEN FAVOR REPAID

MY FEET STARTED HURTING SOON AFTER I RETURNED TO Camp Evans. At first, I didn't pay too much attention. But after a few days the pain got so bad I had to do something. My feet looked all right, so I assumed there was something wrong with my boots and drew a new pair from the supply officer.

The soreness didn't go away, which worried me. I was barely able to walk.

Finally, I did what I should have done all along and turned up for sick call one morning in the aid tent. I can't remember if I saw a medic or a doctor, but he knew what was wrong as soon as I described the symptoms. I had a form of foot immersion, aggravated by my being wet so long during Tet. He gave me a tube of silicon paste, which solved my problem within minutes. When I retired, this foot problem entitled me to a partial disability—about eighty untaxable dollars a month.

Our battalion surgeon was top-drawer, but we did have a problem with his religious counterpart, the battalion chaplain, Dan Clem. Later I learned that Sweet had relieved Clem—fired him, in effect. I should have suspected there'd be problems after the incident with Helvey before he went on the reconnaissance mission behind NVA lines.

Apparently, Clem was more upset than any of us realized by the casualties we took during Tet. Part of his anguish was understandable: he knew many of the men personally and, in some ways, better than the rest of us. That was part of his job.

In Clem's case, however, he couldn't accept growing casualty lists, and one day the pressure got to him. He took his grievances to Sweet, advising the battalion commander to change his tactics so there'd be fewer casualties. Tactics is out of bounds for a chaplain. But Clem had been in trouble before. I learned later he had twice been relieved for insubordination and inability to adjust.

I was saddened to hear of Clem's death in Germany a few years ago, long after the incident in Vietnam was forgotten. He was killed in a helicopter crash on his way to minister to soldiers on a field exercise. There's no doubt his calling was genuine.

The commander of Company D also gave Sweet some problems and had to be relieved. The officer was indirectly responsible for the drowning death of several soldiers in a stream-crossing mishap. Sweet had put him in command on my recommendation. I was sorry for the recommendation when the officer claimed racial discrimination after Sweet relieved him. The actual reason, according to Sweet, is that he ignored an order to personally supervise the stream crossing.

Colonel Ross heard I was at Camp Radcliff and about to leave for the States.

He invited me to spend my last night at Evans in his private tent, with a farewell dinner in the general's mess. I told the guests about what had happened at TFP, providing the earliest firsthand account they had received. I also told them that someday I'd write a book about my experiences. I think they believed me . . . but I got no encouragement.

After stopping at Camp Radcliff near An Khe to collect my moldy baggage and civilian clothes, I arrived in Saigon with a Listerine bottle filled with scotch. For me, Vietnam was over.

There were perhaps two hundred of us waiting for a boarding pass at the departure counter when the sergeant briefing us stated that no more planes were expected to leave for four days. Actually, there were planes leaving every day, he explained, but they were filled by people who arrived in Saigon before we did.

After he finished the announcement, I heard my name called over the loudspeaker. I was directed to report to the office behind the ticket counter for additional instructions. Somewhat puzzled and a bit annoyed that I was probably going to be put in charge of some detail— perhaps the urine collection detail, part of the drug suppression program—I reported to the office defensively. Behind the desk was the sergeant. I started to think of reasons why he should pick someone else.

"You're Captain Krohn?" he asked. I nodded. "You don't remember me, do you?" I didn't. "I used to be with the 2/12th Cav, and we were together at TFP. The night before we attacked you gave me your last can of C-rations when I was looking for something to eat. I didn't want to ask an officer for anything, but I was so hungry. . . ." His voice trailed off. I said a few things to him about some of the things we had done together.

After a moment, he turned his head aside and reached into his desk. He handed me an envelope. "Here's a ticket," he said. "You're leaving tonight."

This incident, maybe as well as any I can think of, dramatizes the tender and lasting bonds of comradeship between men who have risked everything together.

CHAPTER 28

VIEW FROM THE OTHER SIDE

I'D LIKE TO SAY THAT THE 2/12TH CAV WAS MENTIONED in some of the NVA documents captured later as the most ferocious unit they encountered, that we almost upset their plan to attack and hold Hue. In fact, the Army's Center of Military History has two captured plans, but I couldn't find anything in them that specifically identifies our battalion.

The NVA did a certain amount of gloating. It was justified from their point of view. They knew they caught us with our pants down and were proud of it. The reports acknowledge resistance from the north, but they were prepared. "We were ordered to resolutely stand firm against enemy counterattacks." And they did, according to the document "Achievements in Hue City and surrounding districts during one year of the general offensive and uprising," dated December 1968.

Parts of the document are gross exaggerations, but parts are not. The following is pretty good:

> In the small hours of the 31st of January 1968 we launched attacks on Hue City. At 0230 on January 31st, attacks were conducted in all directions, simultaneously, inside and outside the city and coordinated rhythmically. These surprise attacks confused the enemy . . . but our reserve forces were insufficient. . . . The motivation of the masses was not deep enough. Therefore we were not able to overrun the town. . . . The competent coordination of direct operations . . . [and] continual attacks on the enemy . . . [forced] many of the enemy to coordinate widely with our operations. It made the enemy lose the direction and confused his command. Therefore, for a long period the enemy was not able to organize effective counterattacks on Hue City.

Another document captured in April 1968, just a few months after the battle, shows how well the NVA understood our weaknesses. The overall size of our force was considerable; the numbers actually in the foxhole much less.

> Though the enemy strength was large, his actual combat strength was low. Only 7,000 soldiers out of 25,000

were able to fight successfully. Furthermore, it consisted of diversified army branches that would be confused in combat.

The same document indicates that the attack was originally planned for March 1968, "but the opportunity presented itself and we could not miss it. . . . Our soldiers had practiced 26 attack exercises which gave them good experience."

The report notes that the NVA campaign can be divided into three phases.

During the first phase, from January 7 to 27, they "infiltrated the masses to propagandize among the people . . . motivated the people to kill tyrants . . . attacked the communications lines between Da Nang and Hue . . . [and] occupied a number of districts." The attack on LZ Ross near Da Nang would certainly fit into Phase I, as reported.

Phase II was the attack on Hue. Phase III was to hold the city "so that a revolutionary administration could be established. We had to resist all enemy attacks from 1 February to 23 February before we withdrew. . . . In only a few days, our forces had destroyed three enemy battalions, four artillery weapons, and one platoon of U.S. soldiers." Could any of these be the 2/12th Cav?

The summary states that eleven battalions of the United States and "puppet troops" were completely destroyed, as well as twenty-six companies, including "one air cavalry company." Five battalions of U.S. air cavalry are listed as "worn down."

The report also notes the "elimination" (that is, murder) of "1,892 administrative personnel, 38 policemen, 790 tyrants, 6 captains, 2 first lieutenants, 20 second lieutenants, and many NCOs." Assuming the administrators, police, and "tyrants" were civilians, the total acknowledged murdered is 2,748. Mass murderers, history suggests, like to keep careful records. The official U.S. Army figure of civilians massacred is 2,786, almost exactly the same number. No American soldiers are proud of My Lai. One wonders if anyone in Hanoi still recalls Hue.

I recognize that enthusiasm for communism is waning in Vietnam just as it is in almost all countries that once extolled the scientific glories of Marxist doctrine. The Soviets now acknowledge the horrors of the Stalinist era, which smooths the path for reconciliation with the West. The dialogue with Vietnam is just beginning, although General John W. Vessey, Jr., a former chairman of the Joint Chiefs of Staff, has been visiting Hanoi for years to discuss the missing-in-action issue. Whether or not the agonizing over MIAs is worthwhile only history will judge, the suffering of next-of-kin notwithstanding.

It is easy for me to admit we lost the war. I even acknowledge that someday we will reconcile our lingering feud with Vietnam. Whether it is one Vietnam or two Vietnams makes little difference to me. But I personally will never be able to accept a solution that maintains people in power who can look back to the Hue massacre and gloat. Never.

My respect for the professionals in the North Vietnamese Army has been recorded, and I harbor no bitterness against soldiers who fought us fairly . . . and all those who faced us abided by international conventions, so far as I know. If they didn't, I would have said so. For murderers and war criminals, there is no statute of moral limitations. They are no better than Nazi war criminals and should be hounded to their graves without pity or remorse, certainly without a diplomatic delegation of U.S. mourners.

It was always my opinion that we won the Battle of Tet 1968 militarily but lost politically. Despite how the campaign ended on the battlefield, the American public withdrew what little support we had left. Clark Clifford became Secretary of Defense to help pull Johnson's Vietnam chestnuts out of the fire, but was soon converted by the antiwar camp early into his tenure. Helvey and I were working in the Pentagon together at the time and watched the secretary's about-face nearly firsthand. We were upset with his new attitude, because we still had troops in Vietnam fighting the war, and believed the secretary of defense should be more supportive.

Our private nickname for him was "Benedict Clifford." Many years later I somewhat regretted our harshness, because it was obvious that Mr. Clifford was, presumably, one of Washington's most clear-thinking personalities, with a reputation beyond reproach. I acknowledge that his biographer one day may draw conflicting conclusions based on the BCCI scandal. Maybe our original judgment was justified after all.

I should point out that military thinkers are still divided on how they describe the Tet uprising. Most people tend to agree that Tet cost the support of Congress and the people, but the damage inflicted on the NVA made Tet a military victory for us. In a 1985 interview for an Army oral history collection, General Tolson noted that we really hurt the enemy considerably in the Tet offensive in the I Corps area. "They lost a lot of people and a lot of equipment, weapons, and everything." He acknowledged that the NVA miscalculated the amount of public support they'd receive, thinking erroneously that the Saigon government would collapse.

His closing comment is somewhat cryptic, and I wish the interviewer had asked a follow-up question to pin down his position: "The Tet offensive really didn't pan out at all like the North Vietnamese had anticipated," Tolson concluded. "We were very fortunate in the way things turned out."

CHAPTER 29

WHO WON? WHO LOST?

THERE ARE MANY WAYS TO EVALUATE THE SUCCESS OR failure of a military operation. Accomplishing the mission is usually the most valid indicator, but consider Pyrrhic victories where the cost of life required to win makes the notion of victory questionable. Other yardsticks relate to the success of the tactics employed, acts of gallantry that serve to inspire others, and other events that help define an army and the nation it represents. Another test is how well the component parts of a military force function together—a reflection on how efficiently the machinery operates as a whole.

There are many parts to a military machine. A non-exclusive list includes the combat maneuver elements of infantry, armor, and artillery, as well as combat support elements of engineer units, aviation of all kinds, communications networks, and logistics-based combat service support units. The maneuver units can't do it all by themselves, any more than a car can be operated without gas stations, garages, or wreckers, not to mention road builders, training schools, engineers, designers, developers, and all the others who contribute to the final outcome.

A nation may rally around a gallant commander, very visible in his own way.

The infrastructure behind the scenes, however, is just as important. When the supporting systems fail to support the commander, as they did during the 2/12th Cav's attack on Hue, there's not a whole lot left to boast about. Shortfalls of that magnitude cannot be overcome by any leader, however brilliant. Ironically, a mediocre commander may appear larger than life when the supporting systems work smoothly enough to mask his intellectual or moral shortcomings.

THE 2D BATTALION, 12TH CAVALRY COULDN'T HAVE BEEN trapped, lost, and subsequently cut loose without a countrywide uprising like Tet '68. It simply shut down U.S. military operations, especially in the northern part of the country where the supporting logistical infrastructure collapsed completely. Our taking the truce seriously, as a gesture of goodwill if not peaceful intent, gave the NVA the opportunity to surprise us. Only at Tet—during a truce—could any combination of North Vietnamese Army units have successfully surrounded a U.S. infantry battalion for more than a few minutes. At any other time help would have come from U.S. bases around the country—reinforcement, artillery, air strikes, whatever it took. No cost would have been too great. There would even have been some rejoicing that the NVA was willing to fight in a fixed position, so we wouldn't have to waste effort finding them. At any other time, we would have destroyed them at our leisure because they would have had nowhere to hide and no way to protect themselves. They would have become, in effect, sheep in wolves' clothing.

Only during truces did we suspend continuous operations, taking advantage of the lull to give ourselves a guarded breather. During Tet '68 the NVA took advantage of the weather, which they couldn't manipulate, and our complacency, which they could, to drive a wedge between our army and the matériel it needed to wage war. Our supporting systems collapsed, because we weren't ready for either the weather or the NVA. It didn't take long for the NVA leadership to exploit the unique opportunity to hit us when we couldn't hit back.

CHAPTER 30

WE'LL NEVER KNOW

THE SUPPLY SITUATION THROUGHOUT THE 1ST AIR Cavalry Division during the Tet period was one helluva mess. There is, surprisingly, universal agreement on this point. Charges as to who is responsible, however, range from Cushman to Tolson to God. Everyone but God was willing to discuss their recollections for the record.

My first instinct is to hold Tolson liable for the situation that sent us toward Hue without artillery support, and for the shortage of artillery ammunition when the tubes finally arrived at PK-17. Shortages stemmed from the fact that the supplies based at Hue-Phu Bai were not moved with Tolson's headquarters when he displaced to Camp Evans from Hue-Phu Bai. The decision not to move the supplies was based on the assumption that the division would continue to have unrestricted access to

Hue-Phu Bai by truck or air, an assumption unjustified by facts.

Ordering the 2/12th Cav to move north without ammunition was also ill-advised, but I cannot pinpoint who first assumed that we would be resupplied with fresh stocks once we reached Camp Evans, the G-4 (supply officer, or Geezus-4) of the 1st Air Cav or the G-4 of the III MAF responsible for supporting our division.

During Tet, when nearly every normal supply channel collapsed, the III MAF did their best to supply the 1st Cavalry Division, but "they didn't know how to handle us," Collier Ross later recalled. The division G-4, Lieutenant Colonel Robert D. Vaughn, thinks the III MAF just wasn't prepared to provide the vast amounts of supplies on short notice the 1st Cav required to keep its men and equipment, particularly hundreds of helicopters, operational. We also used up artillery ammunition a lot faster than the Marines were accustomed to, rarely putting constraints on how much the tubes could fire in support of wide-ranging ground operations, whether or not in actual contact with the enemy.

During the early stages of Tet, fuel and artillery ammunition were very critical for the division, as Tolson admitted. Vaughn agrees. "Every night I had to report [to General Tolson] how many shells we had per tube. It was about seventy or eighty or something like that." The division had plenty in storage at Hue-Phu Bai, but considering there was no way to move ammunition by truck or air, "it might as well have been in Timbuktu."

III MAF supply procedures were also foreign to the 1st Cav, which tended to move things around without worrying too much about accountability. The Marines, on the other hand, were strict bookkeepers, going so far as to ask Colonel George W. Putnam, Jr., the division's chief of staff, to sign for the 150 or so torn-up tents and other minor items they left behind at Camp Evans when we moved in. Putnam told the Marines to deal with Vaughn, whose reaction was the same as Putnam's: "You gotta be kidding!" Throughout the period the division signed for everything it got from III MAF sources. There was no malice involved, it's just that the Army and Marines operated differently.

The system was defeated to some extent by the pilots from the 1st Squadron, 9th Cavalry, who flew scout missions for the division after they located three Navy barges filled with JP-4 jet fuel docked for the duration of the Tet campaign at the mouth of the Perfume River just outside Hue. Helicopters were able to land on the barges and swapped VC flags and other items for fuel with the men manning the barges, recalled Colonel Putnam. "Yes, that's true," confirmed Vaughn. "The 1st of the 9th Cav were, without question, the best scavengers of the whole outfit." So long as the scouts were kept flying, no one in the 1st Cav looked too closely into what was being used as trading material. My hunch is that many of the captured weapons we had hoarded earlier ended up in

Navy or Marine hands, later to be traded throughout the country for souvenirs with men who never experienced actual combat.

The men on the barges were so hungry for souvenirs that they offered beef as well as fuel in exchange for VC flags, Putnam later recalled. So much beef "vanished" from Marine stocks that they sent a team to the 1st Cav to investigate, finally asking Putnam to sign for the beef to make the transfer legal, just as they had asked him to sign for the tents. The investigators, predictably, got the same response.

Vaughn became the G-4 just before Tet, replacing Lieutenant Colonel Roscoe Robinson, who had been selected to command the 2/7th Cav battalion. It saved Robinson a lot of ass-chewing. When Robinson, after taking command, ran into Putnam at Camp Evans, he was told by the chief of staff that "you ought to be glad you're not the G-4 now, because the Old Man [Tolson] has Vaughn for breakfast every day." Vaughn, however, doesn't remember Tolson being "unreasonably" angry. "In fact," he said, "I loved the guy."

Putnam recalls that during the Tet period the 1st Cav received no supplies from III MAF, but that III MAF got supplies from us, although he acknowledged that his expertise in this area was not as great as some others more directly involved. He does remember, however, a visit to the division by the Army Chief of Staff, General Harold K. Johnson. After a briefing that included how the division was moving supplies by truck from Dong Ha to

Camp Evans along Highway 1, and the NVA were bringing theirs in by water, Johnson pointed out that this may be the first time in the history of warfare that the supply routes of two opposing armies intersected.

"That's absolutely right," Vaughn confirmed. "During the day we used the roads; they [the NVA] crossed them during the night."

Vaughn believes that if it weren't for the low clouds and rain, there might not have been a supply problem. "It was hell," he remembers, "because the supply systems were all there, but you couldn't make them work due to the weather." He thinks Tolson's overconfidence was based on how well the division's supply systems operated up to that point, especially in the Bong Son area. Before Tet the 1st Cavalry Division had the best supply system in the Republic of Vietnam, and we got spoiled. If that included Tolson, he wasn't alone, Vaughn recalls. If weather was an impediment earlier, it was never the insurmountable obstacle that it became during Tet.

Putnam says the division staff made sure the supply system worked, and worked well. It wasn't the Americal Division that ensured the 3d Brigade in the Da Nang area was supported to 1st Cav standards, he told me, it was the division staff. I agree with Putnam's assessment and told him so. "In the Que Son Valley we had everything we needed."

Putnam later retired as a major general. Robinson retired as a full four-star general. Vaughn retired as a colonel.

Colonel Campbell recorded his rage over the supply situation in his diary on the day the walls of Hue were finally breached. "If anything can go wrong it will *and it has* for two months," he wrote, referring to inadequate food, water, and ammunition supplies. There is no evidence, however, that he ever took his complaints directly to Tolson. If we had, it wouldn't have made any difference. Tolson couldn't have delivered more at this point, even if he had wanted to.

CHAPTER 31

AMBIGUOUS FACTS

WAS THERE A COVER-UP OF OUR NEAR-MASSCRE NEAR Hue? The answer is ambiguous; the facts are not.

A lot depends on an understanding of the Army culture, and how "untidy" things are handled by its bureaucracy.

On the face of it, there was no cover-up. No one in the battalion was asked to hide the facts of what happened, and my recommendation for the 2/12th Cav's Presidential Unit Citation didn't pull any punches either. Nor did the draft of my written recommendation for Sweet's Distinguished Service Cross suppress controversial information.

But the public doesn't read recommendations for awards, either collective (unit) or individual. So what I wrote disappeared into the archives, perhaps never to be seen again.

Shelby L. Stanton wrote a book about the 1st Cavalry Division in Vietnam, basing it on official accounts, called *Anatomy of a Division*. Although he points out that weather kept the division from providing the customary fire support for the attack on Thon La Chu, he draws no further conclusion, except to note that limited support from two rocket-firing helicopters enabled us to reach the hamlet and secure positions in the woodline. As I have written, however, the helicopters fired on us rather than the enemy. From the documents available to Stanton, he can't be blamed for such errors in an otherwise fascinating account.

Stanton notes that the 2/12th Cav escaped encirclement "before it was annihilated." The issue of being "cut loose" is missing, of course. Leaving the dead behind may be inferred from his statement that the few helicopters that landed were only able "to retrieve the seriously wounded."

There is no mention whatsoever of Major General Tolson's role in ordering the attack, or of what action he took, if any, to help us break out. What more could Stanton write based on the division's own after-action reports? Very little.

If Stanton drew material from the report published in August 1968 by the 31st Military History Detachment, it's easy to appreciate how he could be misled. "Supporting indirect fire artillery, aerial rocket artillery, and helicopter gunships preceded a ground attack [on Thon La Chu] by the 2d Battalion, 12th Cavalry. . . . With the aid of helicopter gunships, they were able to penetrate and clear an area along the northern edge of the settlement." My emotional handwritten note on the margin of this report reads "lies, all lies." Later the report concluded that "the 2/12th Cav had sustained significant casualties and it was decided to move the battalion to a better position on the high ground four kilometers to the south." The facts again are different: it may be true that casualties were high, but the reason we moved is because if we had stayed at TFP for a few more hours, we would have faced annihilation. With luck we might have held on for another day, but not much longer. Our moving may be described as part courage, part desperation.

The most telling document is the Officer's Efficiency Report (OER) that Tolson wrote to grade Sweet's performance. The OER was then and is now the Army's chief means of recording performance and evaluating potential. The system is structured so that anything less than a near-perfect report dooms the officer forever—no promotions, no good assignments, in effect, no future.

OERs are now shown to the rated officer, but in 1968 they were supposed to be confidential in the sense that the rated officer would rarely see his report card unless the rater gratuitously provided a copy. But word gets around fast, particularly at the higher echelons. Survival depends on knowing who is in favor and who's out.

Tolson rated Sweet's judgment as mediocre, checking

Block III. Block I was the highest, Block V the bottom. This was a monumental setback for Sweet, a kick in the groin.

What this report said to the Army establishment was that "I, Major General John J. Tolson III, have determined that Lieutenant Colonel Richard S. Sweet's performance under stress of combat means that he has little potential for positions of greater responsibility." The implied message is more important: "Furthermore, anyone who disagrees with this assessment may have Sweet for a friend but most assuredly will have me for an enemy. Those of you who plan a future in the Army should be on notice of my ability to influence decisions affecting your career."

This kind of fitness report, ordinarily, would have made Sweet a marked man. It also meant that Sweet's past exploits, no matter how successful or commendable, didn't really amount to much because of the curse he was carrying. Why waste time praising a man on the way to the gallows? And since nobody in division headquarters was very proud to remember the Thon La Chu disaster anyway, it was best to forget about the whole incident. It became a nonevent, except to recall the gallantry of everyone who helped oust the NVA from Hue.

Fortunately for Sweet, there were enough people aware of his combat competence to ensure that he received a couple of promotions and was selected to the prestigious schools he would ordinarily be picked to attend. But even his friends took the caution to register their respect in private, lest they be tainted by the Tolson curse, as recorded in the OER. Sweet couldn't expect them to do more, and he finally retired as a brigadier general and Army War College graduate, respectable in any man's book. Still, he spent his career from Tet onward keeping an eye over both shoulders and was never able to shake the Tolson evaluation. That's more than a successful combat commander should have to put up with.

The irony is that Tolson himself selected Sweet to be his G-3, or operations officer, after Colonel Ross returned to the United States. Isn't it odd that Tolson would want Sweet so close to him on one hand while trying to destroy him on the other, basically over Sweet's successes in conducting night operations? Furthermore, Tolson's fear of Sweet's night operations was unfounded, because they were always successful, even after the Hue campaign.

Maybe Tolson selected Sweet because the light of Abrams shined on Sweet, and Tolson knew it. We know, for example, that Abrams was instrumental in expediting Sweet's Distinguished Service Cross. What is not known is why Abrams "locked" Tolson's heels (made him stand at attention) for an ass chewing behind the 1st Cav tactical operations center in mid-February, after we escaped encirclement but before we reached Hue. Was it to tell Tolson how badly we had been handled? That Sweet was one of the best ground commanders Abrams had ever known, and that Tolson would be wise to make Sweet the division G-3 when Ross's tour was up? Unfortunately, my source wasn't close enough to hear the conversation, and Abrams died before I had a chance to ask him.

If Tolson took a different approach, perhaps the lessons, the real lessons, of Thon La Chu would be taught today at the Army's Infantry School at Fort Benning, Georgia. Tolson died in December 1991, and his influence is gone now. But how many opportunities were lost during the Vietnam era in order not to offend the general's sensibilities? Unless he knew better, a young military student today might believe that night operations weren't truly understood until Desert Storm.

History is filled with lessons of mistakes of great combat commanders, but usually superior leadership acted wisely, applying harsh but not terminal punishment on the one who erred.

Eisenhower nearly relieved Patton for slapping a soldier. But he restored Patton to command the Third Army, which helped influence the outcome of the war. That's how things used to be done. Lincoln knew Grant drank heavily, but invested great confidence in the man who won battles.

But Sweet's only error was to stand up to General Tolson, a fact both acknowledge. Was this worse than slapping a soldier? I guess it depends on one's point of view.

Sweet, as I've written, was—and is—irascible. But he knew how to fight and how to lead men in battle by personal example. Fault his personality, but I challenge anyone to dispute his tactics. Tolson, on the other hand, commanded the division and was the final arbiter, the court of last resort. If Tolson didn't want to discuss night operations, Sweet raised the issue at his own peril. Being right or wrong is somewhat beside the point, because commanders don't have to be right. Ideally the senior officer is the most professional, dynamic, and experienced soldier in the command, respected for his tactical and operational insights and for the tough decisions every commander must make. But only a child would assume this always to be the case.

During other wars, men like Tolson didn't survive long as division commanders. His gifts simply weren't adequate to handle the mid-intensity war that Vietnam became during Tet '68. He was competent enough to compete with the Viet Cong, warfare characterized by hit-and-run engagements between small units, company, platoon, or squad. But that changed when major units of the North Vietnamese Army entered the war via the northern provinces in 1968. We were lucky to get through Tet '68 as well as we did. Still, the change in tempo was more than the American public could handle or understand.

The Army had an even tougher time during the Vietnam era finding its proper niche, because the line between war and politics was so blurry. Gradual escalation of force wasn't even contemplated during Desert Storm, but it was a popular notion in academic and political circles during the Kennedy-Johnson era.

Maxwell Taylor was the architect of flexible response, a military notion; flexible response was the father of graduated response, a political derivative. As a military idea, flexible response makes a lot of sense, especially when it was presented as an alternative to the nuclear corner we painted ourselves into during the Eisenhower era. Eisenhower found the idea of massive retaliation appealing, not because he lusted for war, but because it meant we could keep the Soviets at bay by threatening all-out nuclear war if they should cross the "brink," a relatively cheap solution compared to the cost of preparing for land warfare and the large standing armies required to make land warfare credible. The location of the "brink" was carefully painted in vague terms, so the Soviets would never know for sure if they were crossing it or not, and were pressured to keep tensions between us at an absolute minimum. At least that was the theory. As a result, Eisenhower took a lot of money from the Army and gave some of it to the Strategic Air Command, saving the rest and protecting his budget. Taylor saw the folly—and the weakness—of this ploy and postulated the notion that the President should have the capability of responding to various threats in an appropriate, balanced fashion—not all or nothing. In short, Taylor argued for a varied arsenal, so we could react with the military response proportional to the threat. If the United States is threatened, according to the Taylor doctrine, we should respond with just enough force to defeat the threat and not, certainly, plan to use nukes on every occasion. So far, so good. Taylor became Kennedy's confidant, and the Army, having been gutted by Eisenhower, rejoiced. Old soldiers may be proud of Ike as a general, but his presidency was something else.

When Lyndon B. Johnson and Robert S. McNamara got hold of Taylor's thinking, they played around with the numbers and tried to parlay flexible response into graduated response, or sometimes gradual escalation. They used slick words and a fast sell, but the result was a disaster. The reason is that the gradual application of force does not necessarily defeat an enemy; it may make the enemy more determined to hang in for the long haul. Nazi bombing had this unexpected effect on the British during World War II, and our bombing of North Vietnam had corresponding results. As we applied more force, they increased their resolve. In the end, of course, they waited us out. In hindsight, it was bound to happen, considering the cohesiveness of a disciplined Communist society.

As a military doctrine, flexible response makes sense: witness Desert Storm and our ability to pace the battle faster than Iraq could handle. As a political doctrine, however, graduated response is flawed because the winner is the one who cries "uncle" last. We cried out first in Vietnam, not because we were weaker militarily, but because we lost the will and the interest to continue. Graduated response does not incorporate this possibility, and LBJ should have known it.

The problem began when White House experts in the LBJ situation room started picking "targets of escalation" instead of the targets that should have been attacked. Military leadership that knew better succumbed to political browbeating, perhaps because they considered it their duty.

The proper military response would have been "Look, I know that this country is run by elected officials and not the Joint Chiefs of Staff. You give us the orders and we'll carry 'em out. But you can't meddle in operational matters, any more than you can tell a surgeon how to cut."

Much of this is folk wisdom today. I can only guess how hard it was to stand up to Lyndon Johnson, McNamara, his righteous whiz kids, Richard Nixon, and Henry Kissinger. I am sure that history will judge this peculiar aspect of their imperious characters harshly. But I would add that the military leadership that caved in to their whimsical running of the war has a lot to answer for too.

The conduct of Desert Storm proves fairly conclusively that the right lessons were learned from Vietnam, that professional soldiers know something after all. Of course I recall the White House rebuttal to General Schwarzkopf's observation that we might have ended the war a trifle too soon, leaving a little doubt about who actually made the decision to stop the attack before our victory was conclusive . . . but that's another story. The fact is that General Schwarzkopf was in charge of actual military operations from Day One.

Sweet, then, was a good soldier during the Korean War. He became a better soldier in Vietnam because he had studied his profession in the lull between wars. The fact is, however, he was politically incorrect during the Vietnam era because, ultimately, he would have told

Johnson what fighting the North Vietnamese Army was all about . . . in rude words.

I can almost hear it now. "Goddamn it, Mister President, when are you going to learn that we can't win this war if we treat our enemies like idiots in black pajamas. We've got to kick 'em in the balls nonstop every chance we get . . . because that's just what they're doing to us, even though no one wants to admit it."

Tolson, his ear to the ground, made sure that Sweet and LBJ would never meet. Under the circumstances, he may have done them both a favor.

CHAPTER 32

TET, MEET DESERT STORM

All of this is now an indelible part of our history and it will never be forgotten. It will, in some way, no matter how vague, haunt the mind of every man who is ever called upon to bear arms in defense of the United States. It may not have ruined us as a country, though it is having its effects. But it is unsettling. Having now learned that we are indeed, as a country, capable of such behavior, we will always wonder whether we will crack again. And wondering whether we will crack, we will somehow seek to avoid another test, until the test is imposed upon us in such an overwhelming fashion that we will have no choice. . . . Those Americans who fought in Southeast Asia brought honor to themselves and could have brought it to their country if their country had been up to it. For many of those whom we failed this must be a particularly galling time. Having done nothing to contribute to our present predicament, they must nonetheless suffer along with the rest, and, inevitably, they will be called on again so that things, at some desperate moment, may perhaps be put right.

—Charles Homer,
Commentary Magazine,
August 1980

I ALMOST CHUCKED THIS PROJECT IN THE TRASH ON A late afternoon in the early summer of 1991, after I went to the Vietnam War Memorial to look up the hometowns of those who perished during the Que Son–Thon La Chu period. A dark shadow of deep depression stared over my shoulder into my heart as I went through the names, one by one. Left alone, I might have finished the job without losing composure, but other visitors, tourists, I suppose, saw what I was doing and inquired about the project. How do you tell strangers that you are suddenly seeing again the faces of sixty friends, all dead for some twenty-odd years?

The best I could do was mumble something about a book project, but inside my guts churned, and I must have wiped my eyes a dozen times. No one noticed, because it was raining lightly and I appeared to be cleaning my glasses.

Later I took my notes to Clif Berry, an old friend who happened to serve with the 196th Light Infantry Brigade just south of Que Son Valley while I was with the 2/12th

Cav. He liked what he read, except for a missing explanation. In all the time I have turned the Hue episode over in my mind, I never thought about an explanation. Clif couldn't help, but he urged me to think things over again.

He was right, of course, and I intuitively knew there was something missing. Nothing worked until I transported myself back to Vietnam one last time.

QUE SON VALLEY WAS A WRECK WHEN WE LEFT IT. THE ghosts of the dead were invisible, but the hulks of burned vehicles, tanks, and helicopters stood out from the ruined landscape. Despite the casualties, we had done well. The system worked. That we were the apparent victor of the battle was interesting, but somewhat beside the point. It had been a fair fight, where each side gave it the best it had. Casualties on both sides were a misfortune.

Lieutenant Colonel Ross had set the stage by meticulous preparation. Lieutenant Colonel Gregory had personal limitations, but he executed the plan that drove the NVA from the valley. Others might—or might not— have done it with less cost, but there was never a lapse in command and control, nor a shortage of support or supplies. The system that oversaw our efforts worked well throughout the crisis. Individuals may have failed at critical points, but the Army system never did.

Lieutenant Colonel Sweet took over as a more efficient Gregory and did a good job of tidying up the battlefield. The system that worked for Gregory continued to operate for Sweet without a hiccup. The battalion that started off for Hue was the same battalion that left Que Son Valley. It was superbly trained, expertly led, disciplined, and cohesive. Then and now, every soldier and citizen can draw pride from the 2/12th Cav, an Army battalion at its finest.

Being told to move from Que Son to Evans without ammunition was the first indicator of a system failure. The fact that there was no ammunition at Camp Evans when we arrived was proof. From then on, there was one system failure after another until the whole effort collapsed. The moment of the total collapse came when we were told at Thon La Chu that we were on our own, that if our escape turned sour, the system would not accept responsibility. If Que Son was a misfortune, then Hue was a tragedy. Sending us from PK-17 without artillery support was a system failure. So was our lack of ammunition. So was the order to attack with cold steel. So was the failure to reinforce us. Assuming we could get to Hue without a mishap was misjudgment of high order that resulted from the division's obeying orders without thinking. Some errors can be excused by the confusion that immediately followed the beginning of the Tet Offensive, when we were all caught so badly off guard. Being surprised is bad for a professional soldier; but recovery from surprise is the tradecraft of the business. The 1st Cavalry Division failed on both accounts.

There were many talented people in the division who should have been able to recover instantly. People like

Tolson, Putnam, Ross, and Campbell were good men, conscientious professionals. But for all their talent and conviction, the 2/12th was cut loose. Why?

Sweet was a talented soldier who never shunned his responsibilities in the darkest hour. The system that produced him was the same that nurtured the others. That system should have mobilized long before Sweet sent Scudder back to tell Tolson that our world had gone to hell.

We who survived are not heroes because we walked out of encirclement. We are heroes because we accept our status as witnesses of a system that failed momentarily, a system that—whatever its faults—we loved then and cherish now.

Yet, the potential for greater tragedy may triumph through historical, factual neglect—through conspiring to ignore how an Army division momentarily collapsed, as if what happened at TFP will fade away over time. Of course the possibility for repetition of our failure at some future date remains great, almost certain. Hiding the story is like not talking about some dark family secret until it finally disappears, hoping the family will somehow be purified over time when the scandal is forgotten. The differences are great, however. A family scandal concerns few people, and the lessons learned can hardly tell us much about the weaker side of human nature that we don't already know. In the case of military failure, lessons learned provide the very basis of instruction, training the astute student to recall the earlier experiences of others, should he ever find himself in a similar precarious situation.

It should come as no surprise that many "lessons learned" reflect how well commanders, units, and equipment performed in the face of adversity, not how poorly. This happened recently when a few writers working for the Pentagon tried to write an objective account of Desert Storm lessons learned, only to find their manuscript was considered too honest by supervisors, who forced them to review their findings to dramatize the positive. One highly placed Department of Defense official, and the kind of professional I respect, told me that "it is the biggest piece of bullshit" he'd ever examined.

What I find unsettling about General Tolson is that he did not take the high ground and tell the whole truth about what happened at TFP—maybe not the biggest event of the war, but not the smallest either. Neither did others, even years later, after it became obvious that Vietnam, historically, was a national disaster. This is not admirable, it's contemptible. If I judge those harshly who seemingly conspired to protect the record, it isn't because I resent their safeguarding their own reputations. That much I understand. What I deplore is the conspiracy that keeps others from learning later. That issue is central to what kind of a people we are. If I appear to single out Tolson, it's only because he fits into this story. In fact, he was no better or worse than many "professionals" of high and low rank who manipulate their reputations at the price of truth. It may be the job of lawyers to twist information to their client's best advantage, the basis of the advocacy system, but soldiers have a much higher obligation to the truth, and for vastly different reasons. When lawyers bend the facts to help their clients, it's their duty. When soldiers hedge on full disclosure, for whatever reason, it's a violation of trust.

THEORETICALLY, WHAT HAPPENED TO THE 2/12TH CAV couldn't happen, it was too improbable that so many systems could fail at one time. Yet it did happen, not because of an act of God—although bad weather was a factor—but because of the failing of men, singly and collectively. Because I was part of the fiasco, I tend to think of the disaster as unique, but this is arrogance on my part. Much worse things have happened to many more people. While I was writing this account, several friends suggested I read Norman F. Dixon's *On the Psychology of Military Incompetence*. It is well worth reading by anyone looking for the root causes of military failure. Our experience during Tet '68 could easily have been a case study. Dixon points out that soldiers most anxious to succeed or most concerned about failure "will be the very ones who make the biggest mistakes. Conversely, less anxious individuals will act more rationally because they are able to devote greater attention to the realities with which they are confronted" (167).

Dixon might well find in Tolson a suitable subject for psychological examination that could yield clues about his behavior during the Tet period. The fact that Tolson remains a beloved father figure to many should not obscure the need to get to the bottom of what happened to the 1st Air Cavalry Division near Hue in February 1968.

As our society changes, hopefully for the better, we cannot expect soldiers of the future to look back with awe on what we have done. I encourage them not to condemn everything either, and to exercise a little tolerance when reviewing our mistakes. But if their idealism is compromised, as ours was, perhaps for vanity, perhaps for sake of advancement, then nothing will have been learned.

Above all, I encourage future generations of warriors to train hard, because wars will be with us for some time, or so it seems in 2008. But they must also train realistically. This means looking beyond the manuals that often hide the lessons of history. Try training for failure—system failure. Train under the assumption that one or more systems supporting you won't work knowing beforehand it reduces your probability of success. Later this may help assure success. Learn to recognize that some people are more imaginative, resourceful, creative, honest, and hardy than others, and don't cut them out of the system early because they may seem out of step. In time of real stress your survival may depend on their unconventional skills.

CHAPTER 33

PASCAGOULA FLASHBACK

IN THE LATE SUMMER OF 1991, FOUR OF US OLD ARMY vets who actually fought the Battle of Hue were invited, in an ecumenical moment, by the Navy to the Ingalls Shipyard in Pascagoula, Mississippi, for the commissioning of the USS *Hue City.* I flew from Washington, D.C., to Mobile with Bob Helvey and we met Bill Scudder at the airport. His plane from Norfolk arrived just a few minutes before ours. The three of us took a taxi to the hotel and met up with our former battalion commander, Dick Sweet, who reached Mobile via Fort Worth, where he had had a business meeting. We celebrated the reunion at various bars the old-fashioned way, except for Scudder, who doesn't drink.

The weather was skin-pricking hot, even worse than Vietnam just before the summer monsoons, and right up until the ceremony started I wished we'd stayed home. The captain of the new ship, Thomas I. Eubanks, thought to himself, "If the Vietnam veterans want their day in the sun, this sure is it." Sitting directly under the sun, the temperature was easily over 100 degrees. The folding chairs were like griddles, and there was no shade, even under the brilliant blue commemorative baseball caps we were obliged to buy because none of us brought hats. Most of us were still a bit thick from the parties in Mobile the night before. When I finally peeled off my jacket, the suspenders left bright red vertical stripes on my shirt. I was irritated by the clown effect, but there was nothing I could do about it. The locals wore belts and hats.

The ceremony made the two-hour wait worth it, and we soon forgot the discomfort. Well-prepared testimonials about Hue and the sacrifices of the Vietnam War brought tears to my eyes. Thanks to the sweat, nobody could see how emotional we all were, although it did get a little sticky when we were asked to stand and the audience applauded. It got worse when they unfurled from the ship's tallest mast the flag that flew over the MACV headquarters in Hue during the Tet battle, tattered but still proud. Weak from heat and emotion, the four of us filed patiently into a waiting bus and motored to nearby fairgrounds for the reception in a delightfully refrigerated exhibit hall. After two cold beers I was more or less refreshed and set out to meet our hosts, including young members of the new crew who weren't the least bit bashful about standing in line with older folks.

One sailor—I guessed he was about fifteen but in fact he was probably closer to twenty, maybe even a little older—worked up the courage to introduce himself and said he hoped I liked the program, because they'd rehearsed for a long time to get it as perfect as they could. He looked like he'd just shaved for the first time, and his eagerness to please reinforced the impression.

"Good job," I said, "and very moving. Couldn't detect a flaw."

"Why," he asked, "were you there? Were you part of the Hue battle?" At first I wondered if he thought I was a party crasher, but his innocence was so disarming that I answered as best I could without sounding like a braggart. I didn't want to appear like one of those pathetic ponytailed vets who camp out near the Vietnam Memorial selling souvenirs to tourists who allow themselves to get suckered into swallowing a sob story. I explained that I was part of a four-man contingent representing an infantry battalion of the Army's 1st Air Cavalry Division that had been part of the Hue campaign. Slowly the line started bending around and I was soon nearly surrounded by young men who probably weren't even alive during February 1968. Our battalion was sent to relieve the Marines holding Hue, I told them, but we didn't get to the moat or the walls in time to do much good, because we were surrounded by the NVA almost as soon as we started to march toward the city.

"Gee," one said, "that sounds like it was real tough. Can you tell us what it felt like?"

I was silent for a few moments trying to think of what to say, something these boys could relate to. The reply just came out on its own.

"It was thirty days without a hard-on," I whispered, but not too softly. Their faces went blank and the rapport we had disappeared as if I'd made an indecent proposition. I didn't know whether I'd said the wrong thing or they just didn't understand. When I finally smiled, they roared. Not only was it the truth, it was the right thing to say.

For the next quarter hour, bursts of laughter erupted around the room as the story was retold, and I realized that I was, momentarily, a celebrity. My only regret was that I couldn't stick around long enough to tell them the whole story. Not having an erection was the easy part.

AFTERWORD

IN THE EARLIER EDITION OF THIS BOOK I CLAIMED THAT the myths from Vietnam were finally laid to rest in August 1991, when we attacked Saddam Hussein's Iraqi forces in Operation Desert Storm. We proved then, once again, that the United States was able and willing to mount a large-scale overseas offensive operation—when we deemed it was in our vital interest. Until Operations Desert Shield and Desert Storm, many Americans had believed we would never again dip our military toe into infested waters for any reason that didn't relate to our immediate survival. It took twenty years to correct this perception.

Our nation's leaders (wisely, in my judgment) attacked Iraq in Desert Storm with overwhelming force, ensuring the conflict would be quickly resolved in our favor. No gradualism this time, no series of piddling responses enabling our enemy to build up his forces faster than we could deploy ours. Muscular allies joined us. I thought this would set the pattern for the future. I was wrong.

Operation Desert Storm was about oil. There was no doubt Hussein eyed expansion of his energy production facilities at the expense of the emir of Kuwait. The Saudis understood that once Kuwait was conquered, their kingdom (and oil patch) would be next. They joined our coalition and even picked up most of the checks afterward.

When Hussein's forces were defeated in the hundred-hour war, the remnants of his tattered army retreated, leaving hundreds of burning oil wells in their wake. This did not inhibit celebrations, however, because the danger to the Kuwait and Saudi oil fields had passed. We allowed Hussein to keep his job, in effect handing over to him those Kurds and Shia who had voiced support for his overthrow when Desert Storm began. We had the obligatory victory parade in Washington, and General Schwarzkopf became the hero of the day. The Kurds and Shia weren't so fortunate.

In 2003 we attacked Saddam Hussein again, not for oil but for weapons of mass destruction. We would have been better off playing the oil card, once it became obvious the WMD claim was false. Some countered that we rid Iraq of a brutal dictator—a worthy goal, surely—while others recalled cynically (but correctly) that Hussein's brutality was not an issue when we abandoned the Kurds and Shia to his executioners in 1991.

If Desert Storm displayed the U.S. armed forces at the peak of our nation's physical and intellectual powers, we never had the opportunity to experience how Operation Iraqi Freedom might have turned out, absent political interference.

This forces me to retract earlier assertions that we had absorbed the lessons learned from Vietnam into our national security strategy and psyche. Desert Storm was not the rule but an aberration. In fact, we ignored the lessons learned from Vietnam when we kicked off Operation Iraqi Freedom. Leaders who should have known better closed their eyes to lessons learned in Vietnam and Desert Storm, starting again from scratch. They predicted the rapid seizure of Baghdad would be a sufficient exercise of power to put the genie back in the bottle. Wishful thinking along these lines led to disaster in Vietnam, and such thoughts were predictably repeated when we captured Baghdad with minuscule forces in reserve and no serious planning for post-conflict operations. Capturing Baghdad wasn't as easy as we thought at the time, but so be it. Then we discovered things could go from bad to worse, leading to calamity and ridiculous denial. Our most important leaders didn't claim to see light at the end of the tunnel: They claimed we were through the tunnel. Now, some 3,600 lives later (at the time of this writing), it's possible we were never in the tunnel in the first place.

This is not the place to discuss arrogance of the mighty or, as Shakespeare said, "the insolence of office." Rather, let us salute the sacrifice of the fallen who did their duty in Iraq as their fathers did in Vietnam.

I agree there's little use in comparing Vietnam to Iraq,

a device war detractors employ to demonstrate the folly of both enterprises. But they make the wrong arguments. A better case can be made for challenging the blissful assumption that leaders would arise in Iraq to make the immediate transition from tyranny to democracy. We had stronger leaders in Vietnam whom we could work with toward a mutually agreeable end, especially President Nguyen Van Thieu. In Iraq we destroyed vestiges of leadership when we disbanded the Iraqi army, with no Thieu look-alike on the horizon. The manipulative Pentagon favorite, Ahmed Chalabi, had more supporters in Washington than Baghdad. The police force basically melted into the surroundings, while looters and gangs filled the vacuum. This left us holding the bag, its contents broadcast by the smell. Ambassador Paul Bremer's tenure resembled the Brothers Grimm more than Grotius, the legendary European jurist.

There is little hope for a quick restoration of government in Iraq, until a central government can establish its authority and respect. We look for signs of progress, but the evidence so far fails to persuade we are there yet. There is room for hope, but things are far from certain. While elections are a positive step in the right direction, they do not guarantee law or a coalescence of order. Military training programs are useful too, but dissected out of context, they can mask a failure to unify the country in body and spirit.

When we left Vietnam in 1973, the country held together without our presence until 1975, when North

Vietnamese forces attacked en masse with overwhelming power. If we leave Iraq abruptly, I doubt it will hold together for half as long. Civil war and sectarian violence cannot be ruled out, nor can an invasion by Iran. We have few levers left to pull. I hope we stay until the situation on the ground, not politics at home, warrants our withdrawal. If there is a chance of Iraq pulling itself together, it would be folly to abandon a floating ship.

Those responsible for the invasion of Iraq calculated wrongly. When we had leverage, we held back. As bad as that was, failure to recalibrate is worse. Had advice been sought in Washington from those still living who experienced Vietnam, the decision makers would have learned that nation building is a long, difficult, uncertain, and expensive process. They would have learned that terrorists acting alone or in concert can be a significant impediment to progress. Witness the effectiveness of the Viet Cong. Nation building requires—then and now—a committed infrastructure, defense forces, and economic and agricultural development. This is not an inclusive list. Compared to the fractured alliances of Iraq, Vietnam had the advantage of social solidarity. Could anything be more obvious when planning for the post-combat phase (itself an ironic expression of cruel proportions)?

We made a mistake of gradually increasing our forces in Vietnam, hoping the more pressure we applied, the sooner our enemies would cry "uncle." When we halted the bombing of North Vietnam, this was acknowledgment that pain may destroy facilities but not fracture solidarity. General Colin Powell, as chairman of the Joint Chiefs of Staff, codified this experience in the Powell Doctrine.

Our attack of Iraq in March 2003 was made with the minimal forces deemed necessary. This was a conscious decision by Secretary of Defense Donald Rumsfeld to ignore Powell's guidance, and Rumsfeld's senior advisers apparently supported this approach. At least none of them resigned in protest. As late as June 2003 the official position was that there was no insurgency, until the facts (and General Abizaid's statements) made denial untenable. Meanwhile, Baghdad crumbled and burned.

After he left office, Powell encapsulated our failure with the observation that we never imposed our will on Iraq. Yet this is what armies in contact with the enemy are supposed to do as Mission One. While serving as secretary of state, Powell tried to participate in war planning but was apparently rebuffed by others in the White House and Pentagon. He was one of the few figures then serving who had experienced the war in Vietnam and Desert Storm.

When we finally got around to doing things right in Vietnam, it was after the departure of General William C. Westmoreland and the ascendancy of General Creighton Abrams and his co-partner, Ambassador Ellsworth Bunker. When they departed, each had served in Vietnam for about six years. President Nixon deferred to their military and political judgment, and he was well served by his patience. Over time, Abrams and Bunker learned from their in-country experience and applied those lessons effectively. President Thieu was an attentive protégé.

Consider that General Abrams had served with distinction in World War II and the Korean War. He understood warfare from the bottom up, without illusion. We went into Iraq without that reservoir of experience. Those who had it were ignored, by all accounts pushed aside by wishful thinkers.

We learned in Vietnam that gradualism doesn't work. Defeating terrorism is a long, difficult task, and working with a strong central government is critical to success. More than anything else, the people who live in the country must share a common vision.

We went into Baghdad blind, as Jim Fallows reported in a classic article published in the January/February 2004 issue of *Atlantic Monthly*. Until more evidence is put on the table, we may depart as blind as we arrived.

This is not my wish. But it may be the inevitable consequence of inexperience, arrogance, and historical ignorance. The Iraqis will ultimately side with an obvious winner. For better or worse, we and the world will have to live with that decision.

INFANTRY BATTALION ORGANIZATION

This is the story of an infantry battalion organized according to one of the Army's tables of organization and equipment (TO&E). It is supposed to have a total strength of 862, but this is only the authorized strength, not the number actually assigned and available for combat, which is called "foxhole strength."

The important thing to remember is that the 2/12th Cav was a lightly equipped infantry battalion, able to conduct only limited sustained combat. It had to have substantial support and reinforcement from brigade or division assets.

The following table explains how the 2/12th was structured internally, based on the TO&Es current during the Vietnam era.

UNIT	PLUS	TOTALS	COMMANDED BY A
1 rifle squad		10 men	Sergeant
3 rifle squads	1 platoon HQ (3 men) and weapons squad (11 men)	44-man platoon	Lieutenant
3 rifle platoons	1 company HQ (13 men) and 1 mortar platoon (11 men)	171-man company	Captain
4 rifle companies	1 battalion HQ (33 men) and 1 HQ support company (146 men)	862-man battalion	Lieutenant colonel

A typical infantry division of the Vietnam era would have a total of nine rifle battalions, a reconnaissance battalion (squadron), four artillery battalions, plus various combat support and combat service support battalions.

A brigade, if properly augmented by an appropriate "slice" of division support units, is the smallest self-sustaining combat element that can be independently deployed. A battalion may be able to sustain itself for a few hours without external support, but it would not be deployed separately on its own.

WHERE ARE THEY NOW?

Forty years after Tet '68, I still stay in contact with several of the key participants.

Lieutenant General John J. Tolson died in 1991. He had been promoted from the commanding general of the 1st Cavalry Division to commander of the Army's XVIII Airborne Corps at Fort Bragg.

Lieutenant General Collier Ross died in 2007, age 76.

Brigadier General Richard Sweet died in 1994, age 65.

A. Earle Spry is in Colorado Springs, where he taught school for many years after retiring from the Army.

Colonel Hubert "Bill" Campbell died in Florida at age 73.

Major General George Putnam lives in Northern Virginia.

Colonel Bill Scudder lives in the Tidewater area of Virginia and coaches girls' high school field hockey.

I saw Phil Pons in 2007, so I suspect he's still alive, but the Virginia number I have for him has been disconnected.

Maury Cralle, now retired, lives near me in Northern Virginia.

Don Bowman is a certified public accountant in Columbus, Georgia, and he tells me he'll never retire.

Bob Helvey retired from the Army in 1991 as a colonel and lives in West Virginia. He has spent most of his post-Army life trying to restore democracy to countries around the world, notably Burma. Serbs give him credit for organizing the nonviolent movement that unseated dictator Slobodan Milosevic in 2000.

I retired from the Army as a lieutenant colonel in 1984, and have worked in the Washington, D.C., area ever since, with the exception of three months in Baghdad, 2003–2004, and two semesters teaching journalism at the University of Michigan in Ann Arbor, 2004–2005. I'm now the deputy director of public affairs for the American Battle Monuments Commission. We manage the nation's 24 overseas military cemeteries.

THE PRESIDENTIAL UNIT CITATION

I had a hard time writing up the recommendation for the 12th Cavalry's Presidential Unit Citation. It wasn't because the facts weren't available, or because I needed fancy language to make the story sound plausible, but because the standards for the submission were so strict. To start with, I needed lots of supporting official documents—after-action reports and that kind of thing—that hadn't been written. I could write the cover letters and a proposed citation, but I couldn't assemble the entire package in the few days remaining to me before I left Vietnam.

As it was, regulations stated that the recommendation for the award must include casualty lists, operations summaries, and other reports that were already several inches thick when I passed them to my successor. The award was processed through channels and was finally signed by President Nixon on May 20, 1970, some two years after the event it recognized.

It was published by the Department of the Army as General Order 42, dated August 11, 1970.

By virtue of the authority vested in me as
President of the United States
and as Commander-in-Chief of the Armed Forces
of the United States,
I have today awarded
THE PRESIDENTIAL UNIT CITATION (ARMY)
FOR EXTRAORDINARY HEROISM
TO THE
2D BATTALION, 12TH CAVALRY
1ST AIR CAVALRY DIVISION AND TO
TROOP B, 1ST SQUADRON
1ST CAVALRY REGIMENT UNITED STATES ARMY

The 2d Battalion, 12th Cavalry, supported by Troop B, 1st Squadron, 1st Cavalry Regiment, distinguished itself by extraordinary heroism in combat during the period 2 January to 12 February 1968 in countering the North Vietnamese Army's Winter-Spring Offensive in Quang Nam Province, Republic of Vietnam. In five major engagements with enemy battalion or larger size units, the men of the 2d Battalion, 12th Cavalry decisively defeated numerically superior enemy forces. Sacrificing hundreds of men, the enemy attempted, in vain, to hold positions or to seize objectives from the battalion in both defensive and offensive operations. The battalion never faltered in its aggressive assault against a determined and well-equipped foe. Crushing enemy initiative and rupturing enemy lines of communication, the battalion prevented the enemy from driving free world forces from the strategic Que Son Valley which was key terrain in the battle for control of Quang Nam Province. Other heroic assaults against enemy positions in the Que Son Valley prevented the enemy from organizing to reinforce his units attacking the city of Hue. On 4 February the battalion was encircled by the elements of the 6th North Vietnamese Army Regiment. Even though the enemy attempted to annihilate the battalion with human wave assaults near the hamlet of Thon Que Chu, the battalion's battle line held fast and during the night the battalion exfiltrated without detection through the encircling enemy into positions even deeper within enemy lines of communication. This unexpected maneuver completely surprised the North Vietnamese Army forces (estimated at over 2,000 troops) and placed the battalion on commanding terrain inside the enemy rear area. From its new base, the battalion interdicted large enemy forces and continued surveillance on enemy movement to and from Hue. From the Que Son Valley to the outskirts of Hue, the 2d Battalion, 12th Cavalry and Troop B, 1st Squadron, 1st Armored Cavalry Regiment showed their gallant fighting timber during many days of sustained combat. Their outstanding bravery, determination, esprit de corps, and devotion to duty blunted the enemy offensive and brought great credit on themselves, their unit and the United States Army.

Richard Nixon

VIETNAM 2D BATTALION, 12TH CAVALRY KILLED IN ACTION

January 2, 1968, to February 28, 1968

RANK	NAME	DATE	UNIT
SP4	Pine, Frederick Andrew	January 2, 1968	C Co
CPL	Valenzuela, Henry Jr.	January 2, 1968	C Co
SGT	Cooke, Charles Thomas	January 3, 1968	A Co
SGT	Goulet, Ronald David	January 3, 1968	A Co
PFC	Lindbergh, Robert Raymond	January 3, 1968	A Co
CPL	Ray, Darwin Esker	January 3, 1968	A Co
CPL	Coonrod, Arnold Lee	January 3, 1968	D Co
PFC	Dautremont, Dennis Dale	January 3, 1968	D Co
SP4	Ellis, Billy Joe	January 3, 1968	D Co
SSG	Guzman, Juan Araujo	January 3, 1968	D Co
SSG	Price, Rodney Allen	January 3, 1968	D Co
SGT	Rodriguez, Jesse Emiterio	January 3, 1968	D Co
SGT	Smith, Jerry Lynn	January 3, 1968	D Co
CPL	West, Melford Wayne	January 3, 1968	D Co

PFC	Cooler, Sidney Homer	January 5, 1968	A Co
SP4	Desilets, William J.	January 5, 1968	A Co
PFC	Earles, Arthur James	January 5, 1968	A Co
SGT	Bruckner, Donald Richard	January 7, 1968	A Co
SP4	Casilla-Vazquez, Manuel Jr.	January 7, 1968	A Co
PFC	Gonzalez, Conrad Nicholas	January 7, 1968	A Co
CPL	Heller, Robert Lee	January 7, 1968	A Co
SSG	Jones, Delmar R.	January 7, 1968	A Co
SP4	Kearney, Robert Curt	January 7, 1968	A Co
SGT	Reeder, Edward James	January 7, 1968	A Co
SP4	Sutton, Frank	January 7, 1968	A Co
PFC	Trujillo, Robert Steven	January 7, 1968	A Co
SGT	Vaden, Robert William	January 7, 1968	A Co
CPL	Carrillo, Arnoldo Leonel	January 7, 1968	C Co
PFC	Hood, Rufus	January 7, 1968	C Co
SP4	Royster, Hubert Jr.	January 7, 1968	C Co
1LT	Stone, James Marvin	January 7, 1968	C Co
SGT	Wysocki, Wojciech	January 7, 1968	C Co
LTC	Gregory, Bob Leroy	January 7, 1968	HHC
MSG	Keefe, Richard Carlysle	January 7, 1968	HHC
MAJ	Malone, Lawrence Michael	January 7, 1968	HHC
PFC	Herbert, Larry Eugene	January 15, 1968	B Co
PFC	Azzarito, Frank Anthony Jr.	February 3, 1968	A Co
SP4	Cervera, Michael Bernard	February 3, 1968	C Co
PFC	Gray, Harold Leroy	February 3, 1968	C Co
PFC	Higginbotham, Harold S.	February 3, 1968	C Co
PFC	Hughey, Edward Wendell	February 3, 1968	C Co
PFC	Quinones, David	February 3, 1968	C Co
PFC	Lau, Hoi Tin	February 3, 1968	HHC

Appendix 4

PFC	Manowski, Edward	February 3, 1968	HHC
SGT	Treadwell, Eugene Durwood	February 3, 1968	HHC
CPL	Holsinger, Gary Olson	February 4, 1968	B Co
CPL	Knox, Bruce Neal	February 4, 1968	B Co
SSG	Patton, Curtis Ray	February 4, 1968	B Co
SGT	Casias, Henry Eloy	February 4, 1968	C Co
CPL	Genzler, August Henry	February 4, 1968	C Co
CPL	Graham, Charles Herbert	February 4, 1968	C Co
CPL	Diaz, Gary Michael	February 4, 1968	D Co
SGT	Hopkins, Robert E.	February 4, 1968	D Co
SGT	Kephart, Russell Edward	February 4, 1968	D Co
SGT	Loos, Thomas Walter	February 4, 1968	D Co
SP4	Scowden, Curtis Dean	February 6, 1968	B Co
SP4	Allen, Robert John	February 9, 1968	B Co
PFC	Eulitt, Leonard Elzy	February 9, 1968	C Co
PFC	Glesenkamp, John Carr	February 9, 1968	D Co
CPL	Littleton, David Ernest	February 9, 1968	D Co
2LT	Dobrinska, Thomas Earl	February 10, 1968	B Co
SP4	Grandahl, Jack William	February 13, 1968	B Co
PFC	Fedor, Terrence Eugene	February 19, 1968	C Co
PFC	Lanning, Ronald Barry	February 19, 1968	C Co
PFC	Norris, Billy Rayvon	February 19, 1968	C Co
PFC	Contreras, Richard Aguirre	February 22, 1968	A Co
SP4	Powell, Larry Dean	February 22, 1968	B Co
PFC	Betleyoun, Gola Calvin	February 23, 1968	A Co
CPL	Plaep, Alfred Edgar Jr.	February 23, 1968	A Co
CPL	Moore, Randy Cois	February 23, 1968	D Co
PFC	Hilyer, Broadus Dale	February 24, 1968	A Co
CPL	Wolfe, Frank Jesse	February 24, 1968	D Co

PFC	Collins, Noble Jr.	February 25, 1968	A Co
SP4	Skeet, Patrick	February 25, 1968	C Co
SSG	Wesley, Robert Earl	February 28, 1968	C Co

VIETNAM 2D BATTALION, 12TH CAVALRY SUPPORTING UNITS KILLED IN ACTION

January 7, 1968, to February 5, 1968

RANK	NAME	DATE	UNIT	DETAIL
WO	Bahl, Robert F., Jr.	January 7, 1968	3rd Brigade	Air crash, 2/12th Cav C&C LTC Gregory
WO	Ford, Marshall H.	January 7, 1968	3rd Brigade	Air crash, 2/12th Cav C&C LTC Gregory
CPL	Knake, Lloyd E.	January 7, 1968	3rd Brigade	Air crash, 2/12th Cav C&C LTC Gregory

Appendix 5

RANK	NAME	DATE	UNIT	DETAIL
SP5	Lauderdale, Arthur L.	January 7, 1968	3rd Brigade	Air crash, 2/12th Cav C&C LTC Gregory
CPT	Barovetto, John L.	January 7, 1968	Company B, 1 Sqd/1 Cav	Commander of Cav unit, LZ Ross
CPL	Blankenship, Larry J.	February 5, 1968	C Battery, 1/77 Artillery	FO RTO with Company B, 2/12th Cav

Reproduced with written permission from the 12th Cavalry Regiment Association, www.12thcav.us/In_Memory_viet_unit_support.htm.

VIETNAM 2D BATTALION, 12TH CAVALRY DISTINGUISHED SERVICE CROSS

January 2, 1968, to February 21, 1968

NAME	UNIT	DATE
Darrell, John	Co C, 2/12 Cav	January 2, 1968
Dentinger, David	Co A, 2/12 Cav	February 21, 1968
Dobrinska, Thomas	Co B, 2/12 Cav	February 9, 1968
Gaskin, Gorden	HHC, 2/12 Cav	January 3, 1968
Gregory, Bob	HHC, 2/12 Cav	January 2, 1968
Helvey, Robert	Co A, 2/12 Cav	January 7, 1968
Lewis, John	Co B, 2/12 Cav	February 3, 1968
Ring, George	Co C, 2/12 Cav	January 7, 1968
Stone, James	Co C, 2/12 Cav	January 7, 1968
Sweet, Richard	HHC, 2/12 Cav	February 3, 1968
Taylor, Ronald	Co C, 2/12 Cav	January 7, 1968

Note: In the 107-year history of the 12th Cavalry Regiment, 32 of its soldiers have received Distinguished Service Crosses for extreme gallantry in action against an armed enemy. The 11 soldiers named above earned the award during the seven-week period recorded in *The Lost Battalion of Tet*.

Reproduced with written permission from the 12th Cavalry Regiment Association, www.12thcav.us/DSC_List.htm.

SOURCES

DOCUMENTS

Presidential Unit Citation Recommendation. 2d Battalion, 12th Cavalry, 1st Cavalry Division (Airmobile). 1 March 1968.

Combat Operations After-Action Report. 1st Cavalry Division (Airmobile). 2 July 1968. Operational Report, Lessons Learned. Headquarters, 1st Cavalry Division (Airmobile). Period Ending 30 April 1968, 26 August 1968.

The History of the Second Battalion, Twelfth Cavalry, For The Year 1967. By First Lieutenant L. W. Fitzgerald, undated.

"The First Air Cavalry Division History," Vietnam. Volume 1, 1965–1969. *The Air Cavalry Division Magazine*. Volume 1, Number 1, July 1968.

The Battle of Hue. 14th Military History Detachment, 1st Cavalry Division (Airmobile). 19 March 1968.

Sources

Cavalair, newspaper. 1st Cavalry Division (Airmobile). February 14, 21, March 6, 20, and 27, 1968, editions.

Newsweek magazine. January 29, 1968.

Time magazine. December 11, 1967, and February 9, 1968.

Combat after-action interview 5-68. 14th Military History Detachment, 1st Cavalry Division (Airmobile). Undated.

Exit Interview with Major General John J. Tolson III, 14th Military History Detachment, 1st Cavalry Division (Airmobile). 24 June 1968.

Exit Interview with Colonel Hubert S. Campbell, 14th Military History Detachment, 1st Cavalry Division (Airmobile). 12 May 1968.

Oral History, U.S. Army Military Institute. The Battle of Hue, interviews with Lieutenant General John J. Tolson, USA (Ret.), Lieutenant General M. Collier Ross, USA (Ret.), and Brigadier General Richard S. Sweet, USA (Ret.). Project 85-G, 1985.

Captured Document, Attack of Hue City, dated 29 May 1968 (CDEC Document IRR 6 027448568). Combined Documents Exploitation Center.

Historical Study 2-68. Operation Hue City. 31st Military History Detachment, Headquarters Provisional Corps Vietnam. August 1968.

The General Offensives of 1968–69. Colonel Hoang Ngoc Lung. Indochina Monographs. U.S. Army Center of Military History, Washington, D.C.

Vietnam Studies, Airmobility. By Lieutenant General John J. Tolson, Department of the Army. 1973.

Sources

BOOKS

Dixon, Norman F. *On the Psychology of Military Incompetence*. London: Jonathan Cape, 1976.

Oberdorfer, Don. *Tet!*. Garden City, NY: Doubleday & Company, 1971.

Palmer, Dave Richard. *Summons of the Trumpet*. San Rafael, CA: Presidio Press, 1978.

Lieutenant Colonel Phan Van Son, Senior editor. *The Viet Cong Tet Offensive 1968*.

Chief, Military History Division, J-5, Joint General Staff, Republic of Vietnam Armed Forces, July 1969.

Stanton, Shelby L. *Anatomy of a Division*. Novato, CA: Presidio Press, 1987.

INTERVIEWS (rank at time of last interview)

General Roscoe Robinson, USA (Ret.). Interview with author.

Lieutenant General M. Collier Ross. Interview with author.

Lieutenant General James B. Vaught, USA (Ret.). Interview with author.

Major General George W. Putnam, Jr., USA (Ret.). Interview with author.

Brigadier General Mike L. Ferguson, USA (Ret.). Interview with author.

Brigadier General Richard S. Sweet, USA (Ret.). Interview with author.

Colonel Donald C. Bowman, USA (Ret.). Interview with author.

Sources

Colonel Hubert S. Campbell, Jr., USA (Ret.). Interview with author.

Colonel James J. Coghlan, Jr., USA (Ret.). Interview with author.

Colonel Norbert D. Grabowski, USA (Ret.). Interview with author.

Colonel Robert L. Helvey, USA (Ret.). Interview with author.

Colonel Dane Maddox, USA (Ret.). Interview with author.

Colonel Philip E. Pons, Jr., USA (Ret.). Interview with author.

Colonel William I. Scudder, USA (Ret.). Interview with author.

Colonel A. Earle Spry, USA (Ret.). Interview with anthor.

Colonel Edwin S. Townsley, USA (Ret.). Interview with author.

Colonel Robert D. Vaughn, USA (Ret.). Interview with author.

Lieutenant Colonel Maury S. Cralle, USA (Ret.). Interview with author.

Lieutenant Colonel Melvin W. Russell, USA. Interview with author.

Major Lewis I. Jeffries, USA. Interview with author.

Command Sergeant Major Richard Halperin. Interview with author.

INDEX

Index

Index

Index

Index

ABOUT THE AUTHOR

Charles A. Krohn retired from the Army in 1984 as a lieutenant colonel with twenty years' service. He served two tours in Vietnam. During the first tour (1967–68) he transferred to the infantry to serve as intelligence officer of a battalion of the 1st Cavalry Division (Airmobile). During the second tour (1970–71) he was a district senior adviser in Tay Ninh Province. He returned to the Pentagon as a civilian in 2001 as the Army's deputy chief of public affairs, followed by several months in Iraq as public affairs adviser to the office responsible for infrastructure reconstruction. From 2004–2005 he was a visiting professor of journalism at the University of Michigan and is now on the staff of the American Battle Monuments Commission in Arlington, Virginia.